THE UNITED STATES AND THE USE OF FORCE IN THE POST–COLD WAR ERA

A Report by
The Aspen Strategy Group

The Aspen | Institute
Queenstown, Maryland
1995

THE ASPEN STRATEGY GROUP

The Aspen Strategy Group is a bipartisan committee organized under the auspices of The Aspen Institute. The ASG's primary goal is to advance thinking about developments in international affairs and expand the range of views participating in discussions about national security. As a standing body, the ASG contributes to the public debate through reports and other publications; focuses attention to new issues that will likely affect U.S. security; and provides a forum for creative and informal exchange in order to facilitate the development of ideas, consensus, and policy.

(continued)

Mr. David Gergen, *Duke University, Durham, North Carolina*
The Honorable Albert Gore, Jr., *The Vice President, Washington, D.C.*
Mr. William Hyland, *Vienna, Virginia*
Admiral Bobby R. Inman, USN (Ret), *Austin, Texas*
The Honorable Jan Lodal, *U.S. Department of Defense, Washington, D.C.*
The Honroable Joseph S. Nye, Jr., *U.S. Department of Defense, Washington, D.C.*
The Honorable William J. Perry, *U.S. Department of Defense, Washington, D.C.*
Professor George Rathjens, *Massachusetts Institute of Technology, Cambridge, Massachusetts*
The Honorable Alice Rivlin, *Office of Management and Budget, Washington, D.C.*
Dr. Enid Schoettle, *National Intelligence Council, Washington, D.C.*
The Honorable Walter Slocombe, *U.S. Department of Defense, Washington, D.C.*
The Honorable Strobe Talbott, *U.S. Department of State, Washington, D.C.*
The Honorable John W. Warner, *U.S. Senate, Washington, D.C.*
Dr. Albert D. Wheelon, *Los Angeles, California*
The Honorable R. James Woolsey, *Shea & Gardner, Washington, D.C.*
Dr. Charles A. Zraket, *The Mitre Corporation, Bedford, Massachusetts*

Contents

About This Report

This study is part of an ongoing series of reports prepared under the auspices of the Aspen Strategy Group, a program of The Aspen Institute. The ASG is a bipartisan standing committee drawing together members from the American academic, policy, and business communities to relate varying perspectives on international security issues facing the United States in the post-Cold War era.

The papers presented in this report were commissioned for an Aspen Strategy Group conference on "The United States and the Use of Force in the Post-Cold War Era," held at the Aspen Institute's Colorado facility on August 14-19, 1994. Participants from the Aspen Strategy Group included Les Aspin, Bruce Berkowitz, Antonia Handler Chayes, Richard Cooper, Kenneth Dam, Leslie Gelb, J. Bryan Hehir, Arnold Horelick, Robert Hormats, Karen House, David Jones, Lawrence Korb, Jan Lodal, Jessica Mathews, Janne Nolan, Sam Nunn, Joseph Nye, George Rathjens, Enid Schoettle, Brent Scowcroft, John Steinbruner, and William Webster.

Guests at the conference included Andrew Bacevich, Abram Chayes, Steven David, Leon Fuerth, Richard Haass, Jane Holl, John Galvin, Bruce George, Charles Horner, Sergei Karaganov, Andrew Kohut, James Lindsay, Charles William Maynes, Dominique Moïsi, Daniel Schorr, David Speedie, Carl Stiner, Jane Wales, and Edward Warner.

Generous support for the Aspen Strategy Group in this project was provided by grants from the Carnegie Corporation of New York and the John D. and Catherine T. MacArthur Foundation. The Aspen Strategy Group would like to thank Anne Callahan for her assistance in preparing the report, and W. Daniel Wright and Susan Eckhardt Oliver at The Aspen Institute for production support.

The introduction was prepared by Bruce Berkowitz. Readers should note that views expressed in this report are solely those of the individual authors. Members of the ASG, as well as sponsoring organizations of The Aspen Institute, are not responsible for the views or opinions expressed herein.

Notes on Contributors

Andrew Bacevich is executive director of the Foreign Policy Institute at the Nitze School of Advanced International Studies, Johns Hopkins University.

Abram Chayes is a professor of law at Harvard University

Antonia Handler Chayes is president of the Consensus-Building Institute, Inc.

Steven R. David is chairman of the Department of Political Science at Johns Hopkins University.

Bruce George is a Labour MP at Westminster and Senior Opposition Member of the Defence Committee.

Richard N. Haass is director of National Security Programs for the Council on Foreign Relations and was, at the time of the conference, a senior associate at the Carnegie Endowment for International Peace.

Jane E. Holl is executive director of the Carnegie Commission on Preventing Deadly Conflict.

Sergei A. Karaganov is deputy director of the Institute of Europe, Russian Academy of Sciences.

Andrew Kohut is director of the Times Mirror Center for the People and the Press.

James M. Lindsay is a professor of political science at the University of Iowa.

Charles William Maynes is editor of *Foreign Policy.*

Dominique Moïsi is editor of *Politique étrangère* and deputy director of the Institute for Strategic Studies in Paris.

Nick Ryan is a parliamentary research assistant in the office of Bruce George.

Robert C. Toth is a senior associate at the Times Mirror Center for the People and the Press.

Introduction

Few national security issues are as controversial as the use of military force. While virtually everyone would agree that U.S. military forces should be prepared to defend the United States from direct attack, there is much less consensus on whether U.S. forces should be used in situations when the threat to the country is less clear or less dire.

This is understandable; the decision to deploy military forces imposes tremendous risks on both individual U.S. military personnel and the country as a whole. The use of force is also inherently controversial because there are often significant risks if force is *not* used; the United States could lose vital interests and, in some cases, its credibility in international affairs. Finally, there is considerable disagreement over whether military force is effective in many of the situations for which it is proposed.

Military Force and the Post–Cold War Era

If anything, the end of the Cold War has made military intervention even more controversial because the fall of the Soviet Union eliminated the main guidepost that U.S. officials relied upon for planning U.S. military forces and their use. During the Cold War, U.S. policy for the use of military force was linked to U.S. containment policy. Most U.S. military forces were dedicated to deterring a Soviet-led invasion of Western Europe or a nuclear strike against the United States. Even U.S. policy for military operations outside Europe were oriented toward the Soviet threat. U.S. planning considered regional conflicts as the so-called "half-war" the that United States might need to address

xi

at the same time as a war in Europe or as a response to Soviet-inspired "wars of national liberation."

With the loss of the Soviet threat, much of the traditional rationale that underpinned U.S. military policy became invalid. Yet, even before the Cold War ended, there were signs that the United States needed to focus on more than just the Soviet threat. The revolution in Iran in 1979, the resulting oil crisis, and concerns over the security of other oil-producing states in the Persian Gulf highlighted two facts: instability in countries, totally separate from the superpower confrontation, could affect U.S. interests; and medium powers could present significant threats to U.S. interests in distant regions. Iraq's invasion of Kuwait in 1991 reaffirmed these concerns.

A second sign appeared in the 1980s, when "low intensity conflict" (LIC) threats began to attract greater concern. LIC includes missions such as terrorism, peacekeeping, and narcotics interdiction—missions that may require combat forces but that fall short of full-scale war. U.S. leaders soon realized that the forces designed to deter a Soviet threat were often poorly suited for LIC and that such operations require forces with greater mobility in addition to specialized training and equipment.

Most recently, in the 1990s, yet another set of "threats" (at least in the broad sense of the term) has begun to emerge: situations in which the armed forces are called upon to provide noncombat services in the form of humanitarian relief or disaster recovery, taking advantage of the military's logistics, command structure, and rapid response capabilities. Such situations are usually associated with the aftermath of war and the displacement of refugees (as in the case of Kurdistan after Desert Storm), the breakdown of a national government and civil order (as in the case of Rwanda in 1994), or natural disasters.

Potential Post–Cold War Requirements for Military Force

The Clinton administration, in proposing the first national security strategy developed entirely after the end of the Cold War, oriented its military planning around these new threats. The overall strategy aims at "engagement and enlargement."

The administration's strategy assumes that instability abroad threatens the security of the United States and the welfare of Americans at home. To reduce this instability, the strategy proposes that the United States play an active role in international affairs (i.e., engagement). This active role includes, at least in some cases, intervening in regional politics and the internal affairs of failed political systems abroad. The ultimate goal is to increase the number of market democracies in the world (i.e., enlargement), which are assumed to be less likely to start wars and which provide better trading partners for the United States.

The military component of the administration's national security strategy would use military force to defend U.S. interests from regional threats and would use the military in LIC and humanitarian missions abroad. The specific military requirements identified in the strategy include:[1]

- *Dealing with major regional contingencies.* Usually these are assumed to be conflicts in the Middle East and in the Pacific in which general purpose military forces would be used. Current U.S. planning calls this type of conflict a "major regional contingency" (MRC) and assumes that the United States needs to be able to fight and win two MRCs simultaneously.

- *Providing a credible overseas presence.* The continuing "forward deployment" of U.S. forces and joint exercises with foreign military forces are intended to demonstrate the commitment of the United States to maintain stability in a region. In specific cases, U.S. forces may carry out "show of force" operations to underline the point, as in the 1988 deployment of U.S. warships to escort tankers in the Persian Gulf during the Iran-Iraq war.

- *Countering weapons of mass destruction.* The administration's strategy neither explicitly states nor rules out the possibility that the United States will strike during peacetime to prevent a country from developing nuclear weapons or other weapons of mass destruction. The strategy does explicitly state that U.S. policy stresses deterrence, developing defensive systems, and the ability of U.S. forces to attack enemy weapons of mass destruction during wartime.

• *Contributing to multilateral peace operations.* Such operations have greatly increased in number and raise issues such as the role of the United Nations, whether to place U.S. forces under foreign command, burden sharing, and determining when such operations are likely to be effective and, thus, prudent.

• *Supporting counterterrorism efforts and other national security objectives.* During the Cold War, terrorism was often considered an extension of the superpower conflict. Currently terrorism is considered to have many sources and can take a variety of forms. "Other national security objectives" include humanitarian relief missions, hostage rescue operations, and disaster relief.

Just when such operations should be carried out—that is, when U.S. forces should be committed abroad—has been the subject of considerable debate for some time. During the Reagan administration, then Secretary of Defense Caspar Weinberger proposed several conditions to be met before the United States deployed military forces. These conditions were partly a reaction to the 1982–83 U.S. peacekeeping operation in Lebanon in which U.S. Marines originally deployed to monitor a cease-fire became ensnared in the local hostilities and ultimately suffered 268 casualties in the bombing of their barracks in Beirut. The conditions probably also reflected the U.S. experience in Vietnam, which many people believed lacked clear objectives and full commitment.

Since the "Weinberger conditions" were offered, the Bush and Clinton administrations have also addressed this question. The Clinton Administration's conditions for the deployment of U.S. forces consist of four "basic principles."[2]

- National interests will dictate the pace and extent of U.S. engagement; vital interests will dictate decisive and, if necessary, unilateral action; less pressing interests (economic interests, commitments to allies, and situations with the potential for generating refugee flows are cited) will be "targeted selectively."

- The United States will seek the help of allies or multilateral institutions "as much as possible," aiming at a proportional commitment from allies with an interest at stake.

- Questions will be asked prior to committing U.S. forces, including whether nonmilitary means have been considered, whether the American public supports the operation, and whether there are defined measures of success and appropriate exit strategies.

- Any commitment of U.S. forces will have to meet cost and feasibility thresholds.

The Clinton administration's policy for the commitment of U.S. forces has raised several issues in public debates. Several members of Congress expressed concern over U.S. participation in multinational operations because of the possibility that U.S. forces might be required to serve under foreign commanders, who are not directly accountable to the United States, or because U.S. allies might have concerns or objectives inconsistent with those of the United States. Other individuals who took exception to the policy were concerned that the use of U.S. military forces in noncombat relief operations could compromise U.S. capabilities to carry out combat missions effectively. Finally, concerns were expressed over the possibility that an initial commitment of U.S. forces might lead to the unintended escalation of that commitment to more ambitious, riskier objectives—the problem of "mission creep."

In addition to these criticisms of the policy, several specific events also raised questions.

- The loss of thirty-six U.S. military personnel assigned to the UN relief operation in Somalia in 1993 caused critics to question how the initial humanitarian relief mission had escalated into a peacekeeping operation, and whether U.S. forces were adequately prepared.

- The debate over U.S. policy in the former Yugoslavia continues; U.S. allies request that the United States contribute ground troops to the UN peacekeeping forces; the effectiveness of the UN chain of command is being questioned; and, in the end, a major break is occurring between the NATO allies who were carrying most aspects of the peacekeeping operation on behalf of the UN.

- The deployment of U.S. troops to Haiti to restore the regime of Jean-Bertrand Aristide (by force, if necessary) made critics question whether U.S. military personnel should be risked in an operation that many thought was not to be linked to a vital U.S. interest.

- The confrontation with North Korea in 1993–94 about its suspected nuclear weapons program prompted questions over whether the United States had a viable military option to employ in the situation and concerns over U.S. negotiating leverage if it did not.

Whatever the merits of these specific cases, it is clear that questions concerning U.S. policy for committing U.S. forces and how they are to be employed need to be addressed in order to ensure U.S. security in the post–Cold War era.

The Aspen Strategy Group Conference
on the Use of Military Force

The papers in this book were originally presented at the Aspen Strategy Group's annual summer conference on August 14–19, 1994. The objectives of the conference were to identify and analyze the situations in the post–Cold War era in which U.S. military force may be required to protect U.S. interests; to de-

velop guidelines, objectives, and limits for the use of military
force by the United States; and to discuss the process through
which the decision to use force is to be made, ensuring that such
decisions can be made expeditiously while also ensuring effective oversight. In addition, the participants also discussed the
operational requirements for these new missions (both combat
and noncombat) and whether U.S. military services are adequately prepared to meet these requirements.

Question One: When Will the United States Need to Use Military Force and Should It?

In the first paper, Richard Haass, a former member of the
National Security Council staff during the Bush administration,
provides a taxonomy of threats potentially requiring the use
of force by the United States and the types of operations that
U.S. military forces might have to carry out in these situations.
Haass shows that these scenarios can be defined along several
dimensions: the nature of the threat to U.S. interests, the objectives of the United States, the specific function that military forces
are supposed to serve, and so on. He notes that these distinctions
are important, as they have significant implications for U.S.
interests and the ability of military forces to affect the outcome of
a situation.

The next two papers by Charles William Maynes and Steven
David debate whether military forces would be an appropriate
and effective response to such threats. Maynes believes that,
contrary to the expectations of many officials in the early 1990s,
the opportunities for the United States to use military force in the
post–Cold War era are quite limited. Even with the Soviet Union
gone, he writes, there are too many players in the international
community that can prevent the United States from enjoying a
clear field on which to take action. He also believes that military
force rarely leaves a neat solution to a problem, and that this,
combined with the reluctance of the American public to accept
casualties, will further limit the opportunities to use force.
Maynes concludes that, while force might be useful in a small set
of well-defined situations, for the most part, these situations will
be few and far between.

Where Maynes highlights the constraints on the use of force, David highlights the range of situations in which military force might be required. According to David, the post–Cold War world will be full of unstable governments that the United States will be unable to ignore because of the eventual ramifications for U.S. interests. For example, David argues, although intervention may be difficult, the United States may still find it necessary to intervene in the affairs of a collapsing regime that has nuclear weapons because the threat of uncontrolled nuclear weapons is so much greater. The bottom line, according to David, is that the United States will need to develop the capability to defend U.S. interests in an unstable world with military force because the potential economic and strategic risks of not doing so are unacceptably high.

Question Two: How Should the United States Decide to Use Force?

The decision-making process for deploying U.S. forces and, later, controlling their use once deployed, has become a significant issue in the post–Cold War era. During the Vietnam War, Congress asserted that it must have a say in such decisions, and this resulted in statutes such as the War Powers Act that constrain the ability of the president to use U.S. military force.

The executive branch has also struggled with the issue of how it will itself decide when to use military force. As noted, the Reagan, Bush, and Clinton administrations all proposed formal criteria for when military force would be used. In general, these criteria have been more restrictive than expansive, in effect *limiting* the situations in which force could be used. It is important to note that the U.S. military, being most directly affected by the risks and potential costs, have often been the must reluctant segment of the government in decisions to use force and have often asserted the most demanding preconditions.

Decisions to use force have been further complicated by a general acceptance of multilateralism by U.S. leaders, beginning with Desert Shield and affirmed during the Clinton administration in its policy toward military action in Bosnia, Somalia, and Haiti. In effect, the United Nations has been brought into the decision process for deploying U.S. forces. Indeed, the cases of Somalia and Bosnia demonstrate that the UN now often even has a role in decisions affecting the use of these forces once they are deployed.

In addition to the decision-making process inside government, public opinion has become more important than ever in decisions to use force. Modern telecommunications have brought conflicts and the grisly results of combat on U.S. personnel, their opponents, and noncombatants into American living rooms in real time. Many U.S. officials have been concerned that the decision to commit U.S. military forces and decisions concerning their use and withdrawal are being excessively affected by popular opinion driven by the media (i.e., the so-called "CNN phenomenon").

The next three papers examine the different factors that shape the decision-making process for the United States to use military force. James Lindsay, a scholar on Congress, examines the history of relations between the executive and legislative branches of government on the subject of war powers. Lindsay argues that the Cold War increased presidential discretion to commit U.S. military forces because of concerns with the immediate Soviet threat. Thus, the relaxation of superpower tension has been accompanied by Congress reasserting its prerogatives in recent years, as illustrated by the congressional debates over Desert Storm, Somalia, and Haiti. However, Lindsay also argues that there are political and institutional factors that limit the ability or willingness of Congress to confront the president even when it has taken explicit steps to limit presidential authority, as in the case of the War Powers Act.

Jane Holl, a former army officer and, like Haass, a former National Security Council staff member, examines the executive branch process for making decisions to commit U.S. forces and the attempt to define criteria governing such decisions. She notes a basic problem. Traditionally it was argued that U.S. forces should be deployed only to defend vital interests. Because post–Cold War conflicts are inherently less threatening, the United States is more likely to face situations in the gray zone where national survival is rarely at risk.

Holl argues that one cannot avoid the "grayness" of post–Cold War threats and that therefore the United States must be prepared to intervene even in some cases when the stakes for the United States seem less than vital. She believes that there are no hard and fast criteria for deciding when intervention is necessary, and it is the responsibility of the president to make the case. The alternative, she writes, would result in excessive constraints on U.S. options.

Andrew Kohut and Robert Toth of the Times Mirror Center for the People and the Press, a public opinion survey institute, suggest that the president may have difficulty in making the case for intervention in many, if not most, circumstances. Kohut and Toth analyze public opinion concerning intervention and focus particularly on U.S. opinion during the Gulf War, the war in the former Yugoslavia, and the crisis in Somalia.

The conclusions that Kohut and Toth report are at odds with many features of the administration's policy of engagement. They find that the U.S. public supports military action in cases in which clearly vital interests are at stake and is even willing to support providing humanitarian assistance where the risk is low. However, there is significantly less public support for peacekeeping—deploying forces in order to guarantee a cease-fire—and even less for the role of peace*maker*, where the United States would be called upon to impose order on a society that was disintegrating or plagued by civil war.

Question Three: What Are the Limits to the Effectiveness of Force?

The next two papers deal with the implementation of policy. One common problem in government is that, for a number of reasons, real world organizations are unable to implement the carefully considered plans of policy-makers.

Andrew Bacevich, a retired army officer and currently a scholar at the Nitze School of Advanced International Studies, suggests a policy-reality mismatch in many of the current proposals for using military force. It is much easier, he writes, for civilian leaders to devise new missions for the military than for the military to reshape itself to carry out those missions. Operations such as peacekeeping and noncombat humanitarian missions are worlds apart from the assignments that the U.S. armed services have trained for during the past five decades. Bacevich cautions that one cannot simply graft new techniques for limited war and noncombat operations onto military organizations, especially when one considers how military organizations, whose effectiveness is so dependent on institutional culture, are particularly resistant to such changes.

In a second "reality check," Antonia Handler Chayes and Abram Chayes question the basic conceptual model usually used to justify the use of limited military force. According to Chayes and Chayes, U.S. leaders tend to think in terms of an escalation ladder, in which the United States (usually in combination with its allies or an international organization, such as the UN) can respond to a conflict first with diplomatic initiatives, then coercive measures such as economic sanctions, and then, finally, with increasingly intense military action. Indeed, report Chayes and Chayes, this model is even reflected in such institutions as the UN charter.

Alas, according to Chayes and Chayes, such a model usually does not work in practice. It is usually impossible to maintain an international coalition through successive levels of escalation. Often the objectives of the coalition partners are too varied, so while a coalition might support economic sanctions to contain a would-be aggressor, some members might drop out if the coalition tries to move up the next rung and use military force. Still others might be willing to use all-out military measures but might be unwilling to engage in limited measures. Moreover, the use of force may preclude more effective mediation measures later. As a result, Chayes and Chayes argue, the use of military force, the potential use of force, or even coercive measures such as sanctions are narrow, limiting strategies in most post–Cold War crises.

As an alternative, Chayes and Chayes favor a mixed strategy in which diplomacy and mediation play the primary role. They admit that this is not as tidy a response as military action as it does not have a clear-cut objective (other than to avoid violence). However, it can buy time, during which the situation can possibly be defused.

Question Four: What About Other Countries?

The final set of papers provides points of view on the role of military intervention in the policies of Britain, France, and Russia.

Bruce George and Nick Ryan provide a general overview of Britain's experience in military intervention during the Cold War and in the years immediately following. George and Ryan offer insight into the difficulties facing a medium power such as Britain, which has had security interests and commitments throughout the world, and considerably less military capability to protect them. They note that, although experience has repeatedly demonstrated the need for Britain to deploy military forces over far distances (e.g., Southeast Asia, the Middle East, and the South Atlantic during the Cold War and, since the end of the Cold War, the Persian Gulf, Northern Iraq, and the Balkans), budget pressures have constantly left Britain's ability to use military force with little margin to spare. The situation, they say, seems unlikely to improve.

French strategic specialist Dominique Moïsi analyzes France's experience in military intervention in Africa in the relatively short period of the Cold War. According to Moïsi, the issue of intervention must be considered in the context of French colonialism. Indeed, "intervention" is a relatively new phenomenon for France because prior to the early 1960s French military action in the developing world consisted of maintaining civil order in French colonies. In other words, a state has to be independent before other states can intervene in it. Only when it is acknowledged that a state is independent are the controversies associated with intervention encountered, e.g., respect for sovereignty, noninterference in the internal affairs of other nations, the responsibility of developed nations to perform as "caretakers" for "failed" states, etc.

Moïsi goes on to note that France's interests in intervention in its former colonies are, at least in part, an inheritance from the motivations that prompted France to build its colonial empire. French colonies (most of which were in Africa) often had little geopolitical significance and were maintained largely as a result of France seeking to rebuild its national self-esteem after its defeat in the Franco-Prussian War. This connection to the French psyche explains the continuing interest of France in the stability of its former colonies although its recognition of these countries as sovereign states restricts France's actions to circumscribed roles defined by formal treaties.

Moïsi believes that, for the most part, French intervention in Africa has been beneficial, inasmuch as it has generally saved lives, maintained order, and, in some cases, kept former French colonies on course in their development as functioning democracies. However, she also notes that the "times are changing." Younger generations in France are less attached to the former empire than were their parents. Also, the costs of intervention and the attitudes of the rest of the world work against intervention as a viable policy.

Ironically, as the role of intervention in French policy seems to be declining, Sergei Karaganov of the Russian Academy of Science's Institute of Europe suggests that it may be increasing for Russia. In some respects, Russia in 1995 is in a situation similar to France in 1960: it has just lost distant territories formerly under its sovereign control; it continues to have many economic interests in these territories; large numbers of ethnic Russians live in the former territories; and possession of these territories was, at one time, critical to Russia's (in the guise of the Soviet Union) national self-image.

Thus it might not be surprising that Karaganov describes a role for Russia in its so-called "near abroad" that is similar to the role France enjoyed in francophone Africa during the past three decades. Karaganov agrees with the prevailing view that, while the probability of a conflict between the United States and Russia has declined, the world as a whole has become prone to regional conflict. The non-Russian territories of the former Soviet Union have proven especially unstable, with internal unrest or ethnic conflict occurring in Azerbaijan, Georgia, Tajikistan, Armenia, Moldova, and elsewhere.

Karaganov, echoing Moïsi's assessment of French intervention, claims that Russian intervention has "proved to be relatively effective in enforcing and keeping peace in several conflicts that have flared up on the former territory of the Soviet Union." He believes that such intervention has served the interest of the international community as well as that of Russia, and he goes so far as to argue that if Russia is willing to assume the burden of deploying its own forces to these territories, the world community should assist it in funding these expeditions.

Naturally, leaders in some of the countries bordering Russia do not view Russian intervention as benignly as Karaganov. Also Russian intervention raises major issues for U.S. leaders. If they are not willing to accede to a Russian "sphere of influence," are they willing to assume the burden themselves when such unrest may affect U.S. interests or to support local resistance to Russian intervention? Alternatively, if U.S. leaders are willing to accept Russia's claims of a "special interest" in its "near abroad," what are the risks of Russia emerging as a reintegrated superpower that might present a direct threat to the United States?

Observations

Although the participants did not adopt formal conclusions on the basis of the conference, several areas of general agreement emerged on key points. In addition, several differences of opinion are worth citing.

Situations Potentially Requiring the Use of Force. Although the probability of a military conflict with a major power is currently small, most of the participants agreed that, in the post–Cold War era, the United States nevertheless needs the capability to deal with three kinds of situations that might require the use of military forces: a conventional war against a regional threat, low intensity operations, and noncombat operations for which the military have unique organizational or logistic qualifications. This said, however, there was considerably less agreement in prescribing the precise situations in which such forces might be used or whether they would be effective in achieving U.S. objectives.

For example, one of the scenarios that many of the participants agreed might call for the deployment of U.S. military forces into combat is protecting access to natural resources from a regional threat. Yet the participants also noted that, despite concerns over the years that many strategic resources—scarce commodities, rare metals, etc.—could eventually be at risk, so far no one has been able to make a convincing argument that this has occurred or will occur in the near future for any resource other than oil. No other resource presents the same juxtaposition of dependency and vulnerability.

Similarly, while several participants favored developing military capabilities for deterring nations that threaten to develop weapons of mass destruction or, (if such deterrence failed, destroying the facilities associated with these weapons) there was also general agreement that it will be difficult to do so. Detecting covert nuclear weapons programs will require better intelligence capabilities. Developing the capabilities for a credible military option will be even more challenging, and the problem will become worse as countries become more sophisticated in concealing their early efforts to build such weapons. Non-nuclear weapons of mass destruction—namely, chemical and biological weapons—are even more difficult to detect and can even be made by potentially hostile parties other than countries, e.g., terrorist groups and fundamentalist movements.

The participants in the conference did generally agree that little evidence exists to suggest that military intervention can install stable democratic government. Similarly, there is little to suggest that intervention is likely to have much relevance for "green" issues, such as population control or averting environmental damage.

Implications for U.S. Military Capabilities. The "two MRC requirement" is not a perfect yardstick, but most participants seemed satisfied that it embodies the essential characteristics for planning U.S. general purpose military forces. They argued that it is reasonable to assume that if the United States can transport and deploy sufficient forces to win wars in the Middle East and Pacific Rim simultaneously, it should be able to address most other conventional military requirements in the foreseeable future.

In accepting this yardstick, though, some of the participants voiced two concerns. First, they noted, an effective "two MRC force" cannot be built by simply paring down the forces developed to deter the Cold War–era Soviet threat. Some of the requirements for U.S. military forces in regional conflicts are significantly different from those that were needed to deal with the Soviet threat. For example, transportation and mobility will be more important than ever before because pre-positioning of equipment is often not possible, and the potential locations for regional conflicts are widely dispersed.

Second, the "two MRC" requirement" assumes that units are not drawn off from core U.S. forces to carry out other operations. It goes without saying that, if the United States deploys a "two MRC force," and then assigns parts of that force to peacekeeping or humanitarian missions, then it no longer has a two MRC force to deploy in combat operations. Historically, the United States has a tradition of a requirements-reality mismatch in military planning; one particular danger in the post–Cold War era is not counting noncombat operations when planning the size and capabilities of U.S. military forces.

The Role of Multilateralism in U.S. Policy. One point proved as controversial in the conference as in the general public: the role of the United Nations and alliances such as the North Atlantic Treaty Organization (NATO) in U.S. policy. The benefits of cooperation cited by proponents of multilateralism are burden sharing and the "legitimacy" of being sanctioned by an international organization. Skeptics question whether burdens are fairly shared, whether the United States is constrained excessively by having to cooperate in multinational initiatives, and whether U.S. officials responsible for the safety of their military personnel can maintain control of U.S. forces assigned to multinational operations.

The area of agreement on this issue seems to be that, despite the difficulties of assembling and maintaining an international coalition, multilateralism is at least *sometimes* in the U.S. interest. Therefore, the United States has a long-term interest in supporting international institutions at least to the extent that they will be available when needed.

The Relationship between Military Force and Diplomacy. It was also generally agreed that policy-makers often do not fully appreciate the linkage between military force and diplomacy.

However, two very different views were expressed on how they misunderstand the relationship.

According to the first view, policy-makers mistakenly believe that diplomacy and force are rungs on an escalation ladder, with mediation, sanctions, blockades, surgical strikes, and full-scale military operations representing more or less ordinal levels of pressure that can be used to push conflicting parties into a settlement. In fact, according to this view, there usually is no ladder of escalation because real world factors preclude one or more rungs, and, in any case, undertaking one alternative now often prevents the undertaking of one or more other alternatives later.

Moreover, according to this view, multilateral force is likely to be impractical as a means to settle conflicts because of the time required to assemble a coalition and the constraints that the various members will impose on its actions. Unilateral force, on the other hand, is likely to be ineffective (at least in the long run) and will lack international legitimacy. Therefore, say those who hold this position, it is best to intervene early with mediation to settle conflicts, leaving the threat of force in the background, to be used, if necessary, to get the parties to the negotiating table.

Those who hold the second view, also believe policy-makers misconstrue the linkage between diplomacy and military force but in a quite different way. According to this view, policy-makers mistakenly consider military force as a *less preferred alternative* to be used when diplomacy fails.

Quite the contrary, according to those arguing this second position, diplomacy is, in fact *dependent* on the threat to use force. They would likely quote Walter Bedell Smith, who argued "Diplomacy has rarely been able to gain at the conference table what cannot be won or held on the battlefield." Successful U.S. diplomacy thus depends on effective U.S. military capability and the credibility that the United States will use force, if necessary. According to this view, having to resort to military force usually does not imply that diplomacy failed, but rather that military measures were not sufficiently convincing.

Thus, according to this argument, the United States must concentrate its efforts in two areas in order to avoid the need to resort to force: maintain sufficient, appropriate military forces, and conduct U.S. diplomacy in such a way that the United States is convincing when it suggests that it will use force. In this view, if U.S. planning for military action in the post–Cold War era is successful, military action will not be necessary.[3]

The conference did not square this circle. It would appear that the gap is quite large, and there are basic differences in the assumptions by the two sides about the nature of post–Cold War conflicts and the nature of parties involved in such conflicts.

The Importance of Presidential Leadership. No current adversary threatens U.S. interests as clearly as the Soviet Union did during the Cold War. Today, threats to the United States are likely to be longer term, less obvious, and, thus, less convincing. Moreover, as has been seen, the American public is reluctant to send U.S. troops to defend interests that are "less than vital."

In this situation, the participants agreed, the role of the president in making the argument for U.S. intervention when it is truly needed becomes more important than ever. Moreover, because post–Cold War threats will not be linked to a single adversary, as was the case in Soviet expansionism, the president will need to make the argument for intervention case by case, explaining each time why the United States is risking U.S. forces and how the operation will protect U.S. interests.

In order to succeed in this task, the president will need at least two assets, both of which must be prepared in advance: a long-range strategy that puts each individual case requiring the use of U.S. military force into an overall context, and a broad-based consensus among the American public that supports this strategy. Although the Clinton Administration has offered a strategy that attempts to explain the need for U.S. military intervention in the post–Cold War era, it is not at all clear that this strategy enjoys a consensus.

It was this type of broad, long-term consensus that supported the U.S. policy of containment for four decades and enabled it to withstand the stress of time, expenditures, and the inevitable occasional setbacks. As a result, identifying the core set of interests that the public is willing to support in the post–Cold War era may be the most pressing requirement to be met before the United States can develop a coherent, effective policy for the use of military force.

NOTES

1. See Bill Clinton "A National Security Strategy of Engagement and Enlargement" (Washington, D.C.: U.S. Government Printing Office, July 1994),.pp. 6, 18–20. Also see Anthony Lake, "From Containment to Enlargement," speech delivered at Johns Hopkins University School of Advanced International Study, September 21, 1993.
2. See Clinton, "A National Security Strategy of Engagement and Enlargement," p. 10.
3. Kenneth W. Dam, "Law, Diplomacy and Force: North Korea and the Bomb," paper presented as the Wilber G. Katz Lecture at the University of Chicago Law School, November 3, 1994. Also see Richard K. Betts, "The Delusions of Imperial Intervention," *Foreign Affairs*, Vol. 73, No. 6 (November/December 1994), pp. 20–33. Betts analyzes recent experience in peacekeeping, noting that it is least likely to succeed when the peacekeeping mission itself is expected to resolve the underlying difference that led to the dispute without reference as to whether one side or the other has a reasonable expectation of achieving its objectives through continued military action.

1

Military Intervention: A Taxonomy of Challenges and Responses

Richard N. Haass

The post–Cold War world is already proving to be markedly different than the new world order envisioned or at least hoped for by many just a few years ago. The possibility of global nuclear conflict is mercifully more remote, but the specter of frequent armed conflicts involving states or factions within a state is all too real. All of these conflicts will involve interests of some importance to the United States, although the nature and significance of such interests will necessarily vary considerably, as will the nature of any conflict and how it is fought. What is certain, though, is that the emerging world will create numerous and difficult challenges and choices for U.S. foreign policy, one of which will be whether and how to use military force to further U.S. goals.

It is impossible and arguably unwise to try to determine in advance exactly where and how the United States would use military force. But it is possible and valuable to think hard about two sets of questions, if only to make sure that forces and plans are appropriate and adequate and that policy-makers and the public are informed and prepared. First, what sorts of situations are likely to arise in the post–Cold War world in which U.S. military intervention could become a serious policy option? Second, what constitutes the range of possible military responses to such situations? This paper addresses both questions, not to come up with prescriptions for policy, but rather to provide the raw material from which policy judgments can be made.

1

THE RANGE OF THREATS

Potential scenarios for the use of force by the United States in the foreseeable future begin with classic, interstate aggression. For example, it is possible imagining a North Korean invasion of South Korea or an attack by Iran or Iraq upon Kuwait, Saudi Arabia, or several other Gulf states. A third traditional scenario for the potential use of force—although one less likely than those just mentioned—raises more problems given the nature of the potential aggressor: a resurgent Russia bent on reclaiming or reconstructing parts of the former Soviet empire, especially in the Baltics or Eastern Europe.[1]

What all of these possible scenarios have in common is their traditional, interstate character. At issue are specific interests as well as the basic organizing principle of international society, that of defending state sovereignty against external aggression. In all cases there are borders—clear divisions between the territory of the attacking state and the attacked. There is a status quo ante that can be restored.

At the other end of the spectrum (in terms of scale) are potential interventions that are clear in importance and purpose but limited in scope and duration. Under this heading might come hostage rescues, limited punitive reprisals against terrorists or states supporting them, and interdiction on behalf of sanctions, narcotics policy, or for purposes of regulating immigration.

Far more difficult (yet still easy to foresee) are possible calls for military intervention in circumstances sure to be as controversial as they are complex. One set of scenarios involves preventive strikes by the United States against terrorist facilities, or, more likely, against the unconventional military capabilities of another state. This is the sort of situation posed by North Korea today and potentially posed by such rogue actors as Iran, Iraq, and Libya.

A second set of potentially controversial undertakings would involve U.S. participation in peacekeeping missions, especially in the Middle East and Bosnia. A U.S. presence on the Golan Heights to buttress an Israeli-Syrian peace treaty could well be desired by the protagonists. Also sure to be sought—in this case by the European Union and possibly by some of the parties to the dispute—is a U.S. contribution, including ground forces, to any international force sent to Bosnia to monitor and possibly help maintain a political and territorial settlement.

A third set of difficult challenges involves intervening in the internal affairs of others, that is, intrastate scenarios. These would be for humanitarian or political purposes and could include operations to protect or help a population threatened by another faction or the government (as in Rwanda), to overthrow a government (as was done in Panama), to bolster a government (as was done in the Philippines), to establish order and authority where little or none exists (as was tried in Somalia), and/or to rebuild a society (as in Haiti).

THE RANGE OF RESPONSES

Armed interventions can be defined as *the introduction or deployment of new or additional combat forces to an area for specific purposes that go beyond ordinary training or scheduled expressions of support for national interests.* Excluded here are indirect uses of military force, i.e., those involving the provision of military assistance (training, arms, intelligence, etc.) to another party so that it may employ force directly for its own purposes. Military interventions can and do differ in their scale, composition, duration, intensity, authority, and, above all, objective. They need not involve "shooting." As a result, a range of possible military interventions includes the following.

Deterrent

The standard definition of deterrence is "the persuasion of one's opponent that the costs and/or risks of a given course of action he might take outweigh its benefits."[2] The movement and use of military forces are obviously a critical component of a deterrence strategy. Forces can be positioned, deployed, and/or exercised to signal the existence of interests and the readiness to respond if those interests are either threatened or attacked.

Deterrence can be the purpose behind long-term deployments, such as the U.S. military presence on the Korean Peninsula or in Europe since the end of World War II. Such deployments are structural, to remain until the political map or international situation fundamentally changes. The decision to place several hundred U.S. troops in Macedonia in early 1993 and the maintenance of air forces in southern Turkey so as to discourage Iraq from attacking its Kurdish population are more recent examples of this phenomenon.

Deterrence can also take the form of a response to a specific or tactical situation that emerges suddenly, say, the perceived threat to shipping in the Gulf in the late 1980s when the United States decided to "reflag" Kuwaiti vessels or the stationing of U.S. and coalition forces in Saudi Arabia under *Desert Shield* to deter Iraqi aggression against Saudi Arabia or other Gulf countries following the invasion of Kuwait. An unsuccessful example of such "tactical" (as opposed to "strategic") deterrence was the United States and the United Arab Emirates tanker exercise that failed to dissuade Iraq from invading Kuwait. It is also possible to point to situations in which tactical deterrence was not used; for example, forces might have been inserted into Kuwait in July 1990 to deter the Iraqi invasion or into both Croatia and Bosnia in 1991 to deter the Serbs. It is for this reason that United Nations Secretary General Boutros Boutros-Ghali describes such interventions as "preventive deployments."[3]

Preventive

Preventive uses of force are those that seek to stop the evolution of a military capability belonging to another state or party before it becomes threatening or to hobble or destroy it at any time. The intelligence or warning involved is strategic or long-term for the would-be attacker. Preventive attacks are the proverbial "bolt out of the blue" from the perspective of the target country. What Israel did against Iraq's Osirak nuclear reactor complex in 1981 would qualify. Some of what the *Desert Storm* coalition did against Iraqi unconventional warfare capabilities inside Iraq was a preventive employment of force in that the capabilities targeted were not yet in a state of development to affect the course of this battle.

Closely related to preventive uses of force are *preemptive* actions. The difference is one of timing and context. Preemptive uses of force come against a backdrop of tactical intelligence or warning indicating imminent military action by an adversary and constitute actions or attacks before the other side acts or attacks or even after hostilities have begun but the targeted forces have not been introduced into battle. Unlike preventive strikes, preemptive strikes take place in an immediate context in which hostilities are about to begin or are under way. Israel's air strikes against its Arab neighbors in June 1967 are an example. Another example would be what the United States did in 1983 in Grenada (a preemptive rescue mission) and to some extent in Panama in 1989. One reality that preemptive and preventive strikes share is that they can raise political problems with skeptical publics at home and abroad. It is important to be able to demonstrate the necessity of acting, to make the case that the costs and risks of striking were less than those of holding back, and to prepare for any possible retaliation.

Compellent

Compellent uses of force are discrete, consciously limited uses of force designed to sway decision making. Compellent interventions seek to destroy some carefully chosen targets of value (in the eyes of the people or leadership of the targeted country) or at least demonstrate an ability to destroy such targets. The goal is to persuade the adversary to alter its calculus, to reassess whether its offending actions are worth the potential cost, and to change its behavior as a result.

It is important not to confuse compellence with deterrence. Robert Art provides the following guide: "The distinction between compellence and deterrence is one between the active and passive use of force. The success of a deterrent threat is measured by its not having to be used. The success of a compellent action is measured by how closely and quickly the adversary conforms to one's stipulated wishes."[4]

Of the two, compellence generally tends to be the more difficult, both to carry out and to achieve. As Thomas Schelling has pointed out, "Compellence . . . usually involves initiating an action . . . the overt act, the first step, is up to the side that makes the compellent threat."[5] But if compellence (as compared to deterrence) requires more of the doer, it also asks more of the recipient. Here Scott Sagan makes an important observation. "A state that is deterred can deny that it ever had the intention of attacking another; a state that is coerced into changing its behavior, however, often faces the loss of prestige that comes from having publicly succumbed to pressure from another power."[6] As a result, successful compellence can require a complementary set of concessions, real or face-saving, to make it politically possible for the target of the effort to comply.

Historical analysis suggests that compellence is more likely to succeed if the goal is specific and relatively modest—to persuade an adversary to stop doing something—than if the goal is more ambitious, say, to have an adversary reverse what it has already done. Bringing about a change in the adversary's general behavior or in its nature or political composition is that much more difficult to achieve. Other critical factors that appear to determine the prospects for compellence are the perceived balance of interests—compellence tends not to work if the issue is of greater importance to the adversary—and the local or immediate (as opposed to potential) military equation.[7]

A compellent use of force, depending upon the targets selected, may have residual military benefits, for example, in destroying forces that could be brought to bear on a battlefield, but this is secondary. Again, the goal is to target and possibly destroy some of what the other side values. It can be facilities closely tied to the political and/or military leadership, key economic installations, something that would weaken the leadership in the eyes of its public, or simply a demonstration of the willingness and ability to attack successfully any of these things. This is the sort of effort tried (albeit half-heartedly) by the United States in the early 1980s in Lebanon against various militias and the Syrians and is the approach suggested by some for the former Yugoslavia, i.e., air strikes against selected targets in Belgrade. Compellence—to intimidate Haiti's military leaders into stepping down—was also a principal motivation behind U.S. military exercises and preparations undertaken in the summer of

1994. That it appeared to succeed may have reflected the overwhelming force involved.

One characteristic of compellent uses of force and one shared by deterrence is that their success depends entirely upon the target of the intervention. What is relevant is not the force used but the reaction to it. It is impossible to know in advance whether a given use of force will have the desired effect. If it does not and if the unwanted behavior persists, the choice becomes one of admitting failure, with all the immediate and long-term costs this entails, or escalating, be it by resorting to ever greater amounts of force in the hope of achieving compellence or by undertaking another form of intervention.

One traditional example or mode of compellence is gunboat diplomacy. The classic definition comes from James Cable: "Gunboat diplomacy is the use or threat of use of limited naval force, otherwise than as an act of war, in order to secure advantage, or to avert loss, either in the furtherance of an international dispute or else against foreign nationals within the territory or the jurisdiction of their own state."[8] The definition is somewhat too narrow; there is no reason that it be confined to naval forces. Modern air forces can and do perform much the same function as demonstrated by the United States in the Philippines. But the lack of recent case studies suggests that the days of gunboat diplomacy may be waning, possibly because of the proliferation of military power and doubts about U.S. credibility in the aftermath of several unsuccessful interventions (or decisions not to intervene). The likely consequence is that for compellence to work it will require actual uses of military force, and considerable ones at that.

Punitive

Punitive actions are uses of military force designed to inflict pain and cost, that is, to make the opponent pay a price for his behavior. They do not reverse what has been done by the side that is the target of the attack whether because matters cannot be reversed (say, a terrorist incident), because the battlefield is not an area where the direct use of force looks advantageous, or because a restoration of the status quo ante is deemed insufficient. Nor can punitive attacks guarantee any particular future behavior by the target country. Indeed, they can stimulate further hostile action—it is partly for this reason that the Carter administration decided against carrying out punitive attacks against Iran in retaliation for its hostage taking—or they may achieve just the opposite. There is no way that the result can be predicted with confidence.

Punitive attacks require something not always available: clear evidence of who was responsible for the offending action. Such proof is necessary to persuade skeptical publics in the United States and in other countries. It is noteworthy that the Clinton administration eschewed any punitive actions in the wake of the February 1994 bombing of the Sarajevo marketplace when it could not point to evidence that would confirm its suspicions of Serbian responsibility. By contrast, the Clinton administration did undertake a punitive attack against Iraq in 1993 when it received what it believed to be persuasive evidence of Iraqi complicity in an attempt to assassinate President George Bush, just as the Reagan administration bombed Libya in 1986 when it determined that Libya was responsible for a terrorist attack in Berlin.

Punitive actions are quintessentially political in nature. They are designed to make a point, not change the situation created by the adversary's provocation. Unlike a compellent use of force in which the object or target of the exercise in effect determines whether the force used is effective, punitive uses of force leave the initiative in the hands of the party actually intervening. The determination of "how much is enough" becomes arbitrary, designed as much to satisfy oneself (and one's own public) as anything else.

Punitive attacks can be proportionate or disproportionate. In the case of the June 1993 retaliation against Iraq for mounting an attempt on President Bush's life, the Clinton administration chose to emphasize what it judged to be the proportionate nature of its response. (The Clinton administration also threatened extremely modest attacks in the event that its February 1994 ultimatum regarding Sarajevo was violated.) The Reagan administration carried out proportionate strikes against Iran when it interfered with Gulf shipping. That all these cases represent proportionality reflects the realities of coalition politics, as anything deemed disproportionate would have risked creating problems for coalition solidarity. Alternatively, punitive attacks can be larger than (disproportionate to) what was done by the adversary. (For years, this was Israel's stated policy when it responded to terrorist attacks.) In such circumstances, punitive attacks take on something of a compellent or deterrent quality. As a result, public presentation of the purposes behind a punitive attack becomes most important and can be the only thing that differentiates a punitive from a compellent use of force.

Peacekeeping

Peacekeeping involves the deployment of unarmed or at most lightly armed forces in a largely if not entirely peaceful or permissive environment, normally to buttress a fragile or brittle political arrangement between two or more contending parties. Peacekeeping takes place under Chapter VI of the UN Charter involving the "pacific settlement of disputes" as opposed to Chapter VII and its provisions for enforcement involving "action with respect to threats to the peace, breaches of the peace, and acts of aggression." Peacekeepers might be called upon to monitor a separation of forces, monitor or verify troop withdrawals, or supervise or provide security for an election. Peacekeepers are also called upon to perform additional and more demanding functions, but many of these go beyond the traditional definition and capabilities of peacekeepers and therefore deserve separate consideration.[9]

Peacekeepers are impartial. They are also relatively passive, i.e., they are more monitors and observers than true keepers of the peace in that their ability to keep peace depends almost entirely upon consent. Any use of force on their part would come only as a last resort and normally only for purposes of self-defense. As William Durch and Barry Blechman have wryly noted, "Peacekeeping operations cannot get off the ground without the support of the great powers, and can't do well *on* the ground without the support of all local parties."[10] Peacekeeping thus involves the use of force in a largely consensual environment in which *at most* there are periodic, relatively isolated and small-scale breakdowns of the peace. By definition, such challenges are not conducted or backed by governments or principal parties to the agreement.[11] If they were, something more than peacekeeping, namely peacemaking, would be called for.

War-fighting

At the opposite end of the spectrum is war-fighting. This is the high end of intervention and involves full-fledged combat operations. Such fighting is still limited in one or more ways—geography, the means employed, and/or the ends to which they are employed. Nevertheless, what distinguishes war-fighting is that it brings to bear whatever forces are available and deemed necessary to dominate the confrontation by attacking enemy forces on the battlefield and those forces located elsewhere that could be introduced to affect it. Korea was an example of war-fighting although with significant self-imposed restraint; so too arguably was Vietnam although here the restraint was so pronounced that at times the U.S. effort constituted something less, more like peacemaking. More recent and less restrained examples of war-fighting were Grenada, Panama, and *Desert Storm*.

Peacemaking

Peacemaking is an imprecise and misleading term probably because it is associated with both peace and peacekeeping when in fact it has little to do with either. Indeed, some observers have suggested the whole notion be jettisoned because it creates a perception so at variance with reality.[12] Some in the U.S. military prefer the phrase "aggravated peacekeeping."[13] Still others define peacemaking in a manner that encompasses a host of activities, including diplomacy and sanctions, designed to help bring about conditions of peace.[14]

Here, the term peacemaking is used to cover activities falling between peacekeeping and war-fighting. What distinguishes it from both is mostly context. To use U.S. military terminology, peacemaking takes place in an environment characterized as "uncertain" rather than either "permissive" or "hostile." Unlike pure war-fighting or combat where the goal is to inflict significant destruction on the adversary, peacemaking is still carried out with measurable restraint. Much greater emphasis is placed on limiting the scope of the combat (rather than trying to solve the problem with a massive use of force) and on restoring or creating an environment in which resistance to peace becomes marginal and allows peacekeepers to operate.

The reason for accepting military constraints tends to derive from the inherent messiness of the situation and above all from the absence of a single adversary and a defined battlefield in which the adversary can be engaged on a significant scale. The corollary to this is that peacemaking often involves one or more local parties to the dispute that are friendly or neutral and a geographical context in which the hostile parties cannot be isolated from them. The option of war-fighting is thus either not available or brings with it severe costs.

It is no less important to distinguish peacemaking from more modest forms of intervention, particularly peacekeeping. *Peacekeeping* is appropriate where all the major parties to the dispute accept an arrangement and the presence of outside troops; any challenges to the peace will at most be marginal and done without the support of a major protagonist. *Peacemaking* assumes the opposition of at least one of the principal protagonists to the status quo, opposition to the presence of outsiders, or both. As a result, and unlike peacekeepers, peace-makers must be heavily armed and be prepared to overcome considerable resistance. They work in a nonconsensual environment but one of threats that tend to be limited in strength, frequency, and duration. It is a transitional role, one that, if successful, should give way to true peacekeeping and/or nation-building.

It is critical that peacemaking not be underestimated. As one observer correctly notes, "It is in the gray area between peacekeeping and all-out war-fighting that the United Nations has gotten itself into serious trouble. The trouble stems from the fact that the United Nations has misapplied perfectly good tools to inappropriate circumstances."[15] The U.S./UN intervention in Somalia became one of peacemaking in the spring and summer of 1993 but failed in part because the forces were capable of little more than peacekeeping. The same can be said of the second multinational force sent to Lebanon in 1982. Peacemaking is an option in Bosnia, but the requirements for implementing it would be enormous given the nature of the situation.

It is also useful to distinguish between peacemaking and *policing*. Police missions involve the deployment of forces in a quasi-hostile environment in which terrorism and small arms are the essential threats. It does not require consent on the part of any party or parties, nor does it require a peace to keep, enforce, or make. What the British are doing in Northern Ireland is the best example. Policing is a damage-limiting operation, one designed neither to defeat opposition nor to solve underlying causes. As a result, it tends to be open-ended in that it seeks to place a ceiling on violence to provide a constructive backdrop or environment in which diplomacy can operate or at least in which daily life is made tolerable for most of the inhabitants.

Nation-building

Nation-building (or "peace building" in the lexicon of the UN Secretary General) is a highly intrusive form of intervention, one that seeks to bring about political leadership and, more important, procedures and institutions different from those that exist. In the case of the United States, nation-building seeks to encourage and sustain democratic and free-market practices. The effort requires a monopoly on the use of force until local units can be created to assume the responsibility. It can be a purpose of (and require) occupation.[16]

Nation-building is an option for dealing with failed states once any resistance is overcome through peacemaking or exhaustion. Similarly, nation-building is an option for dealing with defeated states; indeed, nation-building is what the United States did in Germany and Japan after the Second World War, and, on a far more modest scale, what the United States did in Grenada and Panama. The Bush administration eschewed this course of action in Iraq in the spring of 1991 and later on in both Somalia and Haiti; the Clinton administration, on the other hand, experimented with this option in Somalia before returning to more modest aims and initiated it in Haiti in September 1994.

Interdiction

This is a discrete use of force to prevent specified equipment, resources, goods, or persons from reaching a battlefield, port, or terminal. Interdiction can be done from the air as well as the sea. It can be for purposes of sanctions enforcement; both the maritime multinational force (MNF) operating vis-a-vis Iraq since the summer of 1990 and the earlier multinational effort against Rhodesia come to mind. It can also be done for purposes of law enforcement and is being conducted by the U.S. Coast Guard and other agencies to limit the influx of narcotics or illegal aliens into the United States. Haiti is an example of interdiction used to keep goods out of Haiti and Haitians out of the United States.

Humanitarian

Humanitarian operations involve the deployment of forces to save lives without necessarily altering the political context. Such operations can entail the delivery of basic human services where the central authority is unable or unwilling to do so, the evacuation of selected peoples—for example, the first deployment of marines to evacuate the Palestine Liberation Organization (PLO) from Beirut—or the protection of a people from governmental or other forces.

Humanitarian interventions can be of two sorts: consensual (requiring unarmed or lightly armed personnel) or imposed (requiring heavily armed troops). A consensual humanitarian operation is one conducted within a permissive environment where uniformed forces are involved only for technical reasons, i.e., they possess skills and capabilities to sustain people in difficult conditions. One sees this after natural disasters; it was also the approach planned but aborted by the Clinton administration in Haiti in the autumn of 1993.

An imposed humanitarian intervention, by contrast, is one that is carried out in an uncertain or hostile environment. It is humanitarian in that its aims are narrow, to provide food and/ or other life-sustaining supplies (as well as protection) to peoples. It does not seek to change the overall political authority, but rather to minimize suffering until either the authority or its policies change. It is a military operation in that force must be available to protect those delivering aid, to deter and defend against attacks on both the forces involved and on civilians, and to retaliate, be it to punish those interfering, reduce, or eliminate their capacity to interfere, and/or deter them from additional attempts at interference. This is the sort of operation being carried out in northern Iraq since mid-April 1991 and akin to what was introduced around Sarajevo in early 1994.

To carry out an imposed humanitarian intervention at an acceptable cost, it can be useful to establish geographic zones or safe havens that provide an environment in which supplies can be introduced and people can be reached—all in an area easily defended. Such safe havens can be created as a magnet for people, or (and this is preferable) they can be established where the endangered people are if they happen to be concentrated in one or only a few places. Air forces and a modest number of ground forces are required to protect the humanitarian area or areas—to make a safe haven safe—and air forces may be called upon to carry out punitive attacks on those who violate its terms.

The models here are northern Iraq and Somalia early on in the course of the U.S. or UN intervention. (The establishment of a no-fly zone over Bosnia-Herzegovina and then an exclusion zone around Sarajevo and other designated cities offers another ex-ample although the effectiveness was mitigated by the delay in introducing safe havens and in the way they were implemented.) The concept has four parts: protection for people who would otherwise be victims—something not to be confused with be-coming a military protagonist or partner in a civil war; separation of the warring parties and moving them beyond a range in which their weapons can reach one another; working around any significant resistance, not overcoming it; and requiring that those being protected forgo using the zones as military bases to change the situation outside lest the forces administering the safe havens find themselves caught in a cross fire.

Obvious costs and drawbacks are associated with this ap-proach. Humanitarian zones are open-ended, offering no guar-anteed exit date for those who maintain them. Such commit-ments necessarily drain troops and equipment that would otherwise be available for other purposes. There will be casualties. Except in those situations where an endangered population already exists in one area, establishing zones can either fail to protect some people or force them to migrate to safety, thereby rewarding the aggressor. Most of all, humanitarian zones are limited in what they propose to and can accomplish. Humanitarian interventions are just that. They should never be confused with more ambitious political interventions, especially peacemaking and nation-building. They are designed to provide a respite from the problem at an affordable cost, not a solution to it. They are open-ended until the politics of the situation evolve, and the aggressor indicates a willingness to change his ways, or the protected party chooses to mount a counterattack rather than accept protection.

The principal alternative to humanitarian interventions of one or another sort (besides doing nothing) is to overcome resistance with one or another form of military intervention, be it peacemaking, compellence, and/or war-fighting. Somalia is a case where the United States undertook a humanitarian operation that then evolved into something more (peacemaking) when resistance was encountered; the problem was the failure of the United States and the United Nations either to scale back the mission or to provide the forces to back up the new mission. The UN mission to the former Yugoslavia was for nearly two years an example of how humanitarian intervention encounters difficulty when it operates in a nonconsensual environment but is unwilling to adopt the means of more aggressive forms of intervention.

Rescue

Rescue operations are a form of humanitarian intervention but sufficiently special to merit separate treatment. They are actions sharply limited in both scale and, more important, purpose, taken in what must be assumed to be a hostile environment, for instance, hostage rescue missions. The failed attempt in 1980 to rescue the U.S. hostages in Iran is an example; so too are extractions of persons viewed as vulnerable to becoming hostages. Liberia is a textbook example. Against a backdrop of escalating civil conflict and mounting threats to the U.S. embassy and U.S. personnel and citizens, the United States dispatched naval and marine forces (some two thousand of the latter) to Liberia in June 1990. Some Americans were evacuated right away using commercial aircraft in a relatively permissive environment; over one thousand others were not evacuated until August in a situation far more complicated—one requiring well-armed marines to assert visible control of the embassy area.[17] What makes the Iranian hostage rescue attempt and Liberia classic rescue missions was the absence of any direct or indirect involvement in internal politics. Rescue missions are narrowly focused; for this reason, Grenada was not a rescue mission but rather something broader.

CONCLUSIONS

As was stated at the outset, the purpose of this paper is to present likely challenges and a menu of potential military responses. This paper does not prescribe particular courses of action in particular circumstances. This said, a number of conclusions with policy relevance emerge that merit highlighting.

First, there will be many opportunities to intervene in the future. Most of these will involve problems within states, which tend to be more difficult and less amenable to being fixed by military force.

Second, consistency of means and ends is essential for an intervention to succeed. It is also essential to take into account the likely political and military environment. Goals, forces, and threats must all be in balance. In many situations, this will require that forces be increased or goals scaled back.

Third, policy-makers must be careful not to underestimate the requirements of peacemaking or confuse it with peacekeeping. Peacekeeping is essentially a political undertaking in a permissive context; peacemaking is a military undertaking in a context that includes active resistance.

Fourth, peacemaking is not the only military option in situations where people are threatened by their government or their fellow citizens. Humanitarian interventions involving the establishment of safe havens until the situation evolves offer an alternative to doing nothing or to more ambitious efforts.

Fifth, some purposes for intervening may be mutually exclusive if attempted at the same time. For example, a compellent use of force may make it impossible to carry out simultaneous peacekeeping or a consensual humanitarian operation. Sequential operations, however, are not only possible but often necessary if a context must be created for an operation requiring little or no local resistance.

One last point deserves mention. The emphasis of this paper on military intervention is not meant to imply that military force is always the most appropriate tool. It may be in particular cases, but it needs to pass muster on its own merits—an intervention must not only be desirable but feasible, both worth doing and doable—and it needs to provide a better ratio of likely costs to benefits than the alternatives. In this, military intervention is no different from any other policy choice except that the stakes tend to be greater.

NOTES

1. It is also possible to imagine Russian military involvement in Ukraine and Central Asia. For a host of reasons, including geography, politics, and the presence of nuclear weapons, these areas would not be good locales for the United States to try to intervene with military force. By contrast, defending either the Baltics or Eastern Europe would be a natural undertaking for North Atlantic Treaty Organization (NATO).
2. Alexander L. George and Richard Smoke, *Deterrence in American Foreign Policy: Theory and Practice* (New York: Columbia University Press, 1974), p. 11.
3. See Boutros Bourtros-Ghali, *Agenda For Peace* (New York: United Nations, 1992), pp. 16–17.
4. Robert J. Art, "The Four Functions of Force," in Robert J. Art and Kenneth N. Waltz, eds, *The Use of Force: Military Power and International Politics*, 4th ed. (Lanham, Md.: University Press of America, 1993), p. 6.
5. Thomas C. Schelling, *Arms and Influence* (New Haven: Yale University Press, 1966), p. 72.
6. Scott D. Sagan, "From Deterrence to Coercion to War: The Road to Pearl Harbor," in Alexander L. George and William E. Simons, *The Limits of Coercive Diplomacy* (Boulder: Westview, 1994), p. 84.

7. See the contributions by Alexander George (especially pp. 124–125) and Bruce W. Jentleson (especially pp. 176–180) in ibid. Also see Barry M. Blechman and Stephen S. Kaplan, *Force Without War: U.S. Armed Forces as a Political Instrument* (Washington, D.C.: Brookings, 1978).

8. James Cable, *Gunboat Diplomacy* (London: Chatto & Windus, 1971), p. 21.

9. A good short introduction to the subject is Brian Urquhart, "Beyond the 'Sheriff's Posse'," *Survival*, Vol. 32, No. 3 (May/June 1990), pp. 196–205.

10. William J. Durch and Barry M. Blechman, *Keeping the Peace: The United Nations in the Emerging World Order* (Washington, D.C.: Stimson Center, 1992), p. ii.

11. See John Mackinlay, "Powerful Peace–keepers," *Survival*, Vol. 32, No. 3 (May/June 1990), pp. 241–250.

12. See, for example, Michael Lind, "Peacefaking," *New Republic*, Vol. 209, No. 19 (Nov. 8, 1993), pp. 14–17.

13. See Barry R. McCaffrey, "U.S. Military Support for Peacekeeping Operations," in Dennis J. Quinn, ed., *Peace Support Operations and the U.S. Military* (Washington, D.C.: NDU Press, 1994), p. 5.

14. See Boutros-Ghali, *Agenda for Peace*, pp. 20–25. This definition of peacemaking, one that encompasses a good deal of diplomacy, is too broad to be of much use. Similarly, the term "peace enforcement" is better left unused. It may reflect a legal and political context in that military force is being employed to bring about or enforce some agreement or resolution, but it says nothing about what kind of force is required or how it is to be employed.

15. John Gerard Ruggie, "Wandering in the Void: Charting the U.N.'s New Strategic Role," *Foreign Affairs*, Vol. 72, No. 6 (November/December 1993), p. 28.

16. See Gerald B. Helman and Steven R. Ratner, "Saving Failed States," *Foreign Policy*, No. 89 (Winter 1992–93), pp. 3–20. The authors advocate re-creating UN trusteeships for failed states, using less tainted terms such as conservatorship or guardianship.

17. For background on the Liberia operation, see T.W. Parker, "Operation Sharp Edge," *U.S. Naval Institute Proceedings*, Vol. 117, No. 5 (May 1991), pp. 102–106. For background on the Liberian situation more generally, see David Wippman, "Enforcing the Peace: ECOWAS and the Liberian Civil War," in Lori Fisler Damrosch, ed., *Enforcing Restraint: Collective Intervention in Internal Conflicts* (New York: Council on Foreign Relations, 1993), pp. 157–203.

2

The Limitations of Force

Charles William Maynes

The combination of the Gulf War and the demise of Soviet communism had a profound impact on U.S. discussions of the use of force. For a while it seemed as though the U.S. military was liberated or at least many observers implied this. The United States, they said, was the world's sole remaining superpower. It could intervene wherever it wished without worrying that another global rival would back the other side and risk escalating a local conflict into a global conflagration.

The demonstration in the Gulf War of astounding new technology contributed to the view that the use of force for policy goals was now much more feasible. Soon-to-be Secretary of Defense Les Aspin noted in a September 21, 1992, speech that in the Gulf War it often took only one bomb to destroy a target whereas in World War II it had required an average of 9,000 and in Vietnam 175.[1] The Pentagon official in charge of estimating casualties in the Gulf War wrote that the experience in Kuwait suggested the possibility of "war without excessive brutality."[2]

The vision was intoxicating. The United States had arrived at its "unipolar moment," according to conservative columnist Charles Krauthammer.[3] Aspin predicted that the United States could now develop a military force "flexible enough to do a number of simultaneous, smaller contingencies."[4]

It should be clear by now that this widely-shared optimism was badly misplaced. It is important to understand why. The reasons are several: The demise of the Soviet Union did not give the United States the clear field internationally that was earlier predicted; the new consensus failed to take into account whether the gains derived from the use of force had remained constant—in fact, they have gone down; and the United States failed to take into account that the very purpose of threatening to use force had changed. Earlier the purpose was deterrence and acceptable external behavior. Now it was compellence and appropriate internal behavior.

A CLEAR FIELD?

Although it is true that the United States no longer has the Soviet Union to worry about, it is not necessarily the case that the United States can intervene wherever it wishes without worrying about the involvement of third parties. The U.S. experience in Lebanon had established that reality. The Reagan administration, believing its own campaign rhetoric about the efficacy of force and the importance of political will, deployed U.S. troops in Lebanon without consideration of Syrian interests. It also believed that the actual use of force would intimidate the opponents of a government that it had decided to favor in a vicious civil war. Within months these costly mistakes had led to a humiliating withdrawal.

Nor, as the current crisis with North Korea is demonstrating, does the United States have a completely free hand in Northeast Asia. There is a limit beyond which the United States cannot push North Korea or it has to worry about the reaction of communist China, Japan, and South Korea. In the current crisis, China has not hesitated to clarify that its alliance with North Korea remains in force. It has threatened to veto proposals for economic sanctions that may come before the Security Council.

Along the rim of Russia, the United States has to worry about the reaction of the Kremlin, which is one reason why the U.S. response to Russian peacekeeping efforts in the "near abroad" has been muted, to say the least. In South Asia, the United States has to worry about India's reaction. That reality was brought home to Americans when the Nixon administration ordered the

USS *Enterprise* to enter the Bay of Bengal during the 1971 Bangladesh crisis. India's strong political reaction made many Americans aware for the first time that India was developing into a serious regional power.

Indeed, in most parts of the world except the Western hemisphere and perhaps the Persian Gulf, there is a regional power whose opposition to U.S. intervention could make the exercise of force much more difficult to carry out successfully unless one assumes that air power alone will be sufficient. While the disappearance of the Soviet Union is an important consideration in calculating the utility of the use of force, there are other actors whose policies must be taken into account.

Nor does greater precision in delivery of weapons necessarily clear the way for a more ready resort to force, for it is not at all clear that others will calculate the costs of resistance as the United States hopes they will. As more developed countries have repeatedly learned, in a struggle between the technically sophisticated and unsophisticated, there is often as large a mismatch in political determination as there is in technical capability. The West in general has a very large capacity to kill but a very low capacity to die. The equation is often reversed among the targets of the West's wrath. The United States learned about the differences between capacity and determination in Vietnam, the French learned in Algeria, and the Russians in Afghanistan. This is the overlooked lesson of U.S. involvement in Somalia. The task that the United States set itself was not undoable, but officials in the Clinton administration grossly underestimated the price that others were willing to pay to stop the United States. CIA officials privately concede that the United States military may have killed from 7,000 to 10,000 Somalis during its engagement there. Meanwhile, the United States lost only 30 soldiers. Notwithstanding that extraordinary disparity, the United States felt it had to leave.

What about the gains of using force? Even if the costs have not gone down as far as many have suggested, the use of force might still become more feasible were the gains to increase.

For most of history, it must be acknowledged, wars have been a paying proposition. The victor gained land, wealth, or trade.

Most of the United States' wars, in fact, have been over land. The United States was either seeking it or trying to bar others from gaining it.

The Cold War was different. That war was a struggle over regimes. The Soviets wanted to change the U.S. regime and the United States wanted to change the Soviet regime. Neither side sought more land, at least after the spoils of World War II had been distributed.

Today, the international system seems structurally stable for the first time since 1815. There are several reasons for this transformation.

The first reason is that despite the many small conflicts around the globe, none of the great powers seeks additional land (although there are very small border disputes like the Kirile Islands.) Nor does any great power challenge the political legitimacy of the others. Some might say that Russia is a possible exception because so many Russians live in neighboring states, and Russia is concerned about their fate. The surprise has been that, thus far, Russia has accepted that its Russian or Russian-speaking brothers and sisters living in the near abroad should become citizens of those countries even if it insists that neighboring states display no discrimination against their Russian speakers and at times has urged the concept of dual citizenship. China has minor border disputes with its neighbors but none of them seems nonnegotiable. The decision of the Clinton administration to renew most favored nation (MFN) status for China and end the link between trade and human rights regarding U.S. China policy was an acknowledgment that even if the United States is not comfortable with China's political system, it does not challenge that system.

The second reason for the overall stability in the international structure is that today most major states seek greater power not through external expansion, the historic route, but through internal development. Models for other countries are no longer expansionist states but nonexpansionist states like Japan, the United States, or some of the Southeast Asian countries.

The ideological crusades are over. The Clinton administration's proclaimed doctrine of democratic enlargement is a hope, not a policy. The United States today largely tends its own garden. So do the other great powers.

Another reason for the historical discontinuity through which we are passing is that the recent record of states seeking greater power through external expansion has been so poor. Argentina failed to seize the Falklands. Iraq failed to seize part of Iran and subsequently all of Kuwait. Libya failed to seize part of Chad, and Somalia failed to seize part of Ethiopia.

Nor does the negative record on the use of force end there. More powerful states attempting to control the internal political structure of key countries through overt force also have failed: the United States in Vietnam, the Soviet Union in Afghanistan, India in Sri Lanka, and Israel and Syria in Lebanon. The only "successful" uses of large-scale military force in recent years have been the U.S. conquests of Grenada and of Panama, and even in Grenada recent press reports suggest that the internal situation is now worse or no better than before the U.S. military intervention.

The inability of conquering states to gain compliance from subject populations also plays a role in the altered nature of the international system. For most of history, when a state conquered a new province, the inhabitants of that province respected the wishes of their new ruler. That practice could even extend into religion. *Cujus est regio, illius est religio.* But today nowhere in the world does such mass compliance now take place. On the contrary, populations struggle on for years, even decades: the Tibetans against the Chinese, the Timorese against the Indonesians, the Palestinians against the Israelis, the Kashmiris against the Indians. Of course if states are allowed to carry out the kind of ethnic cleansing or forced integration that has been the norm in past centuries, then the seizure of land from a neighbor is a rational decision. This is what the settlements issue in the West Bank or the ethnic cleansing in Bosnia has been all about. If ethnic cleansing or forced integration is not possible, then one of the principal objectives of war disappears because today, unlike the past, subjugated populations are not compliant.

Seven Categories of Force

In light of the foregoing, there seem to be seven distinct categories for the possible use of force by the United States.

- Meeting alliance obligations
- Promoting counterproliferation
- Protecting key allies threatened with internal disorder
- Protecting individual Americans
- Supporting democracies abroad
- Countering terrorism
- Assisting peacekeeping and peace enforcement

Of the seven, the last, peacekeeping, is by far the most needed yet it is the category for which the United States is the least prepared, as the following analysis demonstrates.

Meeting Alliance Obligations. In theory the United States is obligated through treaties to protect most of Latin America, much of Europe, and a good part of Asia against external attack. The fact is that none of the allies of the United States is threatened with attack except possibly South Korea. The Russian threat in Europe will not reappear for years even if the worst were to happen in Moscow, which it is hoped will not. Because of draft-dodging, the Russian army may soon end up with more officers than enlisted men. Weapons procurement has been cut back to a fraction of Cold War levels. The Russians would need at least a decade or more to reestablish their internal cohesion before they could again threaten the treaty allies of the United States with a conventional conquest.

Nor is nuclear blackmail a serious worry any longer. Blackmail must have a purpose. As long as the two superpowers were engaged in a global struggle for influence, the United States did have to worry that the Soviet Union would use nuclear blackmail to push European states into a neutral or pro-Soviet stand. But Russia has become a "normal" country seeking normal foreign policy objectives—security and economic development. It is difficult to imagine Russia threatening France with a nuclear strike in order to gain trade privileges. It is true that the United States must worry about new nuclear states such as India, Israel,

Pakistan, and perhaps North Korea, but none of these states has global ambitions. With the possible exception of India, none even has regional ambitions. Most have acquired nuclear weapons in order to combat the overwhelming military or demographic challenge of its neighbors.

What about other security threats to the U.S.? Say, subversion in Latin America? In the Western Hemisphere, the Cuban/Soviet threat is ended. Not only has Cuba lost the support of Moscow, which enabled Cuban officials to develop a continental or even transcontinental reach, but the country has lost its allure as an alternative model. There is no immediate security threat to the treaty allies of the United States in the Western Hemisphere.

There is one clear security threat for the United States today. It is in Asia. North Korea's apparent nuclear ambitions together with the treaty commitment of the United States to South Korea create an explosive situation. The United States has 37,000 troops stationed in South Korea. President Bill Clinton has said that this administration will not permit North Korea to develop a nuclear weapon. This is the most serious immediate crisis in the world for the United States, but it exists in part because recent administrations have allowed partisan politics at home to prevent the United States from looking after its own security interests. It is preposterous that the United States should have to assist in the land defense of a country that is twice as populous and up to ten times as rich as its northern neighbor. Ever since Jimmy Carter reversed his campaign pledge to remove U.S. troops from Korea, which was probably premature, the U.S. ground commitment to South Korea has been politically inviolate. When President Clinton was in South Korea he even went so far as to tell the country's legislators that U.S. troops would remain in South Korea as long as the South Korean people "want and need" them. Once the current crisis is past, the United States should step back from this foolish presidential statement, which places too much of the initiative in Seoul's hands, and press South Korea to assume progressively full responsibility for land defense with the United States progressively fulfilling its treaty obligation through air and sea power.

Indeed over the longer run there is now only one part of the world where the United States must be ready to fight a land war virtually unassisted by the states in the area, and that is the Persian Gulf. None of the states there will be prepared to confront Iraq or Iran for the foreseeable future; and in the wake of the Gulf War, the United States has assumed the role of regional gendarme, which it cannot abandon until the regimes in Tehran and Baghdad either fall or radically change policies.

Counterproliferation. The "Defense Counterproliferation Initiative'" is an important policy priority of the Clinton administration. Clearly, with the end of the Cold War and of the nuclear standoff between the Soviet Union and the United States, the most pressing long-run international security issue for the United States is the proliferation of weapons of mass destruction. These could be the great potential equalizers of international relations, robbing the United States of the benefits of being the sole remaining superpower. If Libya, for example, had a handful of deliverable nuclear weapons, the entire diplomatic relationship between Washington and Tripoli might be transformed. Tripoli probably could not seriously threaten the United States, but it could threaten states closely allied with the United States so that the United States would have to treat the Libyan regime with greater respect. The same could be said about a number of other states that are hostile to the United States.

Would nuclear weapons be more dangerous in the hands of Third World states than in the hands of the great powers? The United States used to believe the answer was yes, but the breakup of the Soviet Union should give Washington pause. Nonetheless, the possession of nuclear weapons by new states would necessarily reduce the margin of U.S. power in the world. There is also the fear, whether valid or not, that a Kim Il Sung or an Iranian ayatollah might not care about the fate of his own country or people and would someday decide to use a nuclear weapon against the United States or one of its allies in a fit of irrationality. Of course the more widely spread nuclear weapons become, the greater the risk someday of an accident. In short, in the post–Cold War period, the United States under any administration will have a very strong nonproliferation policy.

The issue is what can realistically be done about the issue of proliferation in a military sense. States have learned from the Israeli attack on the Iraqi nuclear facilities, which did not succeed in the sense that it persuaded the Iraqis to move their program underground. Now all potential proliferants have learned not to expose their program to preemptive attack. According to most experts, a military answer is difficult in the most immediate crisis involving North Korea. As Peter Rodman, former deputy assistant to the president in the Bush Administration, pointed out, "In the case of North Korea, the use of strikes is complicated by the difficulty of locating the right targets or preventing devastating retaliation by the North Koreans. Some people I respect, who are relatively hawkish on the issue in general, say that the military options are no good."[5] Very senior Pentagon officials confirm that the North Koreans possess deeply protected artillery that could devastate Seoul in the event of war.

In a December 1993 briefing to the press, Pentagon officials hinted that U.S. preemptive strikes against North Korea, similar to those of Israel against Iraq in June 1981, were being considered. But in March 1994 Ashton B. Carter, the assistant secretary of defense for international security policy, stated that those who believed that Washington might bomb nuclear facilities of potential proliferators had "misunderstood" Washington's intentions.[6]

I am not in a position to know the administration's true intentions. I do know that the Clinton administration is pressing ahead with efforts to develop special weapons that can penetrate the kind of concrete bunkers that are used to house nuclear facilities. Certainly, however unpromising now, the United States will continue to keep open the military options for a preemptive strike in the cause of counterproliferation. It will also continue to work on the development of theater antiballistic weapons that could disarm a potential proliferant. At this point a sensible nonproliferation policy would seem to rely more on diplomacy than force. The United States cannot police a noncooperative world. It is in the interest of the United States to strengthen the nonproliferation regime in all its aspects, increasing the incentives for compliance while reducing the benefits from violation. Working for a comprehensive test ban, extending the nonproliferation treaty, and negotiating a compromise with North Korea involving recognition and trade in exchange for a freeze in its nuclear weapons program seem better ways to serve U.S. security interests than any early use of force to further the nonproliferation cause.

Protecting key allies threatened with internal disorder. Some states in the world are so important to the United States that Washington would at least consider the use of military power to preserve the status quo domestically as well as internationally. Former Secretary of Defense James Schlesinger has suggested that the U.S. relationship with Saudi Arabia is now comparable to the U.S. relationship with Germany. Although the United States has no treaty obligation to protect Saudi Arabia from external attack or internal disorder, Ronald Reagan on October 1, 1981, stated that the United States would "never" let Saudi Arabia become another Iran. "There is no way that we could stand by and see that taken over by anyone that would shut off that oil."[7] U.S. policy during the Gulf War confirmed that, whatever the treaty obligations might be, the United States would use force if necessary to protect Saudi Arabia against external aggression. The United States may be prepared to take military action to prevent internal change if a sensible option seems available.

There are other states in the world that the United States, if it had the option, would probably consider using military force to protect even though it has no treaty obligation to do so. The United States has invested close to $100 billion in support of the Middle East peace process. The overthrow of the Egyptian government by Islamic forces would be a diplomatic setback for the United States comparable to the downfall of the Shah of Iran. Particularly with the memory of that setback in mind, the United States could be expected at least to consider using military power to help an imperiled Egyptian government if any option made sense. Of course, the Gulf countries should be added to this list. After the Gulf War, the United States has become the defender of the status quo in the area. The United States certainly would react in the case of external aggression. What it would do in the case of an internal uprising is more unclear.

There are other countries such as Ukraine that the United States might consider so important that it would at least consider some form of military response if internal developments threatened to bring to power a government hostile to the United States. The strong likelihood is that in the end Washington would do nothing of a significant military nature.

The ideal model for assisting an ally faced with internal disorder would be George Bush's decision to save Cory Aquino's regime in the Philippines by ordering U.S. aircraft to fly over Manila on December 1, 1989, in an implicit threat to those threatening to overthrow her. The effort was low-key and successful. No Americans died and few were even at risk. It is doubtful that military intervention would be as successful in the other countries of special concern to the United States. It is even doubtful that the United States could carry out a similar operation in the Philippines today. When Bush gave his order, the United States still had military personnel stationed on Filipino soil. In addition, the United States enjoyed an extraordinarily positive reputation among the Filipino people. In most of the cases in question, the United States enjoys little or no advantage in terms of military intervention. It is instructive that when the Saudi monarch was threatened by religious riots in Mecca in 1979, the king drew on French commandos to help him restore order. Allowing Americans in the holy city would have been too risky.

So while it remains true that several countries in the world are of sufficient geopolitical interest to the United States for U.S. officials to consider using force to preserve the status quo, a hard look at the realities suggests that U.S. options are few.

Supporting Democracies Abroad. When United Nations Ambassador Madeleine Albright delivered the Clinton administration's position on the "Use of Force in a Post–Cold War World" before the National War College on September 23, 1993, she mentioned four problems that might require the use of force: the spread of weapons of mass destruction, terrorism, ethnic violence, and the fall of democracy. She mentioned Haiti as an example of the last.[8]

Among the democracies abroad with which the United States has no formal security tie but that it might well decide to use force to defend is Israel. United by democratic values and intimate intergovernmental and societal ties, these two countries are as close to the status of allies as it is possible to be without the formal designation. Indeed, the lack of that formal designation continues because there are unbalanced advantages and disadvantages to the current arrangement. The lack of a treaty arrangement frees Israel from the obligation to consult with the United States about its own military actions. This deprives the United States of the ability to stop actions that it believes counter to U.S. interests, also sparing it the obligation to confront Israel publicly when the interests of the two countries diverge. For that reason this anomalous arrangement continues.

The Clinton administration has suggested a grander commitment to democracy. Its off-and-on again approach to Haiti ultimately resulting in the deployment of military force on the island has suggested that it would not rule out the use of force to reestablish democracy in a country where democracy has been overthrown. The Clinton administration has suggested in PDD-25[9] that one justification for the dispatch of UN or other peacekeeping troops may be the restoration of democracy. No doubt if a viable military option existed, the United States would intervene to protect democratic forces in Mexico against an authoritarian alternative if that alternative threatened to become anti-American.

A review of U.S. policy toward Haiti suggests that, official rhetoric notwithstanding, the United States will be very reluctant to use force to restore democracy to a friendly country. Over the course of spring and summer 1994, the administration reduced its options to the point where military intervention in Haiti became inevitable. But the cost could be high. The congressional opposition to U.S. military action in Haiti remained robust even after the Haitian government agreed to allow the U.S. troops to land unopposed. It is difficult to imagine how any U.S. administration can build a national consensus for a lengthy occupation of Haiti yet that is what seems to be required. If the United States finds it so difficult to act in Haiti, it is unlikely to act elsewhere to "restore democracy." Beyond a very small circle of states, the use of force to restore democracy is going to be primarily through UN or other types of peacekeeping, and PDD-25 makes it clear that U.S. participation in UN peacekeeping will be minimal.

Protecting Individual Americans and Countering Terrorism. There will always be a military requirement for the United States in the protection of its citizens considered in the broadest sense. Approximately 2.5 million Americans are living abroad, of whom nearly 100,000 reside outside the OECD (Organization for Economic Cooperation and Development) countries. Their protection must lie primarily with local authorities, not the U.S. military.

Terrorism will be another concern of the U.S. military. Except in rare occasions where the U.S. government can trace a pattern of terrorist actions back to an accountable state as it believes it has been able to do with Libya and some cases of terrorism, there is no large-scale military response to terrorism. Good intelligence and police work are more important than military force.

Assisting Peacekeeping and Peace Enforcement. In short, when we exhaust the list of possible requirements for the use of military force in a post–Cold War world, we are left with the irony that the greatest requirement for the use of force is in the one area where the United States is most skittish, namely, peacekeeping and peace enforcement. There has been a veritable explosion of intrastate conflicts in recent years. According to UN figures, since the fall of the Berlin Wall, eighty-two conflicts have broken out around the world, but only three of these have been interstate. Seventy-nine were civil wars. Indeed of the three interstate wars, Bosnia and Nagorno-Karabakh might also be termed as civil wars.

In most of these civil wars one can imagine a constructive role for outside mediation and observation if not peace enforcement. Yet the recent evolution in U.S. policy has made it more and more unlikely that the U.S. military will play a constructive role in this area.

The United States by some estimates will be spending more for defense in the coming four years than the rest of the world combined. Yet its real defense needs do not seem to require this effort unless the United States wishes to become much more directly involved in efforts to curtail the growing problem of intrastate conflict in the form of ethnic strife and civil war.

In this regard, the position of the Clinton administration and the Congress on peacekeeping is scarcely reassuring. The early rhetoric suggested that the United States had a major interest in trying to intervene to manage these conflicts. But the recent PDD-25 is greatly watered down from earlier versions and adopts criteria so restrictive that it is doubtful the United States could vote again even for a UN observer force on the Golan Heights. Yet that very modest document is encountering considerable resistance in Congress, which has been hesitant to fund new peacekeeping operations. Both branches of government have been so timid about peacekeeping that the issue of using U.S. ground troops in NATO for European peacekeeping is ruled out of order unless they operate in circumstances that rule out all risk. It is difficult to see how the United States is going to remain a European power if it refuses to participate in the one form of military activity that is the most needed in Europe today.

In short, the optimism that many commentators on the use of force displayed after the Gulf War is gone. Although Americans do not like to hear it, the United States is "timid," as one unfortunate UN official had the temerity to suggest in a public statement.

THE ISSUE OF COMPELLENCE

A discussion on the use of force cannot end here. It may be true that the greatest need for U.S. forces is now in the field of peacekeeping and peace enforcement in intrastate conflicts, but that fact by itself does not help policy-makers decide when it is appropriate and when it is not appropriate for the United States to intervene in ethnic disputes. To arrive at a greater sense of clarity on this issue, U.S. policy-makers must consider carefully the differences between interstate conflict and intrastate conflict, for they are major.

For most U.S. decision makers, the relevant paradigm is the Cold War with whose rules and regulations they are most familiar because they were similar to those of most earlier interstate conflicts. Accountable governments maneuver around one another using the tools of diplomacy and deterrence. Each side attempts to influence the other through a series of veiled or open threats or bribes. Each side rationally calculates the odds and usually remains "deterred." Military power in steadily increasing amounts seems highly relevant to the conduct of policy because threats and the display of force are designed to influence external behavior. No effort is made to influence internal behavior. Indeed, imagine how much more dangerous the Cold War would have been if either Moscow Washington had threatened to use force to change the internal political order in either country, e.g., an end to the Gulag or immediate equal rights for black Americans.

The kind of struggle carried on during the Cold War is hardly the situation American decision makers face today in places like Bosnia or Georgia or Somalia. These involve intrastate conflicts. Generally speaking, in the case of intrastate conflict, leaders are trying to change internal behavior, not external behavior. In this effort they often are not dealing with clearly accountable actors. Nor are these leaders always rational. It was not rational for General Mohammed Farah Aideed to resist U.S. demands at such a high cost, but he and his people were willing to pay the cost. It has not been rational for the Serbs to carry out many of their actions, but the bitter memory of World War II when so many Serbs died at the hands of Croats and Muslims has driven them into a frenzy. It is not rationale for Armenians to ethnically cleanse all Azeris from Nagorno-Karabakh because it will prolong the war, but the outside world has little influence on the Armenian leadership.

In most interstate conflicts, a limited number of rational and accountable leaders on each side can be identified. They are able to give orders and have them obeyed. They order troops to fight, and they order troops to lay down their arms. Generally speaking, the troops follow the orders given. This fact influences dramatically the way that the international community orchestrates its efforts at preventive diplomacy or humanitarian aid. The United Nations, regional organizations, and neighboring states attempt to bring pressure on a small circle of leaders to persuade them to follow a conciliatory policy. These efforts may or may not be successful, but no one doubts where pressure must be directed. This is what the United States is trying to do in North Korea today. But who are the leaders in Bosnia or Haiti or Somalia? Are we really certain that the Bosnian Serb leaders can succeed in ordering their troops to cease fighting? Can the Bosnian government order its Muslim legions to stop struggling to return to homes from which they have been driven by force.

In many intrastate conflicts, popular passions may be too high to permit elite compromise. Conflicts become less a matter of calculation at the top than mass emotion at the bottom. Popular passions may be so strong that leaders lose control. Leaders rise up to exploit popular passions, but the kind of leadership they display resembles a man running ahead of a stampeding herd while maintaining that he is in charge. He may be able to lead the herd to move to the right or the left, but he cannot stop the herd. If he turns around to stop it, he will be trampled.

In intrastate conflicts, religious or ethnic hatred is often so strong that dialogue becomes nearly impossible. The opposing side is viewed as virtually subhuman. Extermination of the heretic and expulsion of the outsider seems to be God's work or a patriot's duty. It is understood that if the other side prevails, one's own side may well disappear. Only one way of life is likely to survive.

In such situations, all individuals—old or young, male or female—may be seen as combatants. The Indians in the American West knew that the arrival of an unarmed farm family was in effect a declaration of war. It was the advance troop of a larger army to follow that would make the traditional Indian way of life impossible.

In Ireland several centuries ago, the Catholic inhabitants could well have viewed Protestant settlers as constituting even more of a threat to the welfare and security of the Catholic Irish than the British soldiers who protected them. The settlers represented another way of life that would suppress or even eradicate the way of life that was to be displaced. The struggle was therefore one to the knife.

Modern ethnic and religious conflicts regrettably have not lost this savage character. Palestinians on the West Bank or various ethnic groups in Bosnia struggle like the ancient or modern Irish and for many of the same reasons. Each outsider, no matter how young or infirm, is seen as a mortal danger to the way of life of those on the other side. This is the rationale for "ethnic cleansing," which has gone on throughout history.

Another characteristic of such wars is that each side seeks total victory. Surrender is almost always unconditional. Victory for one means oblivion for the other. There is therefore a desperate quality to civil wars that makes them particularly hard to control once they get started.

In such struggles, when accountable actors do step forward and adopt unpopular positions, they often find that their very lives are in danger. The United States suffered terribly from its civil war, but it did have the good fortune that when one side prevailed, the other was able to order its troops to cease fighting and they complied. Robert E. Lee deserves his reputation for greatness because he told his generals it was time to stop fighting and restore the nation. We know that in many other civil wars such calming advice is not given. In Ireland, the leaders of the Irish uprising knew it was risky to seek a compromise with the British. Michael Collins, the Irish guerrilla leader, presciently stated that he had signed his death certificate when he agreed to leave the six most northern counties under British control. He was assassinated a few months later. The Palestinians over the years have eliminated leaders who threatened to compromise with Israel. Today Yasser Arafat himself may be in danger. Afghanistan, Somalia, and Bosnia today suffer in part because it is difficult to identify accountable actors. There are too many who claim to be accountable but cannot deliver their people. Those who truly try may be pushed aside or eliminated. It is instructive that in Serbia Slobodan Milošević is not the most extreme proponent of Serbian nationalism.

Since the main problem in the world today is not interstate aggression, but ethnic or civil conflict, how can it be dealt with? Fundamentally, there are three options for the international community when a civil, ethnic, or religious war breaks out. They are victory, compellence, or power sharing.

The international community could simply let the stronger side win, which is often the most effective option. It is, in fact, the option that the international community has traditionally taken.

Compellence is required, however, if the international community is not prepared to see the stronger side win. Deterrence is unlikely to work precisely because the goal of the international community is to change internal behavior, not external behavior. Such an effort requires either peacekeeping or peace enforcement. In short, it entails risks. If the two sides acquiesce in the peacekeeping force, a cease-fire can be frozen in place, and the risks are relatively low. That is what has happened in Cyprus with the deployment of the UN force there. If the two sides do not agree to the deployment, then a form of UN or other protectorate will have to be established, and the risks begin to rise. Overall, compellence is a daunting task that neither the international community nor the United States will often be willing to undertake. But if the task is never undertaken, then the international community is really saying that allowing the stronger to prevail is the only effective option that the international community is willing to support. It is saying that there are no geopolitical consequences to internal change resulting from ethnic conflict that are sufficiently grave to merit the use of force. The seventy-nine conflicts that the UN Secretariat has identified must simply be allowed to burn out.

Does this mean that the world has no other options for action if it is reluctant to use force? Not at all. A number of the conflicts might be managed through power sharing, which will be accepted once the two sides to a dispute have established some rough balance of power either through their own efforts or outside support. That is what happened in South Africa. There was no way to get a peaceful solution to that crisis except through power sharing. Calling for democratic elections with the winner to take all could not solve such ethnic conflicts, nor could military power unless both sides could be disarmed. Only power sharing could solve the problem.

At the heart of the conflict in the former Yugoslavia is a fear on the part of Serbs of being subject again to rule by the combined forces of the Catholic and Muslim populations. During World

War II these two groups at times did cooperate with German encouragement and the result was a massive slaughter of Serbs, Jews, and other minorities. It may be true that the current governments in Sarajevo and Zagreb have no intention of returning to the World War II policies of ethnic warfare, but the collective memory of the Serbian people necessitates that no political solution in the former Yugoslavia can be achieved without Serbian concurrence. The international community unfortunately ignored this fundamental reality. It recognized Croatia without adequate guarantees for the Serbs and encouraged the Bosnian authorities to press ahead with a referendum for independence that could only traumatize the Serbian population, which refused to take part. War was the result.

Instead of such blind support for majority rule—winner take all—the international community should have pressed all parties to accept the proposition that theirs could not be a unitary state, that they would have to accept power sharing, and that recognition would be denied until arrangements along these lines had been completed. A similar line of reasoning should be followed in most of the ethnic conflicts facing the international community. In some communities, the international community is going to have to face the reality that organized population transfers may be more benign than attempting to force a coexistence that the two populations will not accept. The West Bank is probably an example; under a peace settlement, the two populations will have to be separated. It is probably true of Rwanda.

Other approaches to ethnic conflict must also be explored before force is considered. The problem of Crimea or Kosovo cannot be solved without either suppression or succession, which probably will bring even more violence. To avoid a crisis, new concepts like dual citizenship or shared sovereignty must be introduced into the dialogue. Traditional Cold War tools of threats and deterrence will not work because the relevant capitals are not in control of local forces pressing for change.

In summary, the international community faces a serious problem in attempting to curtail internal conflicts that threaten international stability. It is simply unrealistic to expect that the international community, whether through the United Nations or interested states, will often intervene with sufficient force to smother a civil conflict, no matter how bloody it may be. The best we can hope for is that some regional power may be willing to pay that blood price as Vietnam did in Cambodia, but in such an event the motivation is usually not humanitarian. To increase the pressure on contending parties to behave, the international community is going to have to develop new tools for mediation and intervention. On occasion, because the international stakes are so high, the international community or parts of it may resort to the use of force. For most intrastate conflicts, however, the choices will be between inaction or a much bolder diplomatic approach that has seldom been tried before.

NOTES

1. Les Aspen Speech Delivered at the Annual Dinner of the Jewish Institute for National Security Affairs, The Washington Hilton, Washington, D.C. (September 21, 1992).
2. See John G. Heidenrich, "The Gulf War: How Many Iraqis Died?" *Foreign Policy* (Spring 1993).
3. Charles Krauthammer, "The Use and Usefulness of Military Forces in the Post–Cold War World," *Foreign Affairs*, Summer 1992.
4. Les Aspin, *op cit.*
5. Peter Rodman, "The Counterproliferation Debate: Are Military Measures or Other New Initiatives Needed to Supplement the Nonproliferation Regime?" Paper delivered at Conference on Nuclear Nonproliferation, Carnegie Endowment for International Peace (November 17–18, 1993).
6. Ashton B. Carter in the *Los Angeles Times*, March 14, 1993.
7. Ronald Reagan, *Presidential Papers of Ronald Reagan*, p. 871.
8. Madeleine Albright, "Use of Force in a Post–Cold War World," delivered before the National War College, September 23, 1993.
9. *The Clinton Administration's Policy on Reforming Multilateral Peace Operations*, Presidential Decision Directive (PPD)-25, Department of State Publication 10161, May 1994.

2

The Necessity for American Military Intervention in the Post–Cold War World

Steven R. David

The end of the Cold War will not end threats to U.S. interests nor the need for military intervention to defeat those threats. U.S. policy-makers spent the Cold War worrying about threats such as superpower nuclear war or a Soviet invasion of Western Europe whose probability was small but whose consequences would have been catastrophic. Now the United States confronts threats whose consequences may be less catastrophic but whose likelihood of emerging is great. Simply because the "vital" interests of the United States might not be endangered is no reason to be unprepared to deal with challenges that can and most likely will threaten crucial U.S. concerns.

Since the end of the Cold War, the United States has intervened with large numbers of troops in the Persian Gulf, Somalia, and Haiti. The interventions are significant in themselves but are also important for what they represent. The U.S. intervention against Iraq stemmed from concerns about traditional, tangible interests—to preserve access to oil and to prevent the spread of nuclear weapons to a rogue regime. U.S. interventions in Somalia and Haiti were undertaken primarily for humanitarian concerns. Although the motives, nature, and outcome of the interventions differed markedly, they illustrate the kind of problems that the United States is likely to face in the coming years.

Despite, or in many cases, because of the end of the Cold War, instability, hatreds, and conflict have come to characterize much

39

of the world. International disorder will challenge traditional U.S. interests as well as raise humanitarian concerns to a new level of awareness. Dealing with threats to traditionally important interests will require the United States to be able to intervene militarily to achieve a decisive victory. The costs that the United States will be willing to bear will depend largely on the importance of the interests threatened. If the threatened interests are important enough, virtually any cost will be borne to safeguard them. Intervening for humanitarian purposes is different. The decision about whether or not to intervene will depend less on the scale of the atrocity than it will on the costs believed necessary to deal with it. No matter how terrible or widespread the abuse, military interventions for humanitarian ends will not be carried out if they incur the risk of large numbers of casualties. With a sensible approach, the United States can meet both sets of challenges despite a declining defense budget and a public wary of foreign involvement.

My argument is presented in four parts. I first show why much of the post–Cold War world will be characterized by instability and conflict. Second, I explain how U.S. security and economic interests will be threatened by this disorder, and why the United States needs to be prepared to intervene to meet these threats. Third, I consider the rationale of intervening for humanitarian ends along with different approaches to carry out such interventions at a tolerable cost. Finally, I conclude with some broad guidelines on deciding when to intervene.

WHY INSTABILITY AND CONFLICT
WILL CHARACTERIZE THE POST-COLD WAR WORLD

Conflict and instability will be prevalent because of the nature of most of the world's states. The countries of what used to be called the Third World and many of the newly emerging states of central Europe and the former Soviet Union share characteristics that foster disorder. Most of these states are relatively young. Instead of the four or five centuries of development that the West European countries had, they measure their independence in decades or less. Virtually all are wrestling with problems of political and economic development. Most have experienced the legacy of colonialism with its imposition of arbitrary borders and the exacerbation of ethnic and religious rivalry by colonial leaders. Many of these countries are led by authoritarian leaders who place their own interests over those of the people they purport to lead. The result has been the emergence of states with internationally recognized borders but without the ability (or sometimes will) to control ethnic and religious conflicts that all too often rage within those borders.[1]

The situation is not much better among states as it is within them. Although interstate warfare has not claimed anywhere near the number of lives as conflicts within states, the prospects for the future are not reassuring. Internal instability itself fosters conflict between states in several ways. Neighboring states act to prevent disorder from spreading to them as India did when it supported the efforts of Bangladesh to secede from Pakistan in 1971. Leaders seek to divert attention from domestic difficulties as was the case with Argentina's invasion of the Falklands in 1982. Domestic instability can create the impression that an adversary has been so weakened that a "window of opportunity" for invasion has been opened, as seen in Iraq's 1980 invasion of Iran.

Interstate warfare is also likely because the factors that explain the "long peace" of the developed world do not apply to other states. Most of the world's countries are not democratic, removing any peace-inducing effects that this form of governance provides. Institutional linkages such as the European community and North Atlantic Treaty Organization (NATO) are not as numerous or as effective outside the developed world. Most non-Western states do not have nuclear weapons, eliminating the potent deterrent effect these arms entail. While in Europe and elsewhere, the emphasis on knowledge-producing forms of wealth has lessened the importance of territory as a source of power, this is not the case for much of the world where dependence on agriculture and raw materials makes land an asset that is all too often violently contested.[2]

Attitudes toward warfare also vary markedly among countries. As the political scientist John Mueller argues, developed states may be moving towards a realization that war, like slavery and dueling, is an indefensible form of behavior that is rapidly becoming obsolete.[3] For other countries, however, the glorification of military conflict that some thought was put to rest by the two world wars is alive and well. Ethnic nationalism that was supposed to have been a vestige of primitive societies is exploding not only in Third World countries such as Rwanda and India, but throughout the former communist world as well. Religious extremists, most notably in the Middle East but in South Asia and the former Soviet Union too, routinely commit and support acts of violence against those who do not support their beliefs. Ideologies of expansionism and irredentism (as seen in Iraq, Iran, and North Korea) far more virulent than anything that existed between the United States and the Soviet Union during the Cold War, endanger neighboring states. For much of the world, the view that war is becoming unthinkable is an idea whose time has yet to come.

Nor will the end of the Cold War usher in a new era of peace. To be sure, the superpowers have exacerbated conflict through their profligate arms sales and by dragging countries into an East-West dispute that many just as soon would have preferred to avoid. But the source of most of the world's conflicts are indigenous and will not go away with the absence of great power involvement. Moreover, it was never in the interests of the United States or the Soviet Union to provoke war since that raised the risk of losing a client or even worse, of a superpower confrontation. As a result, the United States and the Soviet Union frequently acted to prevent the outbreak of war as seen in Moscow's restraint of Egypt's Anwar Sadat from 1970 to 1973 and U.S. efforts to prevent Somalia from attacking Ethiopia in the late 1970s and early 1980s. If armed conflict nevertheless did occur, the superpowers often attempted to bring it to a halt as they did in the 1956, 1967, and 1973 Middle Eastern wars. With the Soviet Union gone and the United States increasingly disengaged, the efforts of the superpowers to mitigate conflict will also end. It is at least plausible that if the Cold War had continued, Iraq's invasion of Kuwait, the violent dissolution of Yugoslavia, and the collapse of Somalia would not have been permitted to occur.

WHY CONFLICT AND INSTABILITY THREATEN U.S. INTERESTS AND NECESSITATE PREPARATIONS FOR MILITARY INTERVENTION

Conflict and instability throughout the world are of concern to the United States because their presence threatens U.S. economic welfare and security. Nowhere is this clearer than in the U.S. dependence on imported oil. The United States imports over half of its petroleum needs. U.S. allies are even worse off, with foreign oil accounting for more than 60 percent of West European requirements and almost all of Japan's needs. The demand for oil will in all probability rise due to the rapidly expanding economies of Asia and the decrease in energy efficiency after more than a decade of low energy prices. The supply of oil to meet this rising demand will almost surely fall over time; no new big oil fields are waiting to be exploited, and former major oil producers, such as the United States (which has seen a 25 percent decline in production since 1986) and the former Soviet Union (which has seen its production collapse with the demise of the empire), cannot make up the difference. Major foreign investment in the former Soviet Union may result in increases of production, but no one knows if major deposits exist to be exploited or, if such deposits exist, whether the political climate will allow production to take place. A major portion of the shortfall will have to be made up by the Persian Gulf states that possess nearly 70 percent of the world's excess production capacity and are the likely locale of any new major oil finds.[4]

Those who argue that this dependence on foreign oil, particularly in the Gulf, does not threaten U.S. interests maintain that market forces will protect U.S. concerns. They reason that whoever owns the oil will have to sell it to reap the profits. Boycotting a single state or group of states is no longer possible as the International Energy Agency mandates sharing. Large price increases could also not be sustained, they argue, since that would drive the importers to different exporters, energy alternatives, and conservation. With oil at its lowest price in decades, they assert there is little reason for worry.[5]

This view is mistaken. Precisely because there is so much instability in the Persian Gulf (and elsewhere), oil production may be cut off regardless of the economic costs. There have been sixteen disruptions in the Middle East since 1950, and as the 1991 Gulf War so vividly demonstrated, interruptions in supply are not dependent on the Cold War. Internal instability exists throughout the Gulf. Saudi Arabia, which possesses the world's largest oil reserves, faces a multiplicity of domestic threats, any one of which could disrupt production for long periods of time. They include a potential revolt by the 400,000 Saudi Shiites, a takeover of the government by Muslim zealots similar to a 1979 insurrection, or a civil war between rival Saudi clans. Similar vulnerabilities exist within the other Gulf states as well. The Iraqi invasions of Iran and Kuwait are clear illustrations of the threat posed by external war. Another Arab-Israeli war or renewed efforts by Iran or Iraq to establish its hegemony could also threaten the stability of this vital region. A protracted war within or among states could destroy pumping stations, pipelines, and refineries which could cripple production for months or even years.

The violent nature of so many of the threats to the West's supply of oil requires that the United States be prepared with a military response. The United States must retain the capability of massive intervention in the Persian Gulf both to protect countries from interstate aggression (as was the case with Iraq's invasion of Kuwait) and to suppress a major civil conflict. The 1991 Gulf War deployment included over nine U.S. ground divisions and six aircraft carriers. The United States must keep the ability to intervene on this scale, including the maintenance of adequate air-and sea-lift and supporting air power. Moreover, rapid deployment forces that can respond in a matter of hours to protect a regime from domestic disturbances or to reverse a coup d'état should also be maintained. Forces designed to intervene in the Persian Gulf could, with some modification, be used elsewhere as well, making them insurance for contingencies that are as yet unforeseen. These capabilities are quite modest. They are consistent with deep cuts in the defense budget and are well within the limits projected by the Clinton administration.

Another major threat to U.S. interests stems from the spread of nuclear weapons. Nuclear weapons represent the primary physical threat to the security of the United States. Even a small attack against the United States or its allies would do catastrophic damage, and an effective defense against nuclear attack shows no signs of being developed. The demise of the Soviet Union has hurt the cause of nonproliferation by removing the restraining influence of the Soviet Union and by raising fears that former Soviet scientists may sell their services or fissionable material to would-be nuclear powers. Should they decide to do so, there are plenty of potential customers. Approximately a dozen Third World states have or are attempting to develop nuclear weapons. This group includes avowed enemies of the United States such as Libya, Iraq, Iran, and North Korea. Within central Europe and the former Soviet Union, many other states have emerged with at least the technical capacity to produce nuclear arms.

Arguments that nuclear weapons will be stabilizing because they raise the costs of war to unacceptable levels are not convincing.[6] The prevalence of internal conflict can cause nuclear weapons to fall into the hands of terrorists who would have few compunctions about their use. The lack of sophisticated command and control systems combined with vulnerable nuclear forces could lead to unauthorized launchings and accidental detonations. With many states having nuclear weapons, the source of an attack may be unclear, undermining the deterrent threat of assured retaliation. Different cultures may have different ideas as to what constitutes "unacceptable" damage, further eroding the security of deterrence.[7]

U.S. interests will be hurt if nuclear weapons are used. A regional nuclear conflict can produce severe environmental damage and, if it occurs in an economically critical area such as the Persian Gulf, could cause great economic distress to the United States. U.S. allies such as South Korea, Japan, and Israel are potential targets of a nuclear strike. Given U.S. promises to protect these countries, the United States stands a good chance of getting involved should a nuclear attack be launched against them. Most alarmingly, nuclear weapons might be directed against the United States itself. There is no shortage of countries and groups with grievances against the United States. As increasing numbers of countries acquire nuclear weapons and the means to deliver them (ballistic missiles, cruise missiles, aircraft, boats, even suitcases), the possibility grows of some nuclear attack on the United States itself. The overall likelihood of the United States being subject to a nuclear strike might not be great, but given the number and nature of the potential attackers, it is almost certainly higher than ever was the case during the Cold War. Even if a proliferator has no intention of using nuclear weapons against the United States, there are no guarantees that a successor regime or some other government to which the weapons are transferred would exercise the same restraint. Proliferation begets further proliferation complicating efforts for global stability and raising the prospect of horrific regional wars.

Several responses to the prospect of nuclear proliferation do not involve military intervention. Strengthening the nonproliferation treaty and tightening controls on the export of nuclear materials and technology can work to stem the spread of nuclear weapons. Maintaining an adequate deterrent against nuclear strikes on the United States and on U.S. allies would provide some degree of security against countries who, despite safeguards, develop nuclear arms. For most nuclear threats, an approach of combining actions to halt proliferation and reliance on deterrence if states acquire nuclear weapons will be sufficient.

Nevertheless, the threat or use of U.S. military force also has a key role to play in halting nuclear proliferation. By maintaining a robust military force capable of intervention, the United States helps to convince allies that they can rely on Washington rather than on their own nuclear weapons to meet their security needs. A major reason why Japan and most of the countries in Western Europe have not developed nuclear weapons (despite being able to do so) is the commitment of the United States to protect them in the event of attack.

Military intervention can also play a role in preventing a country from acquiring nuclear weapons. Military force should be considered when the acquisition of nuclear weapons by a specific group or country is deemed to present a clear threat to U.S. vital interests. All potential proliferators are not the same. The prospect of Japan developing nuclear weapons might not be welcomed in Washington, but neither would it prompt considerations of military intervention. Libya's Muammar Kadaffi, Iraq's

Saddam Hussein, and North Korea's Kim Jong II are a different matter. The North Korean case points out a second condition for military intervention, namely that there be a reasonable chance that an attack would successfully destroy the nuclear potential. After the 1981 Israeli raid on Iraq's Osirak reactor, many countries suspected of developing nuclear weapons have dispersed, hidden, and protected (e.g., placed underground) their nuclear facilities. Whether a military strike against North Korea could disarm its nuclear potential remains in doubt. Nevertheless, it is likely that cases will emerge where a preventive strike will be judged to be feasible against a group or regime whose possession of nuclear weapons is viewed as unacceptable to U.S. policymakers. Prudence dictates that the United States be prepared with the necessary plans and forces to address these threats if they arise.

While the *prospect* of nuclear proliferation may increase the probability of U.S. military intervention, the actual *acquisition* of a nuclear weapons capability lessens the likelihood of such involvement. Any decision to use U.S. military forces will consider the potential cost. That cost will frequently rise to unacceptable levels if U.S. troops are threatened with nuclear attack. If, for example, Saddam Hussein had waited until he had nuclear weapons before invading Kuwait, it is not at all certain that the United States would have intervened. The potential deterrent effect of a nuclear weapons capability on U.S. intervention will not be lost on other would-be hegemons who can be expected to press forward with their own nuclear programs before launching an attack on their neighbors.

Aside from the threats posed by conflict in the Gulf and nuclear proliferation, the uncertainty and instability that exists throughout much of the world necessitates that the United States be prepared for a wide range of contingencies that might require military intervention. A consistent U.S. interest since the end of World War II has been to prevent the emergence of a hegemonic power in Eurasia. Although the prospects of this occurring in the near future are small, they cannot be discounted. So long as the United States seeks to remain a world power, it must maintain a robust interventionary capability to dissuade countries from seeking superpower status and to deter those who attain it from threatening U.S. interests.

Of more immediate concern, the United States is committed by treaty to protect many countries from attack, including Japan, South Korea, and most of the West European states. Either Washington should be prepared to act as it promises or to terminate these commitments with all the negative consequences for global stability that would likely ensue. With the United States increasing its dependence on international trade, the need for military intervention to protect U.S. investment may rise. As was reportedly the case in Grenada and Panama, Americans in distress because of civil turmoil or the deliberate actions of a government could require an U.S. interventionary force to rescue them. The United States may need to be prepared to intervene militarily to stem the flow of drugs to U.S. shores. Protracted civil war in Mexico would directly affect U.S. interests and could prompt a U.S. intervention to restore order.

The United States also has commitments to countries based on historical and political ties that might bring about military intervention. The United States maintains close relations with Israel based on shared values, strategic concerns, and a powerful domestic constituency. In the unlikely but conceivable event of Israel needing outside military intervention to protect it from outside attack, the United States needs to be ready to provide it. If U.S. troops are sent to serve as peacekeepers in trouble spots throughout the world (e.g., the Golan Heights between Israel and Syria), U.S. military intervention to rescue the forces in the event of war might become necessary. Long-standing U.S. ties to the Philippines and many Central American countries could provoke U.S. military involvement should they be threatened by domestic turmoil or external attack.

Regardless of the specifics, it is crucial for the United States to be prepared to intervene militarily because it is impossible to identify far in advance which countries and interests are likely to be important. When Secretary of State Dean Acheson excluded South Korea from the range of U.S. vital interests, he did so because South Korea lacked intrinsic importance to the United States. The subsequent invasion by North Korea (probably encouraged by Acheson's action) demonstrated that countries of seemingly small significance can gain in importance when threatened (even indirectly) by a hostile power because the threat calls into question the credibility of the United States as an ally. During the 1980s, few would have predicted that the United States' budding friendship with Iraq would end in war between the two countries. In 1992, Somalia would have been at the bottom of most policy-makers' lists of countries that would provoke an U.S. military intervention. Whether the decisions to intervene in these and other cases were justified is the subject of legitimate dispute, but it is impossible to determine *a priori* where U.S. policy will next be engaged. What is clear is that situations are almost certain to arise somewhere requiring U.S. military intervention, making the preparations for such contingencies prudent and inescapable.

The United States, of course, could choose a path of isolation whereby it would forgo most if not all of these commitments. To do so, however, would destroy what little order and stability exists in the world. Not only would that be an abdication of U.S. values, it could well lead to a world of hostile countries who would eventually turn their wrath on the United States. The United States is fortunate that its basic security and economic well-being are not endangered. In a world where the United States ceases to exert influence, this remarkable state of affairs could very well disappear.

HUMANITARIAN INTERVENTION AND U.S. INTERESTS

In one sense, military interventions for humanitarian ends are not new. In the nineteen century, West European states frequently intervened in Turkey and elsewhere to protect the rights of ethnic and religious minorities. More recently, India attacked Pakistan in 1971 in part to stop the carnage in what is now Bangladesh, Tanzania intervened in Uganda in 1979 to unseat the despotic Idi Amin, and Vietnam (also in 1979) invaded Cambodia to topple the genocidal Pol Pot regime. Rationales for humanitarian intervention are also not new. Hugo Grotius wrote of the right of princes to intervene on behalf of foreign citizens suffering abuse in 1625. The nineteenth century British theorist John Stuart Mill asserted the right of military intervention to deal with a country that commits gross human rights abuses. Contemporary scholars such as Stanley Hoffmann and John Westlake support humanitarian interventions when states take actions that "shock the conscience of mankind."

In another sense, humanitarian interventions are very new. In his 1977 book, *Just and Unjust Wars,* the political theorist Michael Walzer could not cite a single historical case of a military intervention that was primarily driven by humanitarian concerns. Examples such as India and Pakistan, and Vietnam and Cambodia all contained a strong strategic rationale that in itself could explain the military involvement. In the few years since the end of the Cold War, however, there have been at least three clear cases of military interventions that would not have occurred if humanitarian concerns had not been present. In Operation Provide Comfort, the United States, working with the United Nations, established an enclave for the Kurds in northern Iraq to protect them from Saddam Hussein's cruel forces. In Somalia, the United States (also in cooperation with the United Nations) intervened with some 28,000 troops to ensure that food and medicine would reach the Somali people following the collapse of their state. In Haiti, the United States intervened with nearly 20,000 troops to restore democracy and unseat the murderous regime of Raoul Cedras. Moreover, humanitarian interventions in Bosnia (which has already seen the use of NATO aircraft to protect a beleaguered Moslem population) and Rwanda have been seriously considered.

It is no coincidence that humanitarian concerns have prompted so many actual and contemplated military interventions so soon after the end of the Cold War. Because the United States faces no major security threat, it has greater latitude to pursue international challenges that would otherwise be ignored. The end of the Soviet Union has meant that the United States and other powers can intervene militarily without fear of provoking a superpower confrontation. Washington's concerns about its military strength being diverted for peripheral matters are less salient now that no other great powers can challenge U.S. might. The absence of a Soviet veto has also enabled the United Nations to act far more effectively than in the days of the Cold War when every issue (including humanitarian ones) seemed to become a point of superpower conflict. Although not directly related to the end of the Cold War, the increased media coverage of atrocities and suffering throughout the world has galvanized the United States (and others) to try to do something to lessen the scale of global horrors.

The increased significance of humanitarian issues in prompting military intervention has prompted a major debate on the role of the United States in the world. On one side are those who oppose intervention for humanitarian purposes. They argue that U.S. security, economic well-being, and political autonomy are not threatened by human rights abuses elsewhere. Asking Americans to die to protect the human rights of others is unjustified and will not be supported by the American public. If the United States establishes a principle that it will act to end gross violations of human rights, it will be condemned to endless interventions that will sap U.S. strength while leaving untouched the root causes of the abuses. Selective interventions that seek to address only some cases of humanitarian concern may prevent the United States from becoming overextended but raise the critical issue of how the determination to intervene is made— or not made. If Bosnia, why not Rwanda? If Somalia, why not Sudan? The very legitimacy of military intervention for humanitarian ends is also open to question. What right does the United States or any country have to disregard the sovereignty of other states in the name of morality? The opponents of military intervention for humanitarian ends argue that the proper role for the United States and other outside countries is to deal with their own domestic problems, thereby setting an example as to how states should behave, while forgoing interference in the affairs of others.

Despite these cogent views, the United States should be prepared to intervene militarily for humanitarian concerns for two compelling reasons. First, all great powers seek to spread their values to other states in order to make certain that their institutions and ideological outlook are not isolated from the rest of the world. The United States, as did the Soviet Union, has always sought to convince its citizens that its way of life is worthy of emulation by others. In part, this reflects the belief that a nation's strength is not measured entirely by military and economic might, but also by its sense of self-worth. This is especially true for the United States whose commitment to human rights and democracy is inextricably tied up with its identity. If the United States betrays its principles by ignoring the desperate plight of others, U.S. self-confidence—and U.S. power—will be undermined.[8] Second, the United States should be prepared to intervene militarily to prevent gross violations of human rights because it is the right thing to do. As the only surviving superpower, the United States bears a large responsibility for what happens in the world. Washington cannot nor should not attempt to mold the world in its image. Neither should the United States remain aloof from horrific events where it can do much good with little cost.

If a humanitarian interventionist policy is to be effective, the United States must take into account the reservations advanced by responsible critics. Most important is the acknowledgement that with the end of the Cold War, the American people are not willing to tolerate large numbers of casualties for a goal that does not address tangible U.S. interests of security and economic well-being. Most Americans would be willing to overlook interfering in the internal affairs of other states and would accept the view that it is permissible to intervene in some places and not others, provided that the cost (in lives and money) was kept low. The problem confronting U.S. policy-makers seeking to undertake humanitarian interventions, therefore, is to develop an approach that can bring about fundamental change at an acceptable cost to the American people.

Policies of Humanitarian Intervention
The vast majority of human rights abuses will not provoke U.S. military intervention because the costs of dealing with them will be judged as too high. Nevertheless, there are two broad exceptions to this policy of restraint. First, the costs and risks of

some humanitarian interventions can be kept low when the objectives are kept modest. In intervening for humanitarian purposes, the best cannot be allowed to be the enemy of the good. Interventions that provide food for the starving and protection for the persecuted should not be avoided simply because they do not provide a total solution to the problem at hand. In certain situations, limited efforts can do much good, thus justifying their use even if the long-term prospects for the afflicted are uncertain.

Humanitarian interventions should also be considered when outside military force has a reasonable prospect of fundamentally reversing a horrific state of affairs at a small cost to the intervener. When the atrocities are the work of a narrow elite and are not the product of irrevocable and widespread hatreds, an effective low-risk U.S. military intervention might be able to be carried out. Before intervening, U.S. policy-makers would want to ascertain that the scale of the abuses was sufficiently terrible to warrant U.S. involvement, that they were perpetrated by a single leader or a small group, that the removal of that group could be achieved with minimal U.S. casualties, and that new leaders would have a reasonable likelihood of establishing a stable and humane rule.

An interventionist policy that focuses on the leadership committing the human rights abuses recognizes that in many cases, the leaders will not have the support of their people, nor are they acting in any conceivable definition of the national interest. Instead, the overriding concern of these leaders is to guarantee their hold on power. In part, this stems from their own megalomaniacal drives. Equally important, they recognize that in the brutal game of politics played out in their countries, to lose power also means the very real possibility of losing their lives. If their calculus of what it takes to stay in power could be modified to convince these leaders that pursuing policies that violate standards of civilized behavior would weaken their hold on power, it is likely that such policies would not be followed. If the abusive policies continued despite warnings from other states or international organizations, the toppling of the leaders would help ensure that those policies were not pursued by their successors.

If the key towards ending human rights abuses by a leadership is to threaten or remove that leadership, a rethinking of sovereignty is in order. This should not be as difficult as it sounds because, as political scientist Stephen Krasner reminds us, infringements on sovereignty have been the rule rather than the exception throughout history.[9] Moreover, great powers have always sought to mold the construction of sovereignty to meet their particular interests.[10] Given the humanitarian concerns of the United States, it makes sense to consider a reconceptualization of sovereignty in those situations where gross abuses occur that gives primary emphasis to the protection of peoples rather than states. This would facilitate outside intervention to redress barbaric behavior. That such a recon-ceptualization is consistent with recent UN resolutions on Iraq and Somalia as well as earlier manifestations of international law makes its adoption all the more feasible.

There are three broad approaches that the United States can take to remove leaders who engage in gross abuses of human rights. First, the United States might participate in a multilateral intervention to remove the offending regime or individuals. Just what form the multilateral intervention would take varies from situation to situation. Ideally, the United Nations or some other international organization would sanction the intervention, which would be composed of troops from many countries. Soldiers from the region where the intervention takes place would be especially welcome. The role of the United States in international interventions will differ from case to case. Presumably, there would be situations where no U.S. role would be necessary. In other cases, U.S. forces or logistical help would be a requirement for the intervention to succeed. Once the offending leadership is removed, international forces could provide order and oversee elections to establish a new government. If the country needs more time to prepare for elections, a kind of trusteeship can be established to ease the transition from dictatorial to democratic rule.

The advantages of this approach are many. International legitimization minimizes the prospect that states would seize upon a new norm of international intervention to advance their own parochial interests (a matter of particular concern with regards to Russia and its neighbors). The participation of an international force lessens the danger that U.S. casualties would be unacceptably high. The involvement of regional forces involves states who are in a better position to understand the problem and ways of redressing it. Interventions from neighboring countries have already done some good in Liberia and Cambodia, and there is much potential for them to do more. An international force also has the advantage of lessening U.S. domestic political opposition to U.S. participation in the intervention.

There are, however, several problems with U.S. participation in multilateral interventions. Without U.S. leadership, needed interventions might not take place. It is unlikely Saddam Hussein would have been stopped if the United States did not organize the coalition opposing his invasion. Multilateral interventions could turn into tactical and logistical nightmares. Military interventions are difficult enough without having to depend on decision makers from different countries with different agendas and different procedures for command and control. The international division of authority has already complicated interventions in Bosnia and Somalia, with the potential for greater difficulties ahead. While the American people would welcome sharing the risks and costs of a military intervention, they will not permit having foreign nationals determine when United States troops will enter into combat. An already overextended United Nations might not be able to intervene effectively in conflicts where the United States believes it should. The United Nations or the international community in general have not demonstrated an ability to manage successfully other countrys' affairs, making the whole question of trusteeship problematic. The difficulties encountered by the United Nations in peacekeeping operations in Bosnia and Somalia have left Washington with an understandable skepticism regarding the wisdom of working with the United Nations on existing trouble spots, much less expanding the scope of cooperation.[11]

Second, the United States can intervene unilaterally to remove the offending leadership. The United States intervened in Grenada and Panama (albeit not primarily for humanitarian reasons) with reasonable success. Direct intervention offers a quick and effective means for the United States to topple leaders who commit human rights abuses without having to compromise its goals or be paralyzed by an indifferent or hostile international community. Moreover, overthrowing offending regimes can help the United States deal with threats to its interests beyond that of humanitarian concerns. If leaders feared that certain actions would provoke a U.S. response to remove them, they would be less likely to undertake those actions. Developing and using nuclear weapons or invading a neighbor are more likely to be deterred if leaders fear retaliation against them personally as opposed to the country they head. Once the leaders have been removed, either the United States could remain in the state until a new government is formed, or an international authority might be invited in to ease the transition to stable and democratic rule.

This approach also raises many problems. Direct intervention of U.S. forces raises the risk of large numbers of U.S. casualties. While that might be acceptable in operations against regimes who threaten core U.S. interests of security and economic well-being, it will not be countenanced for humanitarian ends. Unilateral U.S. intervention even for noble ends will raise charges of neocolonialism and imperialism. Any military intervention would require the assent of an increasingly skeptical Congress. Although there may be few problems in the actual intervention of U.S. forces, providing for a clear exit strategy can be enormously difficult. Regimes that are left in the wake of U.S. involvement will suffer problems of legitimacy. If a new government is unable to solve the problems that provoked the intervention, future U.S. involvement including occupation may be considered. Protracted occupation is likely to promote opposition both in the state that is being occupied and in the United States itself. Finally, in creating the norm for unilateral intervention, the United States may encourage other states to act similarly, with consequences inimical to U.S. interests.

A third approach is for the United States to back coups d'état against a leadership violating the human rights of its people. Because a coup is a sudden forcible takeover of a government by a small group, backing coups should be able to be accomplished with little cost or risk to Americans. The actual policy could entail several levels of involvement ranging from simple encouragement, to helping in the planning of coups, to material assistance to the coup makers, to the direct use of U.S. personnel in the coup attempt. If the United States concentrates on regimes that are narrowly based with little popular support, the prospects for success in backing coups is high. This is borne out by the historical record where the United States has successfully backed coups against Jácobo Arbenz in Guatemala (1953—direct U.S. personnel and military support), Muhammad Mossadegh in Iran (1954—advice and material assistance), Ngo Dinh Diem in South Vietnam (1963—advice and encouragement), and João Goulart in Brazil (1964—advice and offer of material support). Moreover, it has been alleged that the United States played a role in the coup that toppled Prince Norodom Sihanouk in Cambodia (1970—advice and encouragement) and in creating a climate for a coup that overthrew Salvador Allende in Chile (1973—encouragement).[12]

Backing coups can be defended on ethical grounds. If the regimes that are toppled are truly despotic and abusive (unlike many of the earlier targets of U.S. supported coup attempts) and if they are replaced by governments that are democratic or at least responsive to the basic needs of the people, there is a strong moral justification for the coup backing effort. Washington would simply be helping those who are oppressed remove the source of that oppression at a cost that is likely to be acceptable to the American people. It is noteworthy that President Ronald Reagan's open call for the overthrow of Libya's Muammar Kadaffi and President George Bush's frequent exhortations to the Iraqi military and people to topple Saddam Hussein met with little protest.

This is not to suggest that a coup backing policy, even for humanitarian ends, would be trouble free. With the last successful coup backing effort occurring over twenty years ago, it is not at all clear that the United States retains the capability of backing coups even if it decides to do so. The inability of the United States to back coups against leaders it has sought to topple, such as Fidel Castro, Muammar Kadaffi, Manuel

Noriega, and Saddam Hussein, does not inspire confidence. Neither do the abortive efforts to seize Somalia's Mohammed Farah Aideed. Moreover, the "successful" coup backing efforts by the United States in the past all led to long-term problems that often dwarfed the initial gains.[13]

The problematic nature of each of the approaches does not negate their value in specific cases. Although different policies will be required for different situations, some form of international legitimization and participation combined with overall U.S. control of the intervention will usually be the preferred approach. Although difficulties are likely to be encountered in any type of intervention, they are not so daunting when the alternatives are considered. Doing nothing in the face of publicized moral outrage is increasingly seen as being untenable. Economic sanctions punish the innocent while leaving the guilty untouched. Only by acting against the perpetrators of the abuses themselves can the United States pursue a policy that is morally defensible, highly effective, and able to be implemented at an acceptable cost.

Where Humanitarian Intervention Makes Sense: Somalia and Haiti

The value of a strategy that seeks to reverse human rights abuses by targeting the leadership can be seen in the cases of Somalia and Haiti. Somalia is a clear example of where removing self-styled leaders could have done much to ease the humanitarian abuses against the people. Prior to the December 1992 U.S. intervention, Somalia had become a living hell. Its last powerful leader, Mohammed Siad Barre, had been toppled in January 1991. His departure left Somalia without any central government for the first time since independence in 1960. Five hundred Pakistani troops sent to Somalia under the authority of the United Nations in the summer of 1992 proved incapable of stemming a rising tide of clan based violence that prevented food from being distributed to the Somali people. With the anguish of the Somalis vividly captured on television and the widespread belief that U.S. intervention would be relatively cost free, a strong sentiment to act to halt the violence and help the Somali people gripped the American public. President Bush, with the support of the incoming Clinton administration, thereupon undertook the popular decision to send in U.S. forces.

U.S. military intervention went well at first, but problems quickly developed. For the most part, they stemmed from the decision of one of the sub-clan leaders, Mohammed Farah Aideed, to resist the U.S. and UN presence in Somalia. Aideed turned against outside involvement when it became clear to him that the United Nations and the United States would not support his efforts to become the dominant clan leader of Somalia. Given Aideed's control over critical areas of the capital of Mogadishu, including the harbor, airport, and the site of the UN and relief headquarters, his opposition proved to be critical.

Through hijacking and armed attacks by Aideed's forces, food and other relief supplies were prevented from reaching the Somali people. On June 5, 1993, Aideed's forces were believed to be responsible for killing twenty-four Pakistani troops in a well-planned ambush. This prompted a U.S. backed United Nations resolution calling for Aideed's arrest and an attack by U.S. helicopter gunships on Aideed's headquarters. The United States escalated its involvement with a disastrous raid on a building where top aides to Aideed were meeting that resulted in eighteen Americans killed and seventy-five wounded. In the wake of this attack, the Clinton administration gave up on trying to seize Aideed. U.S. forces were withdrawn on March 31 with Somalia still without a central government.

The problem in Somalia is one of an international intervention gone awry. The intervention in Somalia could have been successful either as a short-term expedient to deal with the immediate crisis or as an attempt to fundamentally reorder Somali politics. Because the United States and the United Nations never settled on which objective to pursue, the intervention ended in what most would call a failure.

If the United States and the United Nations were content with simply alleviating the ongoing suffering in Somalia without getting to the roots of the crisis, they should not have targeted Aideed. There is nothing wrong with such an approach. Despite the criticism of the U.S.-UN intervention, it did save thousands of Somali lives. If the interveners had remained aloof from Somali politics, there would have been far fewer casualties, and the intervention would have ended as a qualified success.

If the United States and the United Nations sought a long-term solution to the Somali situation, they were right to focus on Aideed, but efforts to neutralize the Somali leader should have been carried out earlier and more decisively. Before intervening, the United States and the United Nations needed to have recognized that Somalia was in a state of anarchy with the only real power (and hope for order) resting with the clan leaders. The famine in Somalia was not so much a natural event as it was a weapon in a war waged by a handful of clan leaders whose efforts to enhance their power caused them to create and exacerbate the disaster that befell the Somali people. As the clan leader with one of the strongest followings in the strategic area of south Mogadishu, Aideed was central to the long-term success of the relief effort. It was critical, therefore, to make certain that Aideed (and others) did not actively resist the international intervention. The emergence of a Somali political authority open to humanitarian assistance was the best way the relief effort could have achieved its goals with minimal casualties.

The notion of establishing a strong and humane government in Somalia is not as farfetched as it may sound. From independence until Siad Barre's coup in 1969, Somalia was a democracy in which the clans lived in relative harmony. It is at least conceivable that a resumption of such authority could have been brought about. Following the collapse of the central government in Somalia after the toppling of Siad Barre, the United States and the United Nations needed to seek out responsible leaders who would restore democratic and stable rule to Somalia. If the United States and the United Nations were unable or unwilling to move Somali leaders towards that end, then they should have stayed out of Somali politics totally (being satisfied with simply mounting a modest relief effort) or not have intervened at all.[14]

The U.S. goal in Haiti for both the Bush and Clinton administrations was to restore to power the freely elected president of Haiti, Jean-Bertrand Aristide, and thus to bring about a return of democracy and human rights to this impoverished country. The return of Aristide was also seen as a means to stem the flow of tens of thousands of refugees to the United States, lessen drug smuggling, and protect Americans living in Haiti. Blocking Aristide's return to power were senior military officers who deposed the Haitian leader in 1991. Believing that Aristide's return would threaten their position and perks, the military chiefs resisted U.S. efforts and international sanctions to force Aristide's reinstatement.[15]

Little is clear in the complicated and brutal world of Haitian politics except that Aristide reflects the will of a majority of the Haitian people while the military leaders who toppled him represent only themselves. After overthrowing Aristide (who defeated thirteen opponents with nearly 70 percent of the vote), the military officers quickly established total control of Haiti. Under the command of Lt. Gen. Raoul Cedras, some forty officers ruled Haiti by brutally eliminating any signs of dissent. Political opponents were tortured and killed. Groups of thugs organized by the government terrorized the Haitian population into submission through acts of random violence. Acting more as a criminal gang than a responsible government, the leaders of the regime systematically looted what little wealth remained in Haiti.

U.S. policy-makers correctly recognized that the key to dealing with the Haitian problem was removing the Cedras leadership but pursued policies that were ill-equipped for that task. Following the coup against Aristide, the United States supported a United Nations embargo on fuel and arms against Haiti. The embargo was lifted as a result of a U.S.-brokered agreement in the summer of 1993 calling for the Haitian military leaders to relinquish power to Aristide. The military, however, refused to meet the deadline for stepping down. Instead, they sent armed hooligans to prevent the docking of a U.S. ship carrying some six hundred lightly armed U.S. troops designed to help pave the way for Aristide's return. The United Nations renewed the embargo on Haiti and the United States even attempted to freeze the assets of the Haitian leadership. Aside from adding to the burdens of the Haitian people and contributing to the death of Haitian children, the sanctions had little effect.[16] The U.S. decision to intervene militarily in Haiti in

September 1994 at least had the virtue of targeting the leadership that lay at the source of Haiti's—and the United States'—problems. But the military intervention—even given Cedras' willingness to relinquish power peacefully—saddled the United States with a protracted occupation whose human and financial costs were far greater than the American people and Congress will be prepared to bear.

Instead of a massive military intervention, a covert operation in Haiti made far more sense given the stakes involved. A successful coup that replaced Cedras and his cronies with a government led by Aristide would have given the Haitian people one more opportunity to demonstrate that they could make democracy work, without committing the United States to an open-ended nation-building effort whose outcome was unclear. There is little reason why such a covert operation could not have succeeded. Sanctions had left the Haitian leadership with less money to disburse. Much of the Haitian military, including junior officers, were concerned about the decline in their standard of living and presumably open to the blandishments of Washington. The inability or unwillingness of the United States to back a coup and instead launch a massive intervention indicated that Washington had still not learned that uses of force for humanitarian ends must be kept to a minimum or risk a reaction that will forego involvement in humanitarian crises altogether.

Where American Humanitarian Intervention Should Not Be Undertaken

Knowing when to intervene is only one part of a successful policy of humanitarian intervention. Knowing when not to intervene is equally important. U.S. military intervention should not be undertaken (except as a small part of an international peacekeeping mission) when human rights abuses are committed by large segments of the population who are motivated by deep-seated and widespread hatreds of a long-standing nature. The situations in the former Yugoslavia and Rwanda are cases in point. Serbian efforts at "ethnic cleansing" in Bosnia and elsewhere have clearly met the standards of "shocking the conscience of mankind." The problem is what to do about it. Although Serbian leader Slobodan Milošević bears a good deal of responsibility for exacerbating ethnic hatreds and preventing a settlement from being reached, he is playing upon very real and deeply felt emotions. There is no denying that Milošević commands strong support among the Serbian people. His party has won far more seats in parliament than any other, and no meaningful opposition has emerged. It is not clear how international involvement could bring about the downfall of Milošević or, if it could, that it would halt the fighting.

Once it is accepted that the conflict in the Balkans goes well beyond a single individual or a small group, potential solutions all become costly. Air strikes may force the Serbian leadership to make concessions, but the experience so far of a few symbolic attacks ordered through a maze of international authority does not lend confidence to this approach. If bombing is to be effective, it will have to be massive and directed against targets in Belgrade. That raises the issue of killing many innocent people for a goal that is largely humanitarian. Arming the Moslems may help, but the logistics of delivering the weaponry and providing for training make this a problematic choice. Even if international intervention could bring the fighting to an end, preserving the peace is likely to be a protracted and costly affair.

In sum, barring a diplomatic breakthrough, there are no low cost options for the United States and the international community to take in the Balkans that are likely to be effective. As long as U.S. and European interests are seen as principally humanitarian and there is no political settlement among the belligerents, the prospects of outside intervention to halt the fighting are virtually nonexistent. In the meantime, political efforts to promote a settlement, and peacekeeping forces to protect enclaves of beleaguered civilians are the most that can be reasonably expected.

The situation in Rwanda where the majority Hutus and the minority Tutsis have been engaged in intermittent genocidal conflict is even less susceptible to outside intervention. The latest round of atrocities occurred when the presidents of Rwanda and Burundi were killed when their plane was shot down, probably by members of the Hutu-dominated army. The Hutu presidential guard then exacted its revenge on the Tutsis, which prompted Tutsi counter-massacres of Hutus. An estimated 200,000 Rwandans were killed in a month. Given the long-standing and seemingly intractable hatred that exists between the Hutus and the Tutsis and the seemingly widespread popular support for the atrocities, there appears little the international community can do to reverse the situation at an acceptable cost. It is difficult to imagine how the leaders of the Hutus and the Tutsis could be removed from power, and even if they could, that it would halt the slaughter. Promotion of interethnic dialogue, assistance to neighboring countries for refugee resettlement, international efforts to redraw borders, and aid to nongovernmental relief agencies may help to mitigate the magnitude of the horror. Peacekeeping operations to protect refugees would be welcome once some kind of political authority emerges. Logistical and political support for the French intervention to protect civilians was also in order as was the major American relief effort. Nevertheless, if the fighting resumes, the United States should not intervene militarily to bring it to a halt. This kind of outrage, as painful as it is, should not and will not bring about U.S. military intervention to stop the fighting. Only a massive and protracted U.S. military presence could hold out the hope of producing meaningful change, and that level of involvement would be justifiably rejected by the American people.

Lessons of Humanitarian Interventions and Noninterventions

Several important lessons emerge from the U.S. experience in dealing with humanitarian crises in the post–Cold War world. First, humanitarian interventions can be successful. The U.S. interventions in cooperation with the United Nations in northern Iraq and Somalia have been far more effective than commonly thought. In Iraq, the United States and the United Nations have protected the Kurdish minority from what certainly would have been brutal attacks from the Saddam Hussein regime. In Somalia, because of the military intervention, thousands of people who otherwise would have starved to death were provided food.

The future for both the Kurds and the Somalis remains uncertain. But it is unquestionable that great numbers of innocent people, including children, are alive now because these interventions were carried out. Even where interventions do not bring about fundamental, long-term solutions, they can do much good.

Second, despite these benefits, the United States is unlikely to intervene again purely for humanitarian reasons. This is in large measure due to the Somali experience. The American casualties, problems with coordination with the United Nations, and the continuing uncertainty regrading Somalia's future have soured the United States on humanitarian interventions. The savings of thousands of Somalis was judged not worth the cost in American lives, however small in comparison it may be. The U.S. resistance to intervening in Bosnia and Rwanda and the reluctance to cooperate with the United Nations in peacekeeping operations unless stringent conditions are met all reflect the unacceptablity of even minimal casualties to protect the lives of non-Americans.

Finally, despite the unwillingness to intervene for purely humanitarian reasons, concerns about human rights abuses are likely to play an important role in bringing about U.S. military interventions when other interests are also at risk. In many cases, actions that "shock the conscience of mankind" will take place by regimes that also threaten more traditional interests such as the lives of American citizens, the security of allies, or economic investments. Where these traditional interests are endangered, concerns about human rights can play a decisive role in tipping the scale towards military intervention. The United States intervened in Haiti, for example, in large part due to concerns about an influx of refugees. Nevertheless, if the Cedras regime had not systematically and visibly violated the rights of the Haitian people, it is unlikely that any intervention would have taken place. Similarly, if the United States intervenes militarily in Bosnia, the desire to prevent the spreading of the war into Europe will undoubtedly have played a role. It is unlikely, however, that any intervention would take place in the absence of brutal behavior by the Serbs. Being able to intervene at little cost or risk becomes a necessary but not sufficient cause for humanitarian intervention.

GUIDELINES FOR DECIDING
ON WHEN TO INTERVENE

The preceding analysis demonstrates that intervention is not good or bad in itself but depends on where it takes place and for what reasons. Despite the complexity of the post–Cold War environment where the "rules of the game" have yet to be agreed upon and each case is unique, useful guidelines for deciding on when to intervene can be put forth. Before intervening, some commonsensical questions need to be addressed. Does the United States have a clear set of objectives? Are they achievable with the means employed? Are the objectives worth the lives of Americans (put another way, how comfortable would one be explaining to the parents of dead U.S. soldiers why their children died)? Can the United States accomplish its aims quickly with a minimum of casualties? Once in, is there a clear way out? And how damaging to U.S. interests will it be if events do not unfold as planned? Concerns about domestic support for interventions are also important, but it should be remembered that a quick, successful action will produce support where it might not have existed while a protracted, ineffective effort will undermine the support that may have been present when the decision to intervene was made.

Along with these questions, policy-makers must subject each decision to intervene to a cost-benefit analysis. Are the benefits of the contemplated intervention worth the cost? The decisions will be relatively easy in situations of high cost and low benefit (e.g., few would choose to intervene in Tibet) and in situations of low cost and high benefit (e.g., defending the Persian Gulf from Iraq proved enormously popular—at least after the fact). Decisions, however, will be more problematic in situations of high cost, high benefit (e.g., North Korea) and in situations of low cost, low benefit (e.g., Haiti).

One way to make the difficult decisions easier is to change the cost-benefit calculus. The United States can do little to control the benefits from a given intervention, but Washington can do much to control the costs. There is no reason why military interventions always have to defeat an adversary's army or overcome a mobilized populace. As discussed in this essay, there are many cases in which the harm done to U.S. interests stems from the actions of a single leader or a small group. It makes sense to think of ways that interventions can be carried out that will replace rogue leaders at a minimum risk to the United States. Not every intervention will be subject to this approach, but for those that are, the United States will be able to do much good (for itself and others) at an acceptable cost.

CONCLUSIONS

As during the Cold War, the United States maintains important interests throughout the world that at times will have to be defended through military intervention. Although these threats no longer challenge the basic security and economic well-being of the United States, ignoring them risks serious consequences. Threats to traditional interests, including those from nuclear proliferation or impeding access to oil, are more likely to emerge now than at any time during the Cold War. Human rights concerns have become far more important, both because the demise of the Soviet Union has allowed the American people and policy-makers to pay attention to other matters and because world instability has increased in the wake of superpower detachment.

How the United States deals with threats to its interests will vary greatly. Regarding threats to traditional interests, history has taught us that the nature and source of challenges to the United States are unpredictable. Rather than configuring interventionary forces for any specific contingency, substantial allowance must be made for the unexpected. Military interventions prompted in large measure by humanitarian concerns will require creative thinking. Whether the United States attempts to work within international frameworks, alone, or covertly, effective involvement will only take place in those situations where interventions can be carried out at little cost. It is better to invite charges of hypocrisy by avoiding the difficult cases than not helping where one can.

Reasonable people can and do differ on the degree to which the United States should intervene to protect its interests. The debate about whether the United States ought to be prepared to intervene at all, however, is more a debate about the nature of the United States than it is about intervention. Those who argue against being prepared for any intervention tend to be suspicious of U.S. power, believing that any interventionary capability will be misused as it was in Vietnam. They seek to constrain U.S. might by denying the United States the capability to act or paralyzing it in a web of multilateralism. For those of us who believe that the extension of U.S. influence—with all its faults—benefits the United States and the world community, preserving the position of the United States as the dominant global power is a pragmatic and moral necessity. That position cannot be maintained without the ability to intervene militarily in what remains a threatening and unstable world.

NOTES

1. For more on these themes see Christopher Clapham, *Third World Politics: An Introduction* (London: Croom Helm, 1985); Brian L. Job, ed., *The Insecurity Dilemma: National Security of Third World States* (Boulder: Lynne Rienner, 1992); and Robert Jackson, *Quasi-States, Sovereignty, International Relations and the Third World* (Cambridge; Cambridge University Press, 1990).
2. For why causes of peace in Western Europe will not apply to Asia, see Aaron L. Friedberg, "Ripe for Rivalry: Prospects for Peace in a Multipolar Asia," *International Security*, Vol. 18, No. 3 (Winter 1993/94), pp. 5–33. For why such causes of peace will not apply to the Third World, see Steven R. David, "Why the Third World Still Matters," *International Security*, Vol. 17, No. 3 (Winter 1992/93), pp. 127–159. especially pp. 131–144.
3. John Mueller, *Retreat from Doomsday: The Obsolescence of Major War* (New York: Basic Books, 1989).
4. For a similar view on the Middle East's continuing importance as a source of oil, see Joseph Stanislaw and Daniel Yergin, "Oil: Reopening the Door," *Foreign Affairs*, Vol. 72, No. 4., (September/October 1993), pp. 81–93.
5. For a concise expression of this view, see Stephen Van Evera, "The United States and the Third World: When to Intervene?" in Kenneth Oye, Robert Lieber, and Donald Rothchild, eds., *Eagle in a New World: American Grand Strategy in the Post–Cold War World* (New York: HarperCollins, 1992) p. 128.
6. The best argument in favor of the stabilizing effects of nuclear proliferation remains Kenneth Waltz, *The Spread of Nuclear Weapons: More May Be*

Better, Adelphi Papers No. 171 (London: International Institute for Strategic Studies, 1981).

7. For a good overall discussion of the problems caused by nuclear proliferation, see Lewis A. Dunn, *Controlling the Bomb*, (New Haven: Yale University Press, 1982), especially pp. 69–95. For an intriguing argument that military organizations are unlikely to meet the needs of nuclear deterrence, thus heightening concerns about the prospect of proliferation, see Scott D. Sagan, "The Perils of Proliferation: Organization Theory, Deterrence Theory, and the Spread of Nuclear Weapons," *International Security*, Vol. 18, No. 4 (Spring 1994), pp. 66–107.

8. Robert Tucker makes this point eloquently in "The Purposes of American Power," *Foreign Affairs*, Vol. 59, No. 2 (1980–81), pp. 241-274. Tucker, does not, however, believe it is necessary for the United States to spread its values to the Third World. See also Charles Maynes, "America Without the Cold War," *Foreign Policy*, No. 78 (Summer 1990), pp. 3–25.

9. Stephen Krasner, "Westphalia and All That," in Judith Goldstein and Robert Keohane, eds., *Ideas and Foreign Policy*, (Ithaca; Cornell University Press, 1993).

10. Samuel Barkin and Bruce Cronin, "The State and the Nation: Changing Norms and the Rule of Sovereignty in International Relations," *International Organization*, Vol. 48, No. 1 (Winter 1994), pp. 107–130.

11. Presidential Decision Directive (PPD) 25 severely restricts U.S. cooperation with the United Nations. Before such cooperation would take place, the United States would insist that U.S. interests were being advanced, it had congressional support, there were enough soldiers and funds for the intervention, a clear objective and clear exit were delineated, and acceptable command and control arrangements were made. This would eliminate the possibility of U.S.-UN cooperation for many if not most interventions for humanitarian concerns. See Elaine Sciolino, "New U.S. Peacekeeping Policy De-emphasizes Role of the U.N.," *New York Times* May 6, 1994, p. A1. See also Douglas Jehl, "U.S. Is Showing a New Caution On U.N. Peacekeeping Missions." *New York Times*, May 18, 1994, p. A1. The article relates the refusal of the United States to authorize the sending of 5,500 troops to Rwanda until key details are worked out.

12. Steven R. David, *Third World Coups d'Etat and International Security*, (Baltimore: Johns Hopkins University Press, 1976), especially chs. 2 and 5.

13. Restoring the Shah (Mohammad Reza Pahlavi) to power created resentment against the United States, which helped pave the way for the Ayatollah Ruboliah Khomeini a quarter of a century later. Toppling Jácobo Arbenz contributed to decades of instability and repressive rule in Guatemala. U.S. efforts to depose João Goulart and Salvador Allende called into question the United States' commitment to democracy while tarnishing Washington's image in Latin America. Norodom Sihanouk's downfall brought to power the ineffectual Lon Nol, which in turn led to the seizure of power by the murderous Khmer Rouge. Most damaging was the U.S. success in overthrowing the Diem regime which enmeshed Washington

ever more closely into the affairs of South Vietnam with all the horrendous consequences to follow.

14. For a similar view, see Caleb Carr, "The Consequences of Somalia," *World Policy Journal*, Vol. 10, No. 3 (Fall 1993), pp. 1–4.

15. For a good overview of the problems facing U.S. policy-makers in Haiti, see Pamela Constable, "Dateline Haiti: Caribbean Stalemate," *Foreign Policy*, No. 89 (Winter 1992–93), pp. 175–190.

16. See, for example, Howard W. French, "Study Says Haiti Sanctions Kill up to 1,000 Children a Month," *New York Times*, November 9, 1993, p. A1. See also Howard W. French, "Doctors Question Haiti Health Data: Find Flaws in Projection that Embargo is Causing 1,000 Infant Deaths a Month," *New York Times* November 24, 1993, p. A12. Despite the debate over the number of deaths, no one disputes the fact that innocent Haitians are suffering and dying because of the sanctions.

3

Congress and the Use of Force in the Post–Cold War Era

James M. Lindsay

In mid-September 1994, President Bill Clinton faced a potential constitutional crisis. After months of threatening to use force to restore Haitian president Jean-Bertrand Aristide to power, he had failed to convince Haiti's military leaders to step down. Faced with the need to make good on his threat, he found that a substantial majority in Congress was vehemently opposed to invading Haiti. Leading Democrats and Republicans insisted that congressional approval was necessary for an invasion, and polls showed that three-quarters of all Americans agreed.[1] Despite the opposition, Clinton ordered the Pentagon to begin the invasion. A showdown with Congress was averted only because Haiti's military leaders agreed to step down from power shortly after learning that the invasion had begun.

Clinton's belief that the president has the constitutional authority to order the invasion of another country on his own authority would have shocked the men who wrote the Constitution. They almost all agreed with George Mason of Virginia, who said during the Constitutional Convention that he was "against giving the power of war to the executive" because the president "is not safely to be trusted with it."[2] Yet despite the wishes of the founders, U.S. presidents from Harry Truman onward have effectively claimed the war power for themselves. Indeed, during the 1950s and 1960s members of Congress willingly surrendered the war power to the White House, arguing that the communist

71

threat made attempts to limit the president's authority to use force both unwise and contrary to the spirit of the Constitution.

The end of the Cold War has helped to undermine presidential claims to a monopoly on the war power. As Bill Clinton learned firsthand, with the Soviet threat now a fading memory, members of Congress are much more likely to disagree among themselves and with the president over what constitutes the national interest, and the American public is less inclined to punish members who challenge the president. The result of these developments, as the controversies that raged in 1993 and 1994 over Bosnia and Somalia as well as Haiti all attest, is that Congress has become more willing to challenge presidential decisions to use force. These debates also illustrate several important and enduring lessons about Congress. Perhaps most notably, while members of Congress have become more active on war powers issues in recent years, they still decline to dictate policy to the White House. In large part their reluctance stems not from the oft-cited fear of responsibility but from a widespread recognition that Congress is ill-equipped to run foreign policy.

The resurgence of congressional activism on decisions to use force has rekindled interest in the War Powers Resolution. Although the law is widely regarded as ineffective and fatally flawed, some members hope that it can be repaired, either to enable Congress to regain its control over the war power or to encourage greater consultations between Congress and the White House. Whatever the goal of the reform proposals, they are unlikely to become law, and if they do, they are unlikely to have much impact. The reason is simple: structural reforms cannot solve what is essentially a political problem. As hard as the reformers might try, no law can nullify the inherent advantages that presidents have over Congress.

ORIGINAL INTENT AND PRACTICE

Fathoming the original intent of the founders can be distressingly difficult. Yet when it comes to the issue of which branch of government should control the war power, the founders were unambiguous: Congress should.[3] Article I, section 8 of the Constitution states that Congress shall have the power "to declare War." In recognition that not all hostilities reach the level of full-scale war, the Constitution further assigns to Congress the power to "grant Letters of Marque and Reprisal." In assigning the war power to Congress, the founders explicitly rejected a proposal to lodge the authority to use force (outside of the narrow case of a sudden attack on the United States) in the executive branch. When Pierce Butler moved to vest the war power in the president, none of the other delegates to the Constitutional Convention seconded his motion. The founders made explicit their limited conception of presidential authority in their battle to win ratification of the Constitution. As Alexander Hamilton wrote in "Federalist No. 69," the president's power as commander in chief "would amount to nothing more than the supreme command and direction of the military and naval forces . . . while that of the British king extends to the *declaring* of war and to the *raising* and *regulating* of fleets and armies; all of which by the Constitution under consideration would appertain to the Legislature."[4]

To a remarkable extent, the founders' views on the war power guided political practice over the next one hundred and fifty years.[5] At the start of the "undeclared" naval war of 1798–1800 with France, John Adams called Congress into special session "to consult and determine on such measure as in their wisdom shall be deemed meet for the safety and welfare of the said United States," and Congress subsequently passed more than a dozen laws authorizing hostilities.[6] Half a century later, President James Buchanan wrote that the war power of Congress was "without limitation" and extended to "every species of hostility, however confined or limited."[7] During the latter half of the nineteenth century, Congress's role in foreign policy was so pronounced that the era has been called one of "congressional government," "congressional supremacy," "government-by-Congress," and "senatorial domination."[8] And in the years preceding World War II, isolationists on Capitol Hill fought Franklin Roosevelt's efforts to move the United States closer to Britain and France.[9]

Of course, the original intent of the founders was by no means always followed in the first century and a half of the Republic.

The U.S military on occasion—the exact number is a matter of some dispute—used force without congressional sanction.[10] Yet most of these incidents involved relatively inconsequential attacks on nonstate actors such as brigands and pirates, and they frequently occurred without the benefit of either congressional or presidential authorization. Moreover, "when certain presidents did play a little fast and loose with congressional prerogatives— Polk at the start of the Mexican War; Wilson and Roosevelt, respectively, in the events leading up to the First and Second World Wars—they obscured or covered up the actual facts, pledging public fealty to the constitutional need for congressional authorization of military action."[11] In short, despite some exceptions, presidents from George Washington to Franklin Roosevelt remained true to Abraham Lincoln's belief "that *no one man* should hold the power of bringing . . . [war] upon us."[12]

THE IMPERIAL PRESIDENCY

Alexis de Tocqueville speculated in the 1840s that Congress's relative strength in foreign policy owed to the country's isolation from external threat. "If the Union's existence were constantly menaced, and if its great interests were continually interwoven with those of other powerful nations, one would see the prestige of the executive growing, because of what was expected from it and of what it did."[13] The rise of the imperial presidency in the two decades after the end of World War II proved Tocqueville right.[14] As Americans became convinced in the late 1940s that hostile communist states threatened the United States and the rest of the free world, the president's say in decisions to use force grew while that of Congress faded.

The decline of Congress's war powers began in June 1950 when President Harry Truman informed members of Congress after the fact of his decision to send U.S. troops to repel the invasion of South Korea. Whereas only a decade earlier members of Congress had fought tooth and nail to prevent Franklin Roosevelt from taking any step that might entangle the United States in war, few members disputed Truman's authority to order U.S. troops into combat without congressional authorization. Indeed, when it was suggested to Truman during a meeting with congressional leaders that he might strengthen his political hand by asking Congress to pass a resolution endorsing his decision to defend South Korea, the Senate majority leader and several other senior members argued that such a resolution was unnecessary and might prompt a damaging and divisive debate.[15]

Although Truman's unilateral decision to defend Korea usurped Congress's constitutional authority to declare war, the precedent was not necessarily permanent. Dwight Eisenhower accorded greater respect to Congress's war power than did his predecessor, stating that during his administration there would be "no involvement of America in war unless it is a result of the constitutional process that is placed upon Congress to declare it."[16] When U.S. interests were threatened in Formosa and the Middle East, Eisenhower asked Congress on each occasion to give him authority to respond with U.S. troops. Yet rather than restoring Congress's war power, the debates over the Formosa and Middle East resolutions enhanced presidential power. In both cases, members openly doubted that Eisenhower needed congressional authorization to act, and in the case of the Middle East Resolution, Congress struck language from the draft resolution explicitly authorizing the use of force because members feared the country might be harmed if presidents came to believe they could use force only if they first obtained congressional approval.[17]

The decline of Congress's war power accelerated under Eisenhower's successors. John Kennedy included only one member of Congress in the discussions that led up to the Bay of Pigs operation. When he imposed a naval quarantine on Cuba during the missile crisis he did so on his own authority as commander in chief and without congressional approval or consultation.[18] Likewise, Congress played no role in his decisions to increase the number of military advisers in South Vietnam from 685 at the time of his inauguration to roughly 16,000 at the time of his death.[19] For the most part, members of Congress shared Kennedy's expansive view of presidential authority. When the Bay of Pigs operation failed, for example, only one member complained publicly that the president had exceeded his authority.[20]

Kennedy's decision to send more troops to South Vietnam set the stage for the low point in congressional influence over the use of force: passage of the Gulf of Tonkin Resolution. Unlike either the Formosa or Middle East resolutions, debate on the Gulf of Tonkin Resolution was minimal. The House voted unanimously to support Lyndon Johnson after only forty minutes of discussion. The Senate debated for ten hours and passed the resolution with only two dissenting votes. Moreover, whereas the Formosa Resolution explicitly authorized the president to use force to defend U.S. interests, the Gulf of Tonkin Resolution simply stated that "the Congress approves and supports the determination of the president, as Commander in Chief, to take all necessary measures to repel any armed attack against the forces of the United States and to prevent further aggression."[21] As Jean Smith argues, "the change in wording reflected more than presidential predilections; it involved a fundamental shift in the role of Congress from one of ultimate authority to one of subordinate support."[22]

The willingness of members of Congress to surrender the war power to the executive branch in the 1950s and 1960s reflected a belief widespread on Capitol Hill and among Americans that the president *should* have the authority to initiate the use of military force. For many members, the 1930s had taught that strong presidential leadership was essential if the United States were to meet its new national security challenges. Rep. William Colmer's (D-Miss.) speech during debate on the Middle East Resolution was typical. "We cannot make foreign policy in the Congress of the United States; that would be impossible. You know where that would lead to. So we must rely on the Chief Executive and those who would advise him. In fact . . . it is the constitutional duty of the President to make our foreign policy."[23] Regardless of what the text of the Constitution might say, members of Congress had come to see their role as no more than legitimizing decisions made in the White House.

The willingness of members of Congress to surrender the war power to the executive branch stemmed not only from beliefs about which branch of government was best suited to lead in an uncertain world; it also reflected electoral calculations. Members opposed to presidential decisions to use force often swallowed their objections because they calculated that challenging the White House would make them vulnerable to charges that they were "soft" on communism. The deference given to the president became self-perpetuating; potential critics declined to challenge the president because they believed that few of their colleagues would follow their lead. As Sen. J.W. Fulbright (D-Ark.), the long-time chair of the Foreign Relations Committee, explained his reluctance to challenge the Defense Department: "I have been under the feeling that it was utterly useless and futile, that nothing could be done . . . no matter what I did."[24]

CONGRESS RESURGENT

The deference that Congress accorded the president during the era of the imperial presidency ultimately rested on the belief of the public and the political elite alike that hostile communist states posed an imminent threat to the United States. As the Vietnam War marched to its bloody conclusion, many Americans began to doubt the scope of the threat to U.S. security. The consensus that was fractured by Vietnam fell even further into disarray two decades later when the Soviet Union itself collapsed. The not too surprising result of both events was that members of Congress tried to reclaim the war power for themselves.

By the late 1960s, many members of Congress had come to rue the Gulf of Tonkin Resolution. As a result, they sought to curtail what they saw as the excesses of the imperial presidency. Many of the efforts specifically targeted U.S. involvement in southeast Asia. For example, in the wake of the invasion of Cambodia, the Senate voted to cut off all funds for U.S. military operations in Cambodia, and eight months later Congress repealed the Gulf of Tonkin Resolution. Other efforts, however, were designed more broadly to restrict presidential authority to initiate the use of force. These efforts culminated in November 1973 when Congress enacted the War Powers Resolution over Richard Nixon's veto.

The passions that made the War Powers Resolution possible abated somewhat over the course of the next sixteen years.[25] In some instances—Angola in 1975, Lebanon in 1983 (after much delay), and El Salvador and Nicaragua throughout the 1980s—substantial numbers of representatives and senators mobilized to constrain presidential decisions to use military forces overseas and to support proxy armies. In other instances, however, congressional voices were more muted. When the White House declined to consult with Congress on its decisions to use force against Grenada in 1983, Libya in 1986, and Panama in 1989, most members of Congress accepted the decisions without complaint.

Since the invasion of Panama, members of Congress have become more willing to contest presidential decisions to use force. The rejuvenated belief among members of Congress in the need for congressional participation in decisions to use force first became evident in the debate over the Gulf War. Although members of Congress did not influence President Bush's decision to liberate Kuwait by force and though (for reasons discussed below) they did not vote on George Bush's policy until the United States and Iraq were at the brink of war, the January 1991 debate nonetheless remains remarkable. Faced with a vote on a matter of supreme national importance, forty-seven senators and one hundred and eighty-three representatives publicly and formally rejected the president's request for authority to use force.

Congress's resurgent interest in the war power was evident again in 1993 as it wrestled with President Bill Clinton over policy toward Somalia, Haiti, and Bosnia. In February, the Senate passed a resolution authorizing the U.S. mission in Somalia. The vote, which came two months after President Bush sent U.S. troops into Somalia to prevent mass starvation, was notable because with it the Senate was insisting that its authorization was needed. In contrast, ten years earlier Congress had acted to authorize the U.S. peacekeeping mission in Lebanon only after U.S. forces had become involved in the Lebanese civil war and several U.S. soldiers had been killed. In May, the House approved an updated version of the resolution, this time authorizing U.S. troops to participate in what had become a United Nations' mission in Somalia.

The House resolution never became law because the Senate put it aside after United Nations peacekeepers came under attack from Somali militias. In response to the escalating violence, the Senate in early September attached a nonbinding resolution to the defense authorization bill asking the president to report to Congress by October 15 on the goals of U.S. forces in Somalia and to win specific congressional authorization for the mission by November 15. The resolution, which was sponsored by Senate Majority Leader George Mitchell (D-Maine) and Senate Minority Leader Robert Dole (R-Kans.), was designed as a substitute for a more restrictive amendment offered by Sen. Robert Byrd (D-W.Va.), chair of the Senate Appropriations Committee, that would have terminated funding for the Somalia mission if Congress did not authorize the mission within one month of enactment.[26] The House followed the Senate's lead two weeks later and passed the nonbinding resolution.

The September resolution initially looked as if it would satisfy congressional concerns over Somalia. But only a week after the House vote, eighteen Army Rangers were killed during a raid on a suspected stronghold of Somali warlord Mohammed Farah Aideed. The deaths, the highest suffered by any army unit in combat since the Vietnam War, led to a fire storm of criticism. During debate over the annual defense appropriations bill, Clinton's supporters turned back an amendment sponsored by Sen. John McCain (R-Ariz.) that would have repudiated the administration's policy and required the prompt withdrawal of U.S. troops. Instead, the Senate passed an amendment sponsored by Senator Byrd endorsing the administration's policy. But the victory was a hollow one for the White House. It came only after Clinton agreed to narrow the goals of the U.S. mission in Somalia and to withdraw all U.S. troops from Somalia by March 31, 1994.[27]

Concerned that the House might embarrass the president if policy toward Somalia came to a vote on the floor, the House Democratic leadership worked to keep the issue off the agenda. In early November, a vote was avoided when the House accepted the conference report on the annual defense appropriations bill and with it the March 31 deadline. House Republicans objected to this maneuver and under the leadership of Rep. Benjamin Gilman (R-N.Y.), used a provision of the War Powers Resolution to force the House leadership to schedule a vote on a nonbinding concurrent resolution that would have moved the deadline up to January 31. The outcome of the debate was mixed. Gilman's resolution passed 224 to 203, but because the debate was held under so-called king-of-the-hill rules in which only the last in a series of motions is actually adopted, the Gilman resolution was superseded when the House subsequently voted 226 to 201 to endorse a second resolution that supported the administration's withdrawal date of March 31.

As the congressional debate over Somalia unfolded, Congress also became embroiled in similar debates over Haiti and Bosnia. When armed Haitians prevented two hundred U.S. and Canadian engineers aboard the USS *Harlan County* from landing in Port-au-Prince in mid-October to work on development projects in Haiti, speculation rose that the Clinton administration might use force to restore Aristide to power. Senator Dole responded to the speculation by announcing he would introduce binding legislation requiring the administration to obtain congressional authorization before using force in Haiti unless the president certified that the lives of Americans or national security interests were imperiled.

Not surprisingly, the Dole proposal generated a firestorm of criticism–fueled at least in part by Dole's long-standing record of opposing Democratic attempts to fetter Republican presidents and his own admission that if he were president he would oppose the amendment he was offering. With even his staunch allies in the Republican Party among his critics, Dole withdrew his proposal. Sen. Jesse Helms (R-N.C.), however, stepped in to offer a similar amendment. The Senate rejected the Helms amendment by a vote of 81 to 19. Senators then overwhelmingly adopted two separate nonbinding amendments urging the administration to obtain congressional authorization before using force in either Haiti or Bosnia. (In a speech at the United Nations in September, President Clinton had pledged not to send U.S troops to Bosnia without "a clear expression of support from the United States Congress.")[28]

The Senate revisited the issue of Haiti in the summer of 1994. In June, Sen. Judd Gregg (R-N.H.) sponsored an amendment similar to the one proposed eight months earlier by Senator Helms. During the floor debate several Clinton supporters criticized the administration's policy, but senators again refused to mandate that the White House obtain congressional authorization before using force. Less than a month later, amid renewed speculation of a U.S. invasion, senators turned back another proposal, offered by Senator Dole, to postpone military action until a bipartisan commission had time to study the Haitian crisis. Although a majority of senators once again refused to tie the president's hands, the Clinton administration's margin of support slipped. Whereas the Helms amendment had garnered only 19 votes, the Gregg amendment garnered 34, and the Dole amendment 42.

The issue of Haiti moved to the top of the foreign policy agenda in September 1994 as it became clear that the Clinton administration planned to make good on its threat to use force to restore Aristide to power. Members of Congress from both sides of the aisle denounced the proposed invasion, and many went further to argue that Clinton could not act in the absence of congressional approval. As pressure mounted both inside and outside Congress for a vote on the issue, Democratic leaders in Congress blocked floor consideration of any legislation, nonbinding or binding, on Clinton's policy.[29] On September 16, Clinton told the nation that the time for negotiations had ended, but immediately after the speech, in an apparent bid to derail congressional opposition by showing that he was willing to "go the extra mile," Clinton asked former President Jimmy Carter to lead a high-level delegation to Haiti to persuade the nation's military leaders to step down voluntarily. The success of the Carter delegation derailed the impending clash over the war power, but many members criticized the peaceful insertion of U.S. troops into Haiti. The vehemence of the opposition to the presence of U.S. troops on the ground in Haiti made it likely that the Clinton administration would face a fire storm of criticism if any U.S. soldiers were killed.

The debates over the Gulf War, Bosnia, Haiti, and Somalia attest to the resurgence of Congress's interest in war powers issues. The reason for the resurgence stems largely from the demise of the Soviet Union. Five years into the post–Cold War era, no consensus has emerged regarding what will replace containment as the cornerstone of U.S. foreign policy. Instead, considerable debate rages over precisely where the vital interests of the United States lie and over what means should be used to achieve them. At the same time, the disappearance of the Soviet threat and the perceived absence of any threats of similar magnitude have made many Americans far more tolerant of legislative challenges to executive authority. Legislators who once risked electoral punishment for challenging the White House now often stand to benefit from criticizing the president. As a result, unless a new foreign policy consensus emerges or a clear threat to U.S. national security arises, congressional activism will persist, regardless of whether the occupant of the White House is a Democrat or a Republican.

FIVE LESSONS

The flurry of congressional activity on Bosnia, Haiti, and Somalia fueled widespread doubts about the competence of the Clinton administration in foreign affairs. While the administration did mishandle these issues in several respects, as Clinton and several of his senior advisers subsequently admitted, the fundamental source of executive-legislative conflict was less personal than structural. Indeed, the disputes over Bosnia, Haiti, Somalia, as well as the invasions of Panama and Iraq, point to five key lessons about congressional involvement in decisions to use force. Each of these lessons is likely to hold true regardless of who occupies the Oval Office in the post–Cold War era.

1. *Members of Congress have become more active on war powers issues, but they remain reluctant to dictate policy to the White House.* Although the congressional debates over Somalia, Haiti, and Bosnia attracted considerable attention and commentary, members of Congress stopped well short of taking control of foreign policy. Proposals such as the Helms and Gregg amendments that sought to place binding constraints on the White House suffered

lopsided defeats. In refusing to constrain the president's options through legislation, Congress's fear of constituent wrath played a relatively small role; after all, opinion polls repeatedly showed the American public siding with the administration's critics. Instead, substantial numbers of legislators opposed binding legislation because they believed that such an approach would destroy the president's negotiating leverage and set a dangerous precedent. As Senator McCain, one of President Clinton's harshest critics, put it: "I cannot support any resolution which prospectively limits the powers of the president as commander in chief."[30]

If the *powers* of the presidency emerged unscathed from the congressional debates over Somalia, Haiti, and Bosnia intact, Clinton's *policies* fared less well. In all three cases, Clinton found himself revamping his policies to derail even more intrusive congressional action, and in the case of Bosnia, he went so far as to pledge to seek congressional approval before sending U.S. troops. Clinton made these policy changes because members were using committee hearings, floor speeches, and nonbinding resolutions to pressure the administration to heed their wishes. In short, many members continue to believe (at least for now) that the national interest is best served if Congress persuades presidents to change their policies through political pressure rather than compels them to change their policies through binding legislation.

2. *Not all decisions to use force are equal in the eyes of members of Congress.* Although the demise of the Soviet Union emboldened members of Congress, congressional reactions to proposals to use force are not uniform. Instead, presidents are most likely to command majority support in Congress when they contemplate using force to protect traditional U.S. interests, as happened in both Panama and the Persian Gulf. Conversely, presidents are most likely to confront concerted congressional opposition when they contemplate using force to promote U.S. values (e.g., democracy, rule of law, a halt to genocide), as happened in Bosnia, Haiti, and Somalia.

The reasons for the uneven congressional reactions lie in both beliefs and electoral calculations. Although Americans historically have cast foreign policy in moral terms, no consensus exists today at either the elite or mass level on whether it is appropriate for the United States to use force to advance U.S. values such as democratic rule. In turn, the lack of a public consensus inclines many members of Congress to be skeptical of proposals to use force toward these ends. In contrast, in situations where U.S. troops are being called on to protect U.S. interests, or what are widely perceived as U.S. interests, both beliefs and electoral calculations tend to incline members of Congress toward using force. In this respect, it is notable that members of Congress were much more circumspect in criticizing the Clinton administration's handling of a potential nuclear showdown with North Korea in mid–1994 than they were of the crises in Bosnia, Haiti, or Somalia.[31]

   3. *A vote to authorize the president to use force is a "use it and lose it" decision, which encourages members to delay making a decision.* The ability to pass binding laws is typically taken to be the primary source of Congress's power. Yet when it comes to the use of force, Congress can do no more than give or withhold its permission, and a vote either way is fraught with peril. A vote denying the president authority will destroy any attempt at coercive diplomacy, and as a result, may prevent the president from resolving the crisis peacefully in the favor of the United States. Conversely, once members authorize the president to use force, they cede control over policy to the executive branch. Members are free to hope that the president will use the authority wisely, but as the Gulf of Tonkin Resolution shows, once given the authority to use force a president is not bound by the expectations that members might have about the conditions under which he will use it.[32] The fear of destroying the president's bargaining level combined with the "use it and lose it" quality of congressional authorizations makes many members leery to act on crises until events have made armed conflict likely. By doing so, however, members virtually guarantee, as Sen. Arthur Vandenberg (R-Mich.) once put it, that crises will "never reach Congress until they have developed to a point where Congressional discretion is pathetically restricted."[33]

   The evolution of Operation Desert Shield into Operation Desert Storm illustrates the dilemma. When George Bush sent

U.S. troops to the Persian Gulf in August 1990, some observers urged Congress to strengthen the president's bargaining position by authorizing him to use force against Iraq. At the beginning of October, the House and Senate both passed nonbinding resolutions expressing support for the actions Bush had taken, but neither chamber moved to give him authority to act against Iraq.[34] For members of Congress, passing such a resolution had two distinct disadvantages: defeating it would have undercut the president's bargaining leverage while passing it would have relieved him of any need to include Congress in future decisions on the crisis. Since Bush's stated policy was to rely on economic sanctions to compel Iraq to withdraw from Kuwait, most members believed that any debate over authorizing the use of force would be premature. So long as the president refused to discuss the possibility of liberating Kuwait by force, members were content to accept the status quo.

All that changed in November when Bush announced that the United States was prepared to use force to liberate Kuwait. Although Congress was urged to convene in special session, as had been provided for in the adjournment resolution, the proposal foundered over two problems. One was that no one knew if war was likely; if Iraq backed down when threatened with force, as many believed it would, then congressional authorization would be unnecessary. The other problem was that if members voted in November or December to authorize the use of force, they would have lost control of policy. While there were conditions under which a majority was prepared to vote in December for war, there were also conditions under which a majority would have voted against war. No one knew which set of circumstances would prevail. Thus, as Rep. Dan Glickman (D-Kans.) put it at the time, "No one is interested in a hypothetical vote, and I don't want a hypothetical special session."[35]

By early January 1991 the question of whether to use force was no longer hypothetical. The Iraqi government had refused to make even symbolic concessions, and the Bush administration had given in to public pressure and requested that Congress formally authorize the use of force. At the same time, however, members had only two options. They either could grant the president the authority that he requested and thereby risk a costly war or deny his request and thereby deal him a humiliating public defeat that would severely damage U.S. interests in the region. In the end, practical, normative, and electoral calculations led a majority of Congress, albeit a small one in the Senate, to grant the president authority to wage war.

4. *Framing is an important congressional tool for influencing presidential decisions.* The fact that legislation is often a deficient tool invariably pushes members of Congress toward non-legislative courses of action. Preeminent among these is *framing,* or efforts to package an issue in a way that attracts media and executive branch attention, places the issue on the agenda, and puts the administration on the defensive.[36] Members have many different tools with which to frame issues, including speeches on the floor, testimony at congressional hearings, and appearances on television and radio, to name some of the most prominent examples. For example, after President Bush announced in November 1990 that he was doubling the number of U.S. troops in Saudi Arabia, Sen. Sam Nunn (D-Ga.), chair of the Senate Armed Services Committee and a critic of the decision, chaired highly publicized hearings that featured several former administration officials who criticized the Bush administration's decision to use force to liberate Kuwait.[37]

Members of Congress turn to framing because they understand the disadvantages to legislation and because they recognize that changing foreign policy (or domestic policy for that matter) often requires changing the public and elite opinion that gave rise to it. As such, framing seeks to change policy indirectly. But because framing involves attracting media attention and because individual members may stand to benefit handsomely from their media exposure even if their preferred policies go down to defeat, many complain that members are engaged in nothing more than posturing.

Yet the fact that members of Congress may stand to benefit from their association with a major issue does not diminish the importance of framing to members who wish to change policy. For policy entrepreneurs, playing to the galleries is an essential tool for leveling the playing field with the White

House.[38] Members understand far better than their critics that increasing the scope of the decision-making arena may change the ultimate decision.[39] The media, especially television, give members the means to overcome the obstacles that block attempts to shape policy through legislation. The glare of the spotlight is often the best weapon members have to force the administration to reverse its course of action or to build public support for new policy initiatives.

At the same time, framing is no less useful a technique because it typically invokes simple, if not simplistic, arguments. Dismissing floor speeches that are loaded with impassioned sound bites as political theater misses the point. Not only do presidents themselves indulge in simple and dramatic appeals— recall George Bush's repeated attempts to demonize Manuel Noriega and Saddam Hussein—such appeals are essential to winning the support of the public. A simple, well-framed charge that anyone can understand puts the burden of proof on one's opponents to justify their favored policies.[40]

5. *Congress rallies round in victory and piles on in defeat.* Although it might be preferable if Congress evaluated the merits of decision making procedures independently of the policies they produce, the reality is just the opposite. For most members of Congress, the process by which a decision to use force is reached matters far less than whether the operation itself succeeds or fails. In the case of Panama and the Gulf War, for instance, U.S. forces accomplished their objectives quickly, and members of Congress who opposed the decision to use force swallowed their objections about the lack of executive-legislative consultations. Conversely, when U.S. policy toward Bosnia and Somalia began to go sour, members who had previously supported the Clinton administration's efforts or who had not given them much thought moved rapidly to criticize the administration for failing to consult with Congress.

The tendency of members to rally round in victory and to pile on in defeat is by no means a new development; it is a pattern of behavior that dates back to the earliest days of the Republic. Johns Adams's willingness to call Congress into special session to consider whether to pursue a limited maritime war with

France did not protect him once those congressionally approved policies proved disastrous. More recently, Lyndon Johnson learned the hard way that winning congressional approval in advance does not guarantee congressional support when a policy falters: "I said early in my Presidency that if I wanted Congress with me on the landing of Vietnam, I'd have to have them with me on the takeoff. And I did just that. But I failed to reckon with one thing: the parachute. I got them on the takeoff, but a lot of them bailed out before the end of the flight."[41]

Members of Congress tend to rally round in victory and pile on in defeat because of electoral calculations. After all, there is usually little profit to be made in complaining about decision making procedures that led to a popular war or supporting procedures that led to an unpopular one. This fundamental political reality carries with it an important lesson for the White House: in the final analysis, success matters much more than procedure. A hostile Congress can be won over with a victory and a friendly Congress can be lost with a defeat.

THE WAR POWERS RESOLUTION

Increased congressional activism on war powers issues has focused great attention on the process by which the United States decides to use military force. Throughout much of U.S. history, the shape of that process was governed by custom rather than by statute. By the early 1970s, however, custom had swung so far in the direction of the president that members of Congress sought to reclaim their influence by creating a formal legal framework to govern the use of military force. When the War Powers Resolution was finally enacted, its supporters saw it as reestablishing the constitutional balance that the founders had intended between Congress and the president. In practice, though, the resolution has proved to be a disappointment. Two decades after it was enacted into law, most members of Congress regard it as a dead letter.

Section 2 of the War Powers Resolution states that the purpose of the law is to "insure that the collective judgment of both the Congress and the President will apply to the introduction of United States Armed Forces into hostilities, or into situations where imminent involvement in hostilities is clearly indicated by the circumstances, and to the continued use of such forces in hostilities or in such situations." Section 2 further states that the president may order U.S. troops "into hostilities, or into situations where imminent involvement in hostilities is clearly indicated by the circumstances . . . only pursuant to (1) a declaration of war, (2) specific statutory authorization, or (3) a national emergency created by an attack upon the United States, its territories or possessions, or its armed forces."

To give the demand for executive-legislative consultations bite, the War Powers Resolution has two key requirements. Section 4(a) requires the president to submit a report to Congress within forty-eight hours whenever troops are introduced "(1) into hostilities or situations where imminent involvement in hostilities is clearly indicated by the circumstances; (2) into the territory, airspace or waters of a foreign nation, while equipped for combat, except for deployments which relate solely to supply, replacement, repair or training of such forces; or (3) in numbers which substantially enlarge United States armed forces equipped for combat already located in a foreign nation." Section 5(b) stipulates that if U.S. armed forces have been sent into situations of actual or imminent hostilities, the president must remove the troops within sixty days—ninety days if he requests a delay—unless Congress declares war or otherwise authorizes the use of force. The resolution also provides that Congress can compel the president to withdraw the troops at any time by passing a concurrent resolution.

Despite the hopes of its supporters, the War Powers Resolution has proved to be no more than what Arthur Schlesinger has called "a toy handcuff."[42] The sixty-day clock has never been tested, and many members seem almost pained by the fact that the resolution exists. For example, when Ronald Reagan sent marines to Lebanon in September 1982 to act as peacekeepers in the Lebanese civil war, nine months elapsed before Congress went so far as to direct the president to "obtain statutory authorization from Congress with respect to any substantial expansion in the number or role in Lebanon of United States Armed Forces."[43] Congress finally invoked the War Powers Resolution in late September 1983 but only after several marines were killed and U.S. forces intervened in the civil war in support of the Lebanese government.[44] Even then, Congress gave Reagan authority to act under the resolution for eighteen months and to use "such protective measures as may be necessary to secure the safety of the Multinational Force in Lebanon."[45]

As timid as Congress's actions on Lebanon were, they might have set an important precedent. But such was not the case. In 1987, the Reagan administration sent the U.S. Navy into the Persian Gulf to protect Kuwaiti shipping from attacks by Iran. Although the Defense Department paid "imminent danger" bonuses to U.S. personnel in the Gulf and U.S. forces attacked Iranian ships and staging areas, motions to invoke the War Powers Resolution died on the floor of Congress. Members showed even less enthusiasm for invoking the War Powers Resolution after George Bush sent U.S. troops to Saudi Arabia following the Iraqi invasion of Kuwait in August 1990. Congress adjourned for the year in late October without considering any motions to invoke the War Powers Resolution. The same pattern repeated itself in 1993 after U.S. soldiers were killed in Somalia. As mentioned earlier, the House and Senate both passed nonbinding resolutions asking President Clinton to consult with Congress about the controversial deployment, but neither chamber moved to invoke the War Powers Resolution.[46] And during the weeks leading up to the Clinton administration's showdown with Haiti's military leaders in September 1994, few members from either political party mentioned the War Powers Resolution in public.[47]

The failure of the War Powers Resolution to work as planned might be overlooked if it could be said that the prospect of congressional action has had the effect of forcing presidents to consult with Congress. But such has not been the case. In almost every instance in which the United States used military force between 1973 and 1994, the executive-legislative dialogue consisted of presidents *informing* Congress, usually after the fact, that they had decided to commit U.S. troops. In the case of

Grenada, for example, congressional leaders were not informed of the invasion until two hours after President Reagan gave U.S. forces the final order to proceed.[48] Likewise, in Panama, President Bush informed congressional leaders of the invasion shortly before it began, but more than two days after he decided to order military action.[49] In the case of Operation Desert Shield, Bush consulted with a small circle of executive branch officials when he decided in October 1990 to double the size of U.S. forces in the Persian Gulf and to shift them from a defensive mission to an offensive one; he pointedly avoided discussing the proposed troop increase with even ranking Republicans in Congress, and some congressional leaders learned of his decision only minutes before it was announced.[50] The one exception to this trend was the case of Haiti, in which the Clinton White House held relatively extensive talks with selected congressional leaders. By most accounts, however, President Clinton chose to disregard much of the advice he was given.[51]

Reasons for the failure of the War Powers Resolution abound.[52] One is that members of Congress are of many minds when it comes to the wisdom of the resolution. Some members, "reflecting their constituencies, are loath to second-guess the president or to do anything that might be perceived as undercutting American forces, especially if the administration could blame them for the loss of life."[53] Other members doubt the resolution's constitutionality or are happy to ignore its provisions if they agree with the president's decision to deploy troops. These attitudes give members who doubt the wisdom of the policy or the president's authority to order it good reason to conclude that any effort to invoke the resolution will be futile.

A second reason that the War Powers Resolution has failed to live up to the expectations of its sponsors is presidential defiance. Although every president since Richard Nixon has spoken publicly of the need to work with Congress on war powers issues, none has fully embraced the resolution. Indeed, some have ignored the resolution in situations where it would seem to apply. In the early 1980s, for instance, Ronald Reagan refused to file a report on the activities of U.S. military advisers in El Salvador, even after several were killed, on the grounds that hostilities were not imminent.[54] Moreover, presidents generally have avoided taking steps that might be construed as acknowledging the constitutionality of the War Powers Resolution. Thus when Reagan signed the resolution authorizing the presence of marines in Lebanon, he stated that the signing should not "be viewed as any acknowledgement that the President's constitutional authority can be impermissibly infringed by statute, that congressional authorization would be required if and when the period specified in Section 5(b) of the War Powers Resolution might be deemed to have been triggered and the period had expired."[55] In rejecting the constitutionality of the War Powers Resolution, presidents have stated repeatedly that the commander-in-chief clause gives them independent authority to make war.

The ability of presidents to disregard the War Powers Resolution has been made easier by the law's imprecision. The text of the resolution does not define what constitutes imminent or actual hostilities, and it does not require presidents to state if they are filing their report under provision 4(a)(1), which triggers the sixty-day clock. Thus while presidents filed more than twenty reports to Congress in the first two decades that the resolution was in effect, only Gerald Ford during the *Mayaguez* crisis filed a report that specified section 4(a)(1). (Since Ford submitted his report after U.S. forces had been withdrawn, he conceded little to Congress.) In every other instance, presidents have submitted their reports without mentioning any specific sections of the resolution, thereby shifting the burden for starting the clock onto Congress.

Finally, the War Powers Resolution has failed to work in part because of actions taken by the courts. When the Supreme Court ruled in *I.N.S. v. Chadha* (1983) that most uses of the legislative veto violate the presentation clause of the Constitution, it invalidated part of the War Powers Resolution.[56] Although Congress subsequently passed separate legislation substituting a joint resolution for the concurrent resolution provided for in the War Powers Resolution, the change left Congress in a much weaker position. Unlike concurrent resolutions, joint resolutions are subject to a presidential veto, so opponents now need to muster two-thirds of the members in both the House and Senate to compel a troop withdrawal. Given that Congress has overridden only two foreign policy vetoes in the past twenty-five years, such a prospect seems highly unlikely.

While the Supreme Court weakened the War Powers Resolution with its ruling in *Chadha*, the courts have weakened the resolution even more with the deference they have paid to the president's authority in foreign affairs. In the four instances in which members of Congress sued to force the president to abide by the resolution, the courts dismissed the suits as non-justiciable. In doing so, the courts set a high standard for considering such a suit justiciable. In *Lowry v. Reagan*, for example, a federal district court ruled it would hear the dispute over President Reagan's authority to order the navy to protect Kuwaiti shipping only if there were a "true confrontation between the Executive and a unified Congress, as evidenced by its passage of legislation to enforce the [War Powers] Resolution."[57] Likewise, in *Dellums v. Bush*, a case in which one hundred and ten members challenged President Bush's authority to liberate Kuwait without congressional authorization, a federal district court ruled it would act only if "the plaintiffs in an action of this kind be or represent the majority of the members of Congress."[58] Since a declaration of war requires the approval of both houses of Congress, the courts have effectively shifted the burden of proof from a war's proponents, which is where the Constitution placed it, to a war's opponents.

REPAIRING THE WAR POWERS RESOLUTION

The many failures of the War Powers Resolution have produced widespread pessimism about the law's value. As Senator Nunn put it: The resolution has "never worked in the past [and] it's never going to work."[59] Not surprisingly, such sentiments have prompted a spate of proposals for repairing the War Powers Resolution. To quote Sen. Joseph Biden (D-Del.): "It's time to give it up and get something that works."[60]

One possibility, favored by many conservative Republicans, is to repeal the War Powers Resolution outright.[61] The argument for repeal builds on both prudential and constitutional grounds. Proponents of repeal argue that the sixty-day clock diminishes the president's credibility to act abroad because it encourages adversaries to believe that stalling tactics will work to their benefit. At the same time, they argue that the War Powers Resolution impermissibly infringes on the president's constitutional powers as commander in chief. Although repeal of the War Powers Resolution might be taken as a sign that Congress has surrendered its war power, proponents argue otherwise. As Dick Cheney writes: "Congress has plenty of constitutional and political power to stop a president whenever it wants to. Anyone who doubts this should look at the long list of foreign policy limitation amendments to the appropriations acts of the past decade."[62]

Rather than repeal the War Powers Resolution, some critics call for strengthening the law.[63] The underlying assumptions here are twofold: Congress can and should participate in decisions to use force, and the current balance of power on war power questions leans far too heavily in the direction of the White House. The remedy, then, lies in crafting legislation that promotes "a genuine war-powers relationship between the President and Congress."[64]

Some proposals for strengthening the War Powers Resolution focus on closing loopholes in the original language. For example, to make it harder for presidents to circumvent the spirit of the resolution through semantic subterfuge, the War Powers Resolution could be rewritten to specify precisely what constitutes "hostilities," "imminent hostilities," and "consultation." Likewise, sections 4(a)(2) and 4(a)(3) of the resolution, which require the president to submit a report but which do not trigger the sixty-day clock, could be repealed. With these provisions removed, the submission of any report would automatically start the clock in motion. (The justification for repealing sections 4(a)(2) and 4(a)(3) rather than merely requiring presidents to specify the section under which they are filing their reports is that in the latter case defiant presidents almost certainly would file under either section 4(a)(2) or 4(a)(3) and shift the burden onto Congress to demonstrate that it should be otherwise.)

Other proposals to strengthen the War Powers Resolution target its enforcement provisions. To give sharper teeth to the sixty-day time limit, several commentators have proposed amending the resolution to require that once the clock expires, all funds to support the troops must be cut off. Making a funding cutoff automatic would relieve members of Congress of the politically unpalatable burden of voting not to support U.S. troops that are under fire. To further enhance the enforcement provisions of the War Powers Resolution, proponents argue for making it easier for members of Congress to seek a remedy in the courts if a president violates the terms of the law. By cajoling or compelling the courts to enter the fray—proponents differ on what can be done to force judicial participation—Congress would presumably shift the burden of proof back onto the president as the sponsors of the War Powers Resolution intended.

Somewhere between calls for repealing the War Powers Resolution and strengthening it lie proposals to keep some parts of the resolution and to jettison others. The most prominent of these efforts is a bill sponsored by Senators Byrd, Nunn, and John Warner (R-Va.).[65] (Rep. Lee Hamilton [D-Ind.] is the sponsor of companion legislation in the House.) In criticizing the War Powers Resolution, Senators Byrd, Nunn, and Warner have focused their complaints on the effectiveness and prudence of the law rather than its constitutionality. As Senator Byrd has put it, the War Powers Resolution is an "unworkable" law that "robs the President of . . . credibility."[66]

The Byrd-Nunn-Warner proposal would change the War Powers Resolution in two main ways. First, to make it more likely that the president will consult with Congress on decisions to use force, the Byrd-Nunn-Warner proposal specifies precisely whom in Congress he is expected to consult. The proposal directs the president in every possible instance in which the use of force is contemplated or actually used to consult with the Speaker of the House, the president pro tempore of the Senate, and the majority and minority leaders in both chambers. Together with the chairs and ranking minority members of the Foreign Affairs Committee, the Foreign Relations Committee, the armed services committees, and the intelligence committees, these congressional party leaders would form the "permanent consultative group." The president would be required to consult with the permanent consultative group if a majority of that body so requested. In the event of "extraordinary circumstances," the president would be empowered to exclude the committee chairs and to restrict the consultative process to congressional party leaders.

Second, the Byrd-Nunn-Warner proposal would repeal the mandatory sixty-day time limit. With such a change, Congress would retain its constitutional power to pass a joint resolution authorizing the use of force or requiring the withdrawal of U.S. troops.[67] To ensure that such a resolution does not become sidetracked by procedural wrangling, the Byrd-Nunn-Warner proposal stipulates that it must be accorded expedited consideration in both chambers, provided that it has been approved by a majority of the eighteen-member permanent consultative group. By substituting an optional joint resolution for the sixty-day time limit, the Byrd-Nunn-Warner proposal reverses the presumption of the War Powers Resolution that troops should be withdrawn unless Congress gave its permission. Instead, troops would be allowed to stay unless Congress votes (over an inevitable presidential veto) to remove them.

In sum, while a consensus exists that the War Powers Resolution has failed to work, no consensus exists on how to repair it or if it even should be. Some critics, including many Republicans in Congress, argue that the resolution should be repealed and Congress forced to rely on its existing constitutional powers if it wishes to challenge the president on decisions to use force. Other critics, most notably Senators Byrd, Nunn, and Warner, have abandoned hope that the sixty-day time limit can be made workable but remain optimistic that the objective of ensuring that decisions to use force reflect the collective judgment of both Congress and the president can be achieved. Still other critics believe that current practice gives the president authority that the founders never intended and must be stopped by a strengthened War Powers Resolution.

LIMITS TO REFORM

Proposals to rewrite (or repeal) the War Powers Resolution have provided ample fodder for law journals and academic conferences. But are any of these proposals likely to be adopted, and if so, will they alter the balance of power between Congress and the president? The answers to these two questions call for pessimism.

One obvious problem with efforts to rewrite (or repeal) the War Powers Resolution is that while members of Congress may agree that the resolution does not work, they disagree on how to fix it. Yet without a consensus on the proper solution, any attempt to revise or repeal the War Powers Resolution is likely to spark bitter debate. As Les Aspin observed during his confirmation hearings to be Secretary of Defense: "It's always been assumed that to try and amend [the resolution] would be such a humongous fight and raise such enormous hackles, and in the end it's not clear whether you'd get anything much better."[68]

The obstacles that stand in the way of rewriting the War Powers Resolution are made all the more difficult by the fact that there is no politically ideal time for Congress to act. As one Senate aide described the problem: "Legislation on War Powers is a catch-22. When nothing is happening—when there is no ongoing use of force, there's no urge to do something. When something is happening, there's a feeling that action must be taken—later. It produces a perfect catch-22."[69] The fallout from congressional efforts in October 1993 to limit the president's authority to deploy troops in Bosnia and Haiti and to continue their deployment in Somalia is typical in this regard. Aware that Congress "would face this problem over and over again" in the post-Cold War era, Senate Majority Leader Mitchell announced that the Senate Armed Services, Foreign Relations, and Intelligence committees would cooperate with Clinton administration officials to devise a new process for exercising Congress's war power. Despite Mitchell's hope that "a report could be completed and submitted to Congress for action by spring," the spring of 1994 came and went without any progress.[70]

Even if political feasibility were not an issue—and presidents could be counted on to abide by the revised law or the courts counted on to uphold it—no revision of the War Powers Resolution can ensure that decisions to use force will reflect the collective judgment of Congress and the president. The reason is that

Congress will always operate at a disadvantage relative to the president when it comes to decisions to use force. For example, no law, no matter how thoughtful or precisely crafted, can prevent presidents from sending troops abroad without notice and thereby presenting Congress with a *fait accompli*. If the deployment turns out to be for a short duration, as happened in Grenada, Libya, and Panama (among other instances), members have no practical recourse against the president for acting without congressional authorization.

Of course, what presidents intend as a short-lived military venture may lead to protracted combat and the opportunity for members of Congress to become involved in policy making. But even here none of the proposed reforms is likely to do much to give Congress a say in limiting the military operation. To force a troop withdrawal under the Byrd-Nunn-Warner proposal, Congress would have to pass a joint resolution to that effect since the sixty-day time limit would have been repealed. Since the president no doubt would veto such a resolution, no attempt to compel the withdrawal of U.S. troops would succeed unless it enjoyed the support of two-thirds of the members of both the House and Senate.

In theory, Congress would wield a much stronger hand if a strengthened version of the War Powers Resolution were in effect. In this case, congressional inaction by itself would compel the withdrawal of troops (assuming, of course, the president obeys the law, and the Supreme Court does not invoke the doctrine of political questions or find the law unconstitutional). In practice, however, this leverage may well be illusory. The reason is that a strengthened version of the War Powers Resolution would put members in the politically and morally difficult position of allowing funds to be cut off to troops who may be fighting for their lives. Moreover, a president facing a strengthened version of the War Powers Resolution might well respond by asking for a resolution of congressional approval early rather than late, thereby using the rally round the flag phenomenon that often (but not always) follows military operations to force congressional approval.[71] As a result, a strengthened version of the War Powers Resolution is likely to work only in a limited number of situations where presidents have misjudged both the likely success of military operations and the sentiment on Capitol Hill and in the country.

Presidential attempts to present Congress with a *fait accompli* are one matter. What about situations such as the Gulf War and Haiti in which the decision to use force is made over the course of several weeks or months? Since the Byrd-Nunn-Warner proposal and more ambitious proposals for repairing the War Powers Resolution agree on the need to specify both what constitutes consultation and who should be consulted, would not these reforms compel a president slowly building up to war to engage in a sustained dialogue with Capitol Hill?

The answer is almost certainly yes. But the more important question is whether such a dialogue would affect policy. The answer here is another matter entirely. After all, as the case of Haiti vividly demonstrates, the ability of members of Congress to advise the White House depends on the willingness of the president to listen. As the gap between executive and legislative preferences grows—hence, the more important consultation becomes to members of Congress—the incentives that presidents have in order to heed congressional opinion diminish. No legislation can overcome this fundamental political reality.

Legislation is also not likely to have much of an effect on presidents who decline to make a genuine effort to solicit congressional advice. A defiant president usually will be able to take advantage of the fact that members of Congress almost invariably will disagree among themselves over what constitutes adequate consultation, regardless of what the statute might say. In April 1986, for example, Ronald Reagan invited a group of senior members to the White House for a briefing on plans for a U.S. air strike against Libya. The meeting started at four o'clock in the afternoon, two hours after U.S. warplanes had left their bases. Sen. Richard Lugar (R-Ind.), chair of the Senate Foreign Relations Committee, praised the White House for consulting with Congress, "as close in time to the bombing as it was."[72] Democrats, however, complained that the meeting fell far short of true consultation. As one put it, "What could we have done? . . . Told [the president] to turn the planes around?"[73] With many members content to be notified of major foreign policy decisions or willing to come to the defense of a president from their party, presidents generally pay no political price when they fail to consult with Congress.

What about a strengthened sixty-day clock and a slow buildup to war? In theory, this is the reform that has the most potential to increase congressional influence. In practice, however, it may lead to consequences quite different from what its proponents anticipate. The reason is that a fixed clock undercuts presidential attempts at coercive diplomacy because it undermines the credibility of the threat upon which coercive diplomacy rests. (It is for precisely this reason that a strengthened sixty-day clock is the war powers reform that is least likely to be adopted). As a result, if a strengthened time limit were in place, Congress would face considerable pressure to hold an early vote authorizing the deployment of U.S. troops and thereby strengthening the president's bargaining leverage.

The prospect of an early congressional vote on troop deployments no doubt will please many observers. But as mentioned earlier, congressional authorization is a use-it-and-lose-it power; if Congress gives its approval, it loses control of policy. Members might try to make their authorization conditional, but anything other than the most simple condition (e.g., "Unless Iraq withdraws from Kuwait by January 15, 1991") would greatly complicate presidential diplomacy. Likewise, any effort to make the grant of authority narrow in scope would complicate diplomacy and encourage a defiant president to engage in linguistic sleight of hand to read greater authority into the resolution. As a result, if a president enjoys a modest amount of public support when he orders troops overseas, as President Bush did when he dispatched U.S. troops to Saudi Arabia, members of Congress may well find it politically impossible to avoid giving formal authority to the president at the start even if they doubt the wisdom of the operation.

In sum, though efforts to repair the War Powers Resolution are well intentioned, they are unlikely to become law. More important, they are unlikely to ensure that decisions to use military force reflect the collective judgment of Congress and the president. The reason is simple: legislation cannot nullify the inherent advantages of the president and the inherent disadvantages of Congress when it comes to the use of force. Although the founders clearly intended to lodge the war power with the legislative branch, in most situations today members of Congress lack the tools needed to translate their constitutional authority into practical influence, especially given widespread doubts about the wisdom of formally constraining the president's ability to act in foreign affairs.

CONCLUSION

The end of the Cold War has rekindled Congress's interest in reclaiming the war power that it ceded to the White House during the era of the imperial presidency. Members of Congress have been vocal in their criticism of administration policy in the Persian Gulf, Somalia, Haiti, and Bosnia, although thus far they have refused to dictate policy themselves. Even with congressional activism being advisory rather than compulsory, many observers worry that Congress is robbing presidents of credibility abroad. This ongoing debate raises two questions. First, does congressional activism on decisions to use force endanger the nation? Second, given that political obstacles make it unlikely that Congress will overhaul the War Powers Resolution, can some other solution be found to curb the excesses of executive-legislative conflict over the war power?

At one level, complaints about the dangers of congressional activism are understandable. In many instances, debate in Congress does make it more difficult for presidents to accomplish their goals.[74] During the Haiti crisis, for example, Pentagon officials claimed to have intercepted electronic communications that indicated that Haiti's military leaders were counting on Congress to stop the invasion.[75] More generally, the ability of presidents to use coercive diplomacy will always be hampered by the ability and willingness of members of Congress to criticize White House policies they dislike.

At another level, however, complaints about congressional activism are deeply disturbing; they are essentially complaints about the Constitution. After all, the delegates who met in Philadelphia in 1787 *wanted* their new government to be inefficient when it came to war. To quote James Wilson: "This system will not hurry us into war; it is calculated to guard against it."[76] The founders created such a system because they had much less faith than their successors would two hundred years later in the virtue of efficiency. As Alexander Hamilton, himself a strong president man, put it in "Federalist No. 70," "In the legislature, promptitude of decision is oftener an evil than a benefit. The differences of opinion, and the jarrings of parties in the department of the government, though they may sometimes obstruct salutary plans, yet often they promote deliberation and circumspection; and serve to check the excesses of the majority."[77]

Of course, quoting the words of the founders will not sway critics who argue that the distribution of authority intended by the founders is obsolete given the needs and responsibilities of a twentieth century superpower. Thus Robert Bork (normally a fierce proponent of original intent) writes that "the need for Presidents to have that power [to use force abroad without benefit of congressional authorization], particularly in the modern age, should be obvious to almost everyone."[78] Although such arguments may be appealing at first glance, they rest on the dubious assumption that obsolescence can strip Congress of its constitutional powers. Perhaps even more important, the historical record fails to substantiate claims that the Constitution is obsolete when it comes to foreign affairs. Examples in which congressional debate—as opposed to the policy choice that Congress made—unambiguously damaged U.S. interests are hard to find. In contrast, the three biggest foreign policy blunders of the past fifty years—the Bay of Pigs, Vietnam, and the Iran-Contra affair—resulted from too little debate, not too much.

To say that the founders wanted to make it hard to plunge the nation into war and that previous episodes of executive-legislative conflict have not proved catastrophic for the Republic is not to say that bitter conflict is desirable (although it is reasonable to wonder if it is desirable for a democracy to pursue resolutely a policy that deeply divides its people). The country no doubt would be better served if Congress and the president learned to accommodate each other's prerogatives and thereby moderate each other's excesses. The development of such an accommodation was largely prevented during the Cold War era by the increasingly grandiose claims that presidents made for their powers in foreign affairs, a trend best illustrated by George Bush's boast that he "didn't have to get permission from some old goat in the United States Congress to kick Saddam Hussein out of Kuwait."[79] So long as presidents refuse to engage in genuine bipartisan consultation with Congress and thereby acknowledge that Congress has a legitimate role in decisions to use force, they must be prepared to deal with the consequences of potentially bitter congressional opposition.

The ultimate responsibility, then, for genuine bipartisan consultation between the two ends of Pennsylvania Avenue lies with the White House. Congress can help the process along by adopting measures such as the provision in the Byrd-Nunn-Warner proposal to create a permanent consultative group. At a minimum, such reforms deny presidents the excuse that congressional consultations are unnecessary because they cannot possibly consult with every member of Congress. But because the success of any attempt at consultations depends on the willingness of presidents to solicit and listen to advice, the White House ultimately bears the responsibility for opening a dialogue with Capitol Hill.

Genuine bipartisan consultations will by no means eliminate executive-legislative conflict. No amount of consultation can prevent congressional debate on issues that genuinely divide members of Congress. This is particularly so in today's Congress where individual members have much less to fear from party and committee leaders than they did thirty or forty years ago.[80] Indeed, presidents must be prepared for inevitable frustration when talks with congressional leaders fail to quiet criticism on Capitol Hill. But if genuine executive-legislative consultations cannot silence a president's critics, what they can do is to help *minimize* conflict. More important, presidents have a strong incentive to develop a norm of genuine executive-legislative consultations. Given the absence of a foreign policy consensus in the United States, a presidential refusal to consult with Congress on a military venture that turns out poorly may tip sentiment on Capitol Hill in favor of tying the president's hands in the future. Thus, by insisting that they do not need to consult with the old goats on Capitol Hill, post–Cold War presidents may succeed only in curtailing their own powers.

The behavior of the Clinton administration suggests that it understands the importance of consulting with Congress. This is most evident in the area of peacekeeping. Not only did Clinton pledge not to commit U.S. troops to a peacekeeping mission in Bosnia without a clear expression of congressional support, but in May 1994 he agreed to support legislation to rewrite the War Powers Resolution to require that peacekeeping operations be authorized by Congress.[81] In the case of Haiti, Clinton did not ask for congressional authorization to begin the invasion, but he did engage in relatively extensive (at least when compared to the practices of his predecessors) consultations with senior members of Congress. If the Clinton administration continues with its bipartisan consultations with congressional leaders, it will set an important precedent, one that will make for a healthier executive-legislative relationship on foreign policy.

NOTES

1. An ABC poll taken in the second week of September showed that 78 percent of those surveyed believed that the Clinton administration should ask permission from Congress before invading Haiti. See Elaine Sciolino, "Clinton Aides Say Invasion of Haiti Would Be Limited," *New York Times*, September 13, 1994.
2. Quoted in Leon Friedman and Burt Neuborne, "The Framers, On War Powers," *New York Times*, November 27, 1990.
3. The literature on Congress's war powers is voluminous. Among others, see David Gray Adler, "The Constitution and Presidential Warmaking: The Enduring Debate," *Political Science Quarterly* 103, (Spring 1988), pp. 1–36; Arthur Bestor, "Separation of Powers in the Domain of Foreign Affairs: The Intent of the Constitution Historically Examined," *Seton Hall Law Review*, 5 (Spring 1974), pp. 529–665; Charles A. Lofgren, "On War-Making, Original Intent, and Ultra-Whiggery," *Valparaiso University Law Review*, 21 (Fall 1986), pp. 53–68; Charles A. Lofgren, "War-Making Under the Constitution: The Original Understanding," *Yale Law Review*, 81 (March 1972), pp. 672–702; and Peter Raven-Hansen, "Constitutional Constraints: The War

Powers Resolution," in Gary M. Stern and Morton H. Halperin, eds., *The U.S. Constitution and the Power to Go to War: Historical and Current Perspectives*, (Westport, Conn.: Greenwood Press, 1993).

4. Alexander Hamilton, "Federalist No. 69," in Alexander Hamilton, James Madison, and John Jay, *The Federalist Papers*, ed. Garry Wills (New York: Bantam, 1982), p. 350 (emphasis in the original).

5. See Henry Bartholomew Cox, *War, Foreign Affairs, and Constitutional Power: 1829–1901* (Cambridge, Mass.: Ballinger, 1984); Edwin B. Firmage, "Rogue Presidents and the War Power of Congress," *George Mason University Law Review*, 11 (Fall 1988), pp. 79–95; Arthur M. Schlesinger, Jr., *The Imperial Presidency* (Boston: Houghton Mifflin, 1989), pp. 35–126; W. Taylor Reveley III, *War Powers of the President and Congress: Who Holds the Arrows and Olive Branch?* (Charlottesville: University Press of Virginia, 1981); Abraham D. Sofaer, *War, Foreign Affairs, and Constitutional Power: The Origins* (Cambridge, Mass.: Ballinger, 1976); and Francis D. Wormuth and Edwin B. Firmage, *To Chain the Dog of War: The War Powers of Congress in History and Law* (Dallas, Tex.: Southern Methodist University Press, 1986).

6. Quoted in Schlesinger, *The Imperial Presidency*, p. 21.

7. Quoted in ibid. pp. 56–57.

8. Daniel S. Cheever and H. Field Haviland, Jr., *American Foreign Policy and the Separation of Powers* (Cambridge: Harvard University Press, 1952), p. 48; W. Stull Holt, *Treaties Defeated in the Senate* (Baltimore: Johns Hopkins University Press, 1933), p. 121; Gerard Felix Warburg, *Conflict and Consensus: The Struggle Between Congress and the President over Foreign Policymaking* (New York: Harper and Row, 1989), p. 20; and Woodrow Wilson, *Congressional Government: A Study in American Politics* (Gloucester, Mass.: Peter Smith, 1973).

9. See Robert Dallek, *Franklin D. Roosevelt and American Foreign Policy, 1932–1945* (New York: Oxford University Press, 1979).

10. In 1967, the State Department listed 137 cases of unilateral presidential action. Department of State, Historical Studies Division, *Armed Actions Taken by the United States Without a Declaration of War, 1789–1967* (Washington, D.C.: U.S. GPO, 1967). A study subsequently prepared for Sen. Barry M. Goldwater placed the number at "at least 197 foreign military hostilities". Barry M. Goldwater, "The President's Ability to Protect America's Freedoms—The Warmaking Power," *Law and the Social Order: Arizona State University Law Journal*, 3 (1971), pp. 423–424.

11. John Hart Ely, *War and Responsibility: Constitutional Lessons of Vietnam and Its Aftermath* (Princeton: Princeton University Press, 1993), p. 10.

12. Abraham Lincoln to W.H. Herndon, 15 February 1848, in Roy P. Basler, ed., *The Collected Works of Abraham Lincoln*, Vol. 1, (New Brunswick, N.J.: Rutgers University Press, 1953), p. 452 (emphasis in the original.)

13. Alexis de Tocqueville, *Democracy in America* (New York: Anchor, 1969), p. 126.

14. See Schlesinger, *The Imperial Presidency*, pp. 127–207.

15. Dean Acheson, *Present at the Creation: My Years in the State Department* (New York: Norton, 1987), pp. 413–414.

16. For Dwight Eisenhower's deference to Congress's constitutional authority to declare war, see *Public Papers of the Presidents of the United States: Dwight D. Eisenhower, 1954* (Washington, D.C.: U.S. GPO, 1954), p. 306.

17. See Schlesinger, *The Imperial Presidency*, pp. 160–161; James L. Sundquist, *The Decline and Resurgence of Congress*, (Washington, D.C.: Brookings, 1981), pp. 114–116; and U.S. Congress, Senate Committees on Foreign Relations and Armed Services, *The President's Proposal on the Middle East, Part 1*, 85th Cong., 1st sess., 1957, especially p. 118.

18. Shortly before the Cuban missile crisis began, Congress passed a resolution expressing the determination of the United States "to prevent in Cuba the creation or use of an externally supported military capability endangering the security of the United States." The resolution did not, however, authorize John Kennedy to use force; language stating that the president "possesses all necessary authority" to use armed force was dropped at the insistence of senators who argued that it amounted to a predated declaration of war. Kennedy did not cite the resolution in announcing the naval quarantine on Cuba, although it was mentioned in the quarantine proclamation, and Theodore Sorenson writes that at the time Kennedy made it clear he was acting "by Executive Order, Presidential proclamation and inherent powers, not under any resolution or act of Congress." See "Cuba Resolution," *Congressional Quarterly Weekly Report*, September 21, 1962, p. 1565; "House Passes Cuba Resolution, 384–7," *Congressional Quarterly Weekly Report*, September 28, 1962, p. 1691; Schlesinger, *The Imperial Presidency*, pp. 173–175; and Theodore C. Sorenson, *Kennedy* (New York: Harper and Row, 1965), p. 702.

19. Ely, *War and Responsibility*, p. 13.

20. Sundquist, *The Decline and Resurgence of Congress*, p. 116.

21. The text of the Gulf of Tonkin Resolution is reprinted in Ely, *War and Responsibility*, p. 16, and Jean E. Smith, *The Constitution and American Foreign Policy* (St. Paul, Minn.: West Publishing, 1989), p. 235.

22. Smith, *The Constitution and American Foreign Policy*, p. 235.

23. Quoted in Sundquist, *The Decline and Resurgence of Congress*, p. 116.

24. Quoted in Adam Yarmolinsky, *The Military Establishment: Its Impacts on American Society* (New York: Harper and Row, 1971), p. 53.

25. For a list of congressional actions in response to major tests of the War Powers Resolution, see Eileen Burgin, "Congress, the War Powers Resolution, and the Invasion of Panama," *Polity*, 25 (Winter 1992), pp. 225–226.

26. See Elizabeth A. Palmer, "Senate Demands Voice in Policy But Shies From Confrontation," *Congressional Quarterly Weekly Report*, September 11, 1993, p. 2399.

27. See Carroll J. Doherty, "Clinton Calms Rebellion on Hill by Retooling Somalia Mission," *Congressional Quarterly Weekly Report*, October 9, 1993, pp. 2750–2751; Pat Towell, "Behind Solid Vote on Somalia: A Hollow Victory for Clinton," *Congressional Quarterly Weekly Report*, October 16,

1993, pp. 2823–2827; and Pat Towell, "Clinton's Policy Is Battered, But His Powers Are Intact," *Congressional Quarterly Weekly Report*, October 23, 1993, pp. 2896–2901.

28. Quoted in Carroll J. Doherty, "Contrary Paths to Peacekeeping Converge in Wake of Violence," *Congressional Quarterly Weekly Report*, October 2, 1993, p. 2655.

29. See Jeffrey H. Birnbaum and John Harwood, "Clinton Sets Haiti TV Talk Tomorrow; Invasion Idea Has Only Faint Support," *Wall Street Journal*, September 14, 1994; Carroll J. Doherty, "President, Rebuffing Congress, Prepares to Launch Invasion," *Congressional Quarterly Weekly Report*, September 17, 1994, pp. 2578–2583; and Katharine Q. Seelye, "Congress Weighs the Political Profit and Loss," *New York Times*, September 17, 1994.

30. Quoted in Carroll J. Doherty, "Senate Defeats GOP Proposal to Limit Clinton on Haiti," *Congressional Quarterly Weekly Report*, July 2, 1994, p. 1814.

31. See for example Carroll J. Doherty, "Senate Cautiously Prods Clinton on Handling of Nuclear Crisis," *Congressional Quarterly Weekly Report*, June 18, 1994, p. 1639.

32. See Ely, *War and Responsibility*, pp. 21–23.

33. Quoted in Walter LaFeber, *America, Russia, and the Cold War, 1945–71*, 2nd ed. (New York: John Wiley, 1972), p. 60.

34. See Carroll J. Doherty, "Both Chambers Craft Resolutions Backing Bush's Gulf Policy," *Congressional Quarterly Weekly Report*, September 29, 1990, pp. 3140–3142, and Carroll J. Doherty, "Congress Cautiously Supports Bush's Past Gulf Actions," *Congressional Quarterly Weekly Report*, October 6, 1990, p. 3240.

35. Quoted in Carroll J. Doherty, "Uncertain Congress Confronts President's Gulf Strategy," *Congressional Quarterly Weekly Report*, November 17, 1990, p. 3881.

36. See James M. Lindsay, *Congress and the Politics of U.S. Foreign Policy* (Baltimore: Johns Hopkins University Press, 1994), pp. 132–138.

37. See R.W. Apple, Jr., "Remaking of Sam Nunn with '92 in the Distance," *New York Times*, December 20, 1990.

38. See Timothy E. Cook, *Making Laws and Making News: Media Strategies in the U.S. House of Representatives* (Washington, D.C.: Brookings, 1989).

39. E.E. Schattschneider, *The Semisovereign People* (New York: Holt and Rinehart, 1961), pp. 1–3.

40. Roger Hilsman recognized the virtue of simple appeals more than three decades ago. See Roger Hilsman, "Congressional-Executive Relations and the Foreign Policy Consensus," *American Political Science Review*, 52 (September 1958), p. 737.

41. Quoted in Eugene V. Rostow, "'Once More into the Breach': The War Powers Resolution Revisited," *Valparaiso University Law Review*, 21 (Fall 1986), p. 15.

42. Schlesinger, *The Imperial Presidency*, p. 433.

43. "Congress Approves Aid for Lebanon . . . But Demands Role in Troop Decision," *Congressional Quarterly Almanac 1983* (Washington, D.C.: Congressional Quarterly Inc., 1984), pp. 116–117.

44. In theory, Congress is not required to invoke the War Powers Resolution because the law stipulates that the sixty-day clock begins whenever "a report is submitted *or is required to be submitted*" (emphasis added). In practice, however, members have assumed that they bear the burden of starting the clock if the president refuses to file a report specifying section 4(a)(1). See Michael J. Glennon, *Constitutional Diplomacy* (Princeton: Princeton University Press, 1990), pp. 91–93.

45. "Joint Resolution to Keep Marines in Lebanon," *Congressional Quarterly Weekly Report*, October 8, 1983, p. 2101.

46. Clifford A. Krauss, "House Vote Urges Clinton to Limit U.S. Somalia Role," *New York Times*, September 29, 1993; and Elizabeth A. Palmer, "Senate Demands Voice in Policy But Shies from Confrontation," *Congressional Quarterly Weekly Report*, September 11, 1993, p. 2399.

47. See Doherty, "President, Rebuffing Congress, Prepares to Launch Invasion," p. 2581.

48. Michael Rubner, "The Reagan Administration, the 1973 War Powers Resolution, and the Invasion of Grenada," *Political Science Quarterly*, 100 (Winter 1985–86), p. 630.

49. Burgin, "Congress, the War Powers Resolution, and the Invasion of Panama," pp. 232–233.

50. Doherty, "Uncertain Congress," p. 3880; and Christopher Madison, "Sideline Players," *National Journal*, December 15, 1990, p. 3025.

51. See Michael Wines, "Clinton Corners Himself, Along with His Quarry," *New York Times*, September 18, 1994. Not all members were satisfied with the degree of executive-legislative consultation. See the remarks by Rep. Lee Hamilton (D-Ind.) in Jeffrey H. Birnbaum and Thomas E. Ricks, "Clinton Must Persuade Haiti's Dictators to Leave or Convince Americans That U.S. Should Invade," *Wall Street Journal*, September 15, 1994.

52. The literature on the War Powers Resolution is voluminous. Among others, see Ellen C. Collier, "Statutory Constraints: The War Powers Resolution," in Stern and Halperin, *The U.S. Constitution and the Power to Go to War*; Ely, *War and Responsibility*, pp. 48–67; Glennon, *Constitutional Diplomacy*, ch. 3; Michael J. Glennon, "The Gulf War and the Constitution," *Foreign Affairs*, 70 (Spring 1991), pp. 84–101; Robert A. Katzmann, "War Powers: Toward a New Accommodation," in Thomas E. Mann, ed., *A Question of Balance: The President, the Congress, and Foreign Policy* (Washington, D.C.: Brookings, 1990); Rostow, "'Once More into the Breach'," pp. 1–52; "Separation of Powers in Foreign Policy: Do We Have an 'Imperial Congress'?" *George Mason University Law Review*, 11 (Fall 1988); Marc E. Smyrl, *Conflict or Codetermination? Congress, the President, and the Power to Make War* (Cambridge, Mass.: Ballinger, 1988); and Warburg, *Conflict and Consensus*, pp. 119–151.

53. Katzmann, "War Powers," p. 57.

54. Ibid., p. 60.

55. "Resolution on Lebanon Signed into Law," *Congressional Quarterly Weekly Report*, October 15, 1983, p. 2142.

56. On the legislative veto and foreign policy, see Thomas M. Franck and Clifford A. Bob, "The Return of Humpty-Dumpty: Foreign Relations Law After the Chadha Case," *American Journal of International Law*, 79 (October 1985): 912–960, and Martha Liebler Gibson, *Weapons of Influence: The Legislative Veto, American Foreign Policy, and the Irony of Reform* (Boulder, Colo.: Westview, 1992).
57. *Lowry v. Reagan*, 676 F. Supp. 333 (D.D.C. 1987), p. 339.
58. *Dellums v. Bush*, 752 F. Supp. 1141 (D.D.C. 1990), p. 1151.
59. Quoted in Carroll J. Doherty, "The Reluctant Warriors," *Congressional Quarterly Weekly Report*, February 13, 1993, p. 323.
60. Quoted in Towell, "Clinton's Policy Is Battered," p. 2896.
61. Among other proponents of repeal, see Dick Cheney, "Congressional Overreaching in Foreign Policy," in Robert A. Goldwin and Robert A. Licht, eds., *Foreign Policy and the Constitution* (Washington, D.C.: American Enterprise Institute, 1990); Rostow, "'Once More into the Breach'," pp. 1–52; and Robert F. Turner, "Separation of Powers in Foreign Policy: The Theoretical Underpinnings," *George Mason University Law Review*, 11 (Fall 1988), pp. 97-117.
62. Cheney, "Congressional Overreaching in Foreign Policy," p. 120.
63. For example, see Joseph R. Biden, Jr., and John B. Ritch III, "The War Powers Resolution at a Constitutional Impasse: A 'Joint Decision' Solution," *Georgetown Law Journal*, 77 (December 1988), pp. 367–412; Ely, *War and Responsibility*, pp. 115–138; and Glennon, *Constitutional Diplomacy*, pp. 111–122.
64. Glennon, *Constitutional Diplomacy*, p. 121.
65. *Congressional Record*, 101st Cong., 1st sess., 1989, 135, pt.1, pp.465–466. For scholarly endorsements of the Byrd-Nunn-Warner proposal, see Katzmann, "War Powers," pp. 67–68; and James A. Nathan, "Revising the War Powers Act," *Armed Forces and Society*, 17 (Summer 1991), pp. 513–543.
66. Quoted in Glennon, *Constitutional Diplomacy*, p. 119.
67. Because the sixty-day time limit is the core provision of the War Powers Resolution that (in theory at least) puts teeth into the demand for consultations, some critics dismiss the Byrd-Nunn-Warner proposal as nothing more than "disguised repeal." Ely, *War and Responsibility*, pp. 65, 189–191.
68. Quoted in Doherty, "The Reluctant Warriors," p. 323.
69. Quoted in Burgin, "Congress, the War Powers Resolution, and the Invasion of Panama," pp. 228–229.
70. Helen Dewar, "Senators Act to Rewrite Resolution on Troop Deployment Policy," *Washington Post*, October 23, 1993.
71. The classic study of the rally round the flag phenomenon is John E. Mueller, *War, Presidents and Public Opinion* (New York: John Wiley and Sons, 1973).
72. Richard G. Lugar, *Letters to the Next President* (New York: Simon and Schuster, 1988), p. 48.
73. Quoted in Carroll J. Doherty, "Consultation on the Gulf Crisis Is Hit or Miss for Congress," *Congressional Quarterly Weekly Report*, October 13, 1990, p. 3441.

74. For a discussion of the factors that determine whether congressional debates complicate the work of the White House, see Lindsay, *Congress and the Politics of U.S. Foreign Policy*, pp. 176–178.

75. Birnbaum and Ricks, "Clinton Must Persuade Haiti's Dictators."

76. 2 Debates in the Several State Conventions on the Adoption of the Federal Constitution 528, ed. J. Elliot, 1863.

77. Hamilton, Madison, and Jay, *The Federalist Papers*, p. 358.

78. Robert Bork, "Erosion of the President's Power in Foreign Affairs," *Washington University Law Quarterly*, 68 (1990), p. 698.

79. *Public Papers of the Presidents of the United States: George Bush, 1992–93*, Vol. 1 (Washington, D.C.: U.S. GPO, 1993), p. 995.

80. On the problems that party and committee leaders encounter when attempting to speak on behalf of Congress, see Thomas M. Franck and Edward Weisband, *Foreign Policy by Congress* (New York: Oxford University Press, 1979), pp. 211–213.

81. "Clinton Peacekeeping Plan to Involve Congress More," *Wall Street Journal*, May 6, 1994.

4

We the People Here Don't Want No War: Executive Branch Perspectives on the Use of Force

Jane E. Holl

War works. At least it often seems to for the other guy. Bosnian Serbs have muscled their way to exclusive sovereignty over half of a country whose land they formerly shared for centuries with Muslims and Croats. Warlords in Mogadishu control the tempo and rhythm of almost everything in Somalia except the rains. With relentless reckoning hardly noticed by observers outside of the region, Armenians have nearly swallowed Azerbaijan whole. Hutu warriors sliced their way to control in Kigali only to be beaten back by Tutsi militias while millions suffered.

But Americans do not seem to think that war works for them. They hesitate over Bosnia. They argue over Somalia. They try to substitute civilians in Nagorno-Karabakh. They negotiate with North Korea. They ignore Rwanda, and Sudan, and Georgia, and countless other conflicts and conflicts-in-waiting. They wring their hands over Haiti.

Even when Americans do use force or military assets and even when they use them well, they temporize over the results: the successful Bosnian airlift and airdrop operations are criticized as "well-fed dead" policies; eighteen lost lives in Mogadishu have obscured the fact that before the international intervention led by the United States, one thousand people a day were dying in Somalia. Even the sweeping victories in Panama and Desert Storm continue to haunt Americans as inadequate.

111

What is it about Americans' view of force that seems to acknowledge it as a successful (if illegitimate) strategy for others yet so unfulfilling—if not a plan for outright failure—for themselves? If force works so well for the bad guys, why does it not seem to work for the good guys?

In this paper I examine presidential foreign policy decision making to determine, in part, how the United States can think more sensibly about the use of force in the post–Cold War world. I consider briefly the conflicts generated in the transition from the Cold War and why the established democracies have eschewed involvement in these conflicts. I then focus on a key aspect of this tendency toward avoidance, i.e., the strong and consistent military counsel in crisis decision making against the use of force and I examine how the effects of this advice, combined with other factors, can lead to blurred strategic vision, policy incrementalism and missed opportunities. I suggest that as a general rule in dealing with some post–Cold War crises, force today is best applied on set clear limits to intolerable behavior, and I conclude with a modest recommendation of four rules of thumb to guide presidential thinking on the use of force.

PUTTING THE COLD WAR ON ICE

For the United States in particular, the "lessons" drawn from Vietnam and from the Cold War experience have generated a gospel regarding the use of force, which continues to dominate U.S. foreign policy decision making in the post–Cold War era. This gospel has four main tenets that provide for the use of force only

- when vital interests are threatened;

- for objectives that have been clearly defined and enjoy popular and Congressional support;

- with sufficient resources to do the job and only when the way out is as clear as the way in; and

- only as a last resort and when other means to achieve the objectives have failed.

These attitudes and inclinations regarding the use of force reflect not only the experiences of the Cold War years but also deep societal changes that militate against fighting and dying for anything except the most vital interests that ensure the life and cherished values of Americans.[1]

The lessons of the Cold War still condition the habits of thinking of Americans regarding the uses and limitations of various diplomatic, economic, and military policy instruments. Lately, however, these tools seem to have lost their edge as the international community struggles with conflicts that would not have emerged or would have been easier to handle in the shadow of the superpower antagonism.

In the five years since the Berlin Wall fell, some eighty-four conflicts have been documented, and of these, seventy-nine are conflicts within states.[2] Taken individually, the conflicts that characterize the post–Cold War world do not directly threaten our vital interests. However, they have assumed international importance simply because so much conflict and violence affecting so many people is happening at the same time. Many observers argue that the very profusion of conflict poses a direct threat to the collective interests of the established states, and that it is in the enlightened self-interest of responsible states to act to prevent these conflicts from escalating unacceptably, to prevent new conflicts from breaking out, and to restore norms for international behavior based on the rule of law.[3]

If the United States is to act effectively in preventive ways, its familiar dicta that counsel the use of force only in service of vital interests and only as a last resort, no longer serve it well. Yet we continue to use these guidelines and find it difficult to use military assets more creatively to prevent or control conflict. I turn now to an examination of one aspect of the foreign policy decision-making process to help understand why this difficulty persists.

HELL NO, WE WON'T GO

It *ought* to be hard to go to war. Foreign policy decision makers in the United States in both post–Cold War administrations have generally had the right instincts in this regard. They have avoided precipitous falls into war, and even when decisions were made to use force, decision makers have, for the most part, hewed to one Pentagon mantra: "No more Vietnams" which is shorthand for: be clear, be massive, and be quick. In Panama, Kuwait, and in Northern Iraq, the use of force was decisive, the objectives clear, and the military means adequate to the task. These administrations also have been criticized by some for their share of misjudgments regarding whether, when, and how to use force and, indeed, on balance, have been criticized more heavily for failing to act than for having acted.[4]

Of the many factors that bear on U.S. foreign policy decisions regarding force, perhaps none is more important than the president's general attitude toward military force and his specific inclinations regarding the use of force in the context of a particular foreign policy problem. Other commentators have documented how various individual, generational, and historical factors work to influence presidents as they have considered the use of force in foreign policy. George Bush was influenced by his personal experiences during World War II as a navy pilot and Bill Clinton by his generation's battle with Vietnam. Munich has historical significance less as a place than as a synonym for appeasement to many students of foreign policy, just as to others Khe Sanh or Beirut connote the purposeless applications of military power. No doubt personal and historical experiences influence how presidents receive and interpret information, particularly in the early stages of an administration or as they confront a new and unfamiliar crisis.[5]

The president gains experience over the course of a crisis, and as this experience cumulates, it may come to have a greater influence on his thinking than other factors noted above.[6] In other words, as the president starts to deal with a Bosnia or a Haiti, he may at first be inclined to draw on personal or historical analogies to help guide his thinking. However, as the president and his key advisers go through the process of decision making in an actual crisis, that crisis operates more prominently on their thinking: President Clinton's thinking on Bosnia in 1994 was shaped more by his experience with Bosnia in 1993 than by any historical analogies.[7]

Since the process itself may shape presidential choices as much as the options available, it may be interesting to examine one practice evident in a number of post–Cold War crises where the use of force has been at issue: the practice by the professional military to advise strongly and consistently against the use of force. Indeed, this practice was seen in such wide-ranging contexts as Desert Shield/Desert Storm, Somalia, Bosnia, Haiti, and Rwanda.[8]

As noted earlier, U.S. national experience and societal and cultural development have broadly conditioned the United States against using force to achieve its foreign policy objectives.[9] One of the ironies of the post–Cold War world may be the reversal of the siren song of the sixties, when Americans were cautioned against the danger of the "military-industrial complex" driving them into wars they should not want; today U.S. military leadership seems most comfortable with its foot resting on the brake. Today, military leaders to whom decision makers turn for expert advice routinely, strongly, and consistently counsel against the use of force. They mount a convincing case: conditions are not right, costs are too high, the political objectives are not clear, exit strategies are ill-defined. Even as the crisis develops, they continue to argue that the potential for things to go wrong remains.

Not surprisingly, the president and his key advisers become educated over the course of a crisis not to use force—to be risk averse. Risk aversion regarding the use of force induces decision makers to try and retry alternative methods: impose and then tighten economic sanctions, berate and then isolate outlaw regimes diplomatically. If such policies prove unsuccessful, headroom invariably exists to try again. To be most effective, however, economic and diplomatic measures often need to be backed by threats or use of force. Embargoes require enforcement. Diplomatic lines drawn in the sand need muscle to make them stick. Yet the military continues to argue against such piecemeal application of force. The crisis unfolds, however, particularly in situations in which the protagonists have used force or have threatened to use force, and alternative options, such as economic measures and diplomatic pressure, come to reveal their inadequacies. (Both of these approaches are time-consuming, politically difficult to sustain, and frequently yield minimal demonstrable results on adversaries' policies.)

The case of Bosnia provides a useful example. The Serbian war effort in Bosnia consists of two essential elements: the fighting at the front and the continual resupply of war materials by Belgrade. Economic sanctions have curtailed Serbia's ability to sustain its rate of supply by creating shortages in commodities and fuel and by forcing Serbia to use its hard currency assets to purchase consumer goods to deflect the potential for popular discontent. Sanctions alone cannot end Serbia's role in the war in Bosnia, although they have eroded its ability considerably.

Without a corresponding strategy to affect the consumption rate of supplies at the front, however, Bosnian Serbs simply calibrate their war effort based on the supplies available. Just as the North Vietnamese had done, the Serbs control the timing, intensity, and duration of their engagements. Although they have had to react to Muslim and Croat advances, the initial military superiority they enjoyed as the arms embargo went into effect continues to give them the upper hand. Western governments have been united in opposition to undertaking any strategy that would have them join the war on the ground; thus sanctions operate on Belgrade essentially unsupported by other means and fall prey to criticisms of inadequacy.

As a crisis drags on then (and we saw this development in Haiti as well) and as other options are demonstrated to be ineffective, expectations grow that the use of force is the only strategy that will "work." Military and civilian leaders do develop options to use force although the options evolve in relative isolation from rather than in conjunction with other non-force options.

Rising expectations regarding the use of force prompt decision makers to begin to prepare the public for military measures, both at home and, especially in the post–Cold War, on the international front. This process often entails garnering public support to do far more than the purpose for which force is designed.[10] Marshaling this support takes time and opens the policy to scrutiny and criticism by the legislative branch as well as domestic and international publics. Even Desert Storm had its firebrand critics who wondered why the Bush administration had allowed things with Iraq to get so out of hand.

One effect of this criticism is that use of force options become pitted against alternatives rather than considered in context with them. Indeed, even the maxim that force be used only as a last resort suggests that there is a "natural order" to the process—that policy options be sequenced rather than coordinated. During the debate on the Gulf War, for example, those who opposed the use of force argued in favor of giving sanctions more time to work. The same principle applied to Haiti where for months the administration deflected pressure to use force, arguing that sanctions need more time to work.

The decision finally to use force—when, and if, it is eventually made—comes at a time in the crisis when patience already is worn thin and criticism, particularly regarding "missed opportunities," has begun to mount. Consequently, force is expected to do more than is realistic or more than it should ever be designed to do.

Force is most effective when used in conjunction with other foreign policy tools. To isolate consideration of military options from the broader calculus can lead to important policy inconsistencies and disjunctures. Moreover, because the use of force is held in reserve as a last resort, it is expected to deliver success after other options have failed. These expectations place an unfair (but to a certain extent self-imposed) burden on only one of the various arrows in the foreign policy quiver. Even the massive victory in Desert Storm did not obscure the limited utility of war for achieving wider foreign policy objectives, in particular the removal of Saddam Hussein. No wonder the military often oppose the use of force, and no wonder the American people and their governments do not place great store in military options.

The efficacy of the case against the use of force has two other potential self-defeating consequences: first, the risk aversion it induces often serves to prolong crises while decision makers seek more information, often adopting delaying strategies while they try alternative options (and expose themselves to more criticism in the process). Second, it constrains options rather than preserves flexibility. By not considering how limited uses of force and sufficiently credible and potent threats of this kind might have a salutary effect on a conflict, decision makers are constrained to consider first non-force options and only after they seem headed for failure, to consider forceful options. In consequence, decision makers often respond to these constraints by trying piecemeal strategies to achieve their objectives.

In short, systematic advice against the use of force and the withholding of forceful options until the policy landscape is riddled with failure contribute to a decision-making process that is hamstrung, perhaps unnecessarily prolonged, and prone to ad hocery. If this practice is so dysfunctional, why does it happen?

It would be facile to attribute the military's reluctance to advocate use of force exclusively to their repudiation of the way in which the United States waged war in Vietnam. Vietnam had the impact it did because it reinforced military experts' own firsthand knowledge and understanding regarding the limits of force and the relationship of force to other policy instruments.

Soldiers know, for example, that despite a persistent, intuitive belief that decisive success on the battlefield confers victory in war, ample evidence suggests that there is no clear and consistent relationship between successful warfare and the achievement of war aims. In Vietnam, for example, the United States won most of its battles yet lost the war. There are at least four reasons why military activity, even if successful, can fail to deliver the objectives for which it is applied.

First, states are more sensitive to the costs of military action when they are fighting for causes at the margin of their interests rather than situations where vital interests are at stake. Decision makers' preoccupation with the potential casualties of any military engagement—rightly if the public reaction to the recent experience of the United States in Somalia is a guide—makes the point. Thus, if today the United States operates in an environment where vital interests are not clearly threatened, every conflict is open to potential compromise, and no conflict is worth the loss of American lives. Somalia, Haiti, Bosnia, and Rwanda, the argument goes, lie only at the margins of U.S. interests and consequently do not justify U.S. military engagement.

Second, force is often reserved until Americans have their goal line at their backs. The road back from an acute crisis after other policy tools have failed can be a long and difficult one, and the military effort will bear the full burden of delivering success. This standard for success may be impossible to meet.

Third, over time, other domestic and international factors (e.g., elections, reputational concerns, economic interests, other crises) arise that often undermine the military effort. When coupled with concerns about the operation's cost in lives and national treasure as well as with unrealistic expectations about the efficacy of the military instrument, these concerns can lead easily to disillusionment with the whole endeavor.

Fourth, most of today's conflict occurs within states, rather than between them, and states' traditional disinclination to meddle in others' internal affairs inhibits the kind of steps that may be necessary to control conflict or prevent its outbreak. To be sure, there are good reasons not to get involved in internal conflict. Civil wars often drag on for years and are characterized by bloody fighting over irreconcilable differences, a combination that makes them less susceptible to negotiated settlement.[11] Moreover, while the causes of many civil wars may be traced to relatively straightforward power sharing differences between rival groups within a state, they often are sustained by obscure motivations or by desires to settle the still-accumulating score. For these reasons, the "success" of an outside intervention in internal conflict will be hard to measure, making such interventions often ill-advised.

With no apparent threats to U.S. vital interests—save a hostile North Korean regime's possession of nuclear weapons—under what conditions and for what objectives does it make sense to use force? There are important indications of a shift in thinking on how military assets can be used more effectively in the post–Cold War world. The U.S. Army devotes considerable attention to its latest doctrinal manual on what it styles "operations other than war."[12] Internationally, the Partnership for Peace and the successful military-to-military contacts between East and West may fundamentally shift the orientation of East European militaries to think of their role first in terms of peacekeeping and peace support operations and only secondarily, if at all, as armies to mass for land warfare.[13]

However, the United States continues to use Cold War rules regarding the use of force that do not serve it well in the post–Cold War world where conflicts abound that individually do not threaten the narrow self-interests of the United States, but when taken together do threaten the stability of the international system even as they wreak havoc on millions of lives and destroy the fabric of societies around the world. Perhaps the United States can do better.

WHERE SHOULD ALL THE SOLDIERS GO?

The foregoing discussion has argued that the very profusion of conflict in the post–Cold War world threatens the collective interests of the established states. I also have argued that it is in the enlightened self-interest of responsible states to consider more timely action that may well employ threats, and if necessary, use of limited force to bolster diplomacy to prevent and control these proliferating small conflicts

A number of alternative uses for military forces and assets short of outright armed conflict, can help reduce the potential for conflict and control conflict once it has emerged. An incomplete list includes confidence building measures (including comprehensive military-to-military contacts), security and defense guarantees, crisis management procedures, peacekeeping and peace support operations, humanitarian assistance and protection (e.g., safe havens), arms embargo and economic sanctions enforcement operations, show of force demonstrations, observer missions and on-site monitoring, early warning and forward presence, limited-duration governance, etc.[14] But how do Americans get themselves to act?

Perhaps the United States can think afresh about how it might use force in limited ways, in conjunction with others and with other policy tools, to counter the threat posed to the stability of the international system by rampant conflict. Force can play a useful role as an instrument of prevention, but it cannot play that role by itself. Just as harsh diplomatic messages must be backed up with threats of force that are sufficiently credible and potent, so too must the use of force be an integral component of a coherent diplomatic strategy.

In the current international environment, there will continue to be occasions, as in Bosnia, where threats of force will not be sufficiently credible or potent enough to reverse such situations, but, as in Bosnia, force can still be used effectively to set limits on unacceptable behavior. This will require drawing clear lines to show what the responsible members of the international community will not tolerate and to give the offending party incentives to adhere to those lines. This is not a doctrine that says, "This will not stand," but rather one that says, "You have gone too far." This approach to the use of force may not avenge or reverse the violence and destruction that occurs up to the point when the lines are drawn, but it does provide a closer match between the interests that states have in controlling conflict and what they are prepared to do to protect those interests.[15]

It ought to remain difficult to go to war, but it ought not be difficult to use limited force as part of the fair share of the United States to help ensure the stability of the international system.

Arguments against such limited uses of force emphasize the need for worst-case planning and preparation in the event U.S. strategy fails. No one should discount the need for such worst-case planning; neither should worst case planning supplant the development of strategies to help ensure that desired outcomes are achieved. The presidential directive on U.S. participation in UN peacekeeping operations imposes very stringent conditions for U.S. participation in these operations in an effort to guard against the potential downside that can result when military assets fail to achieve their objectives.[16] The directive focuses on avoiding the worst outcomes of intervention but gives little attention to how to achieve better outcomes. Equal emphasis should be placed on shaping modest but useful goals and developing strategies that will help promote the probability of success.

Again, Bosnia serves as a useful example. Every time, and only when, the West has made specific, limited demands on the Bosnian Serbs, backed up with unified determination (usually, although not always via UN Security Council resolutions) and credible threats of force, the Serbs largely have adhered to the lines that were drawn. When the West moved to open Sarajevo airport for humanitarian deliveries, critics charged that the Serbs would retaliate; they did not. Similarly, when the United States called for the establishment of the no-fly zone over Bosnia, observers feared the Serbs would retaliate; they did not. The same is true when no-fly enforcement went into effect, when airdrops were begun, when a no-fly enforcement action was successfully completed, and when ultimata were finally laid down regarding Sarajevo and the safe havens. Just as Bosnia may be an example of the international community's failure to respond to the challenges of the post–Cold War world, so too may it illustrate how limited force can be used successfully to limit unacceptable behavior.

The point to be emphasized is that threats of force were credible and potent enough *only* when issued on behalf of quite limited demands. The international community was not able to convey coercive threats that were credible and potent enough on behalf of more ambitious objectives, e.g., forcing the Serbs to relinquish territory they had seized by force.

Indeed, the U.S. preventive deployment to Macedonia and participation in Operation Provide Comfort are two other examples where limited use of military assets can help limit unacceptable behavior: in these cases preventing the spillover of war from Bosnia or Kosovo (should it come) into Macedonia and preventing Saddam Hussein from attacking the Kurds in northern Iraq. Moreover, the comparative ease with which Americans accepted the tragic loss of life in a friendly fire incident where two U.S. helicopters were shot down over northern Iraq in spring 1994 should be noted. This acceptance of a tragic incident that involved loss of lives comparable to those lost through friendly fire during Desert Storm may be a sign of the legitimacy that people ascribe to this mission. Americans also seemed to take in stride the winter 1993 cruise missile attack on Iraq. Here, too, this general acceptance of a decisive military action to limit the threat posed by a pariah state may reflect the fact that Americans perceive U.S. military participation in Operation Provide Comfort as their fair share in preserving the common international interest of holding Saddam Hussein in check.

INTERESTS, IMPERATIVES, AND INSTRUMENTS

How then, should Americans think about the use of force in the post–Cold War world? As noted earlier, the president's attitude toward the use of force ranks among the most significant factors that determine whether, when and how the United States will use force. I have suggested that "rules" that hold that force should be reserved as a last resort and only when vital interests are threatened no longer effectively guide presidents who must deal with proliferating conflicts in the post–Cold War world.

Decisions regarding threats or use of force must operate in the context of a coherent global strategy. With this in mind, I offer four rules for the presidential thumb regarding the use of force.

1. Force is a legitimate policy instrument for some circumstances.

It might strike some observers that today, responsible states should reject the use of force for any purpose other than self-defense against an overt attack. Presidents should not be bound by such restrictive conditions, however. Moreover, while success cannot be guaranteed, fear of failure should not cause leaders to ignore one of their most effective instruments. Force and military assets are legitimate tools for use in advancing U.S. foreign policy interests. Force has an acknowledged utility in deterrence and conflict prevention.

In Desert Storm, for example, the war was designed, in part, to remove Saddam Hussein's forces from Kuwait. It was also designed to help ensure regional security and stability. To achieve this rather amorphous objective, the war effort sought to cut Saddam Hussein's war making capability—conventional and unconventional—down to size. The war, in fact, could not hope to ensure regional security and stability; it could only remove one significant obstacle to that stability: Iraq's predominant military posture.

2. Force should not be used simply as a last resort.

I have argued that force can be an effective adjunct to economic and diplomatic strategies and should not simply be held in reserve. Preserving force as a last resort implies a lockstep sequencing of the means to achieve foreign policy objectives that is unduly inflexible and relegates the use of force to in extremis efforts to salvage a faltering foreign policy. Conversely, limited use of force early in a crisis can have a salutary affect on unfolding events, and presidents should be attentive to these opportunities.

3. Each case is unique.

The search for universal truths regarding the use of force will be futile. One additional consequence of so much conflict happening simultaneously has been to blur in people's minds a number of starkly different situations into one undifferentiated foreign policy mess. It is routine to speak these days of Somalia, Bosnia, Korea, and Haiti as if they were all part of a seamless whole. To be sure, concurrent events often have reciprocal effects on each other that make it hard to keep them apart. Clinton policy aides take pains to point out that any peacekeeping operation in Bosnia will not repeat the mistakes of Somalia, for example. Indeed, in the closing months of his administration, some observers interpreted the action that George Bush took in Somalia as compensation for his failure to act in Bosnia.[17]

Again, any guide for when the United States should be willing to use force only makes sense in the context of a global strategy. In the closing days of his administration, George Bush highlighted "collective engagement" as the organizing principle for his national security strategy. In his view, effective

U.S. leadership in the post–Cold War world would require work in three essential areas: support for the stability and economic and political reform in Eastern Europe and the former Soviet Union; bilateral and multilateral efforts to support, encourage, and consolidate democracy elsewhere around the world; and, support for a fair and politically sustainable international refugee and immigration regime in this transitional period. Bush also promoted new regional thinking and improvements in the U.S.-UN relationship and called for U.S. leadership to "inhibit the forces of fragmentation that threaten order, peace, and stability."[18]

The Clinton administration echoed many of the same themes but with a different emphasis. In September 1993, National Security Adviser Anthony Lake outlined a strategy of "enlargement" that has four components: strengthen the community of major market democracies; foster and consolidate new market democracies, especially in states of special significance and opportunity; counter aggression of states hostile to market democracy while supporting the liberalization of these states; and pursue a humanitarian agenda with aid, democratization, and development.[19]

What is striking about the Bush and Clinton strategies is the degree to which both post–Cold War administrations articulated the need for an active U.S. role in global affairs. While both administrations were careful to note explicitly that the United States would not become the "world's policeman," it is clear that both anticipated that the United States would retain its position of leadership in the world.

In short, the U.S. post–Cold War agenda rests on three pillars: nuclear, chemical, and biological containment; "anchored" regionalism; and responsible internationalism (including humanitarian assistance and aid for development and democratization). Given this vision of U.S. involvement and the broad responsibilities it conveys to the United States, it makes sense to use all of the tools at the disposal of the United States to consolidate the gains of the last fifty years as well as the gains of the last five years.

Because of the common tendency to group problems together, presidents continually must stress the unique characteristics of each situation for which force is contemplated. It is in the context of each particular case that the design of the force option, including clear military objectives, adequate resourcing, rules of engagement, and "exit strategies," manifests its importance to the successful achievement of policy objectives. Haiti is Haiti, not Somalia, not Vietnam, not even Panama, or the Dominican Republic.

4. Decisions to use force demand committed and sustained Presidential leadership.

Controversy surrounds every decision to use force. Indeed, in every post–Cold War situation where the United States has used or contemplated the use of force, the public debate has been fierce and comprehensive. If an administration is disinclined to use force, it is easy to point to the general and even specific reluctance of the American people to support such a decision. Both the Bush and Clinton administrations, for example, have been quick to highlight the lack of public support for putting U.S. ground troops in Bosnia.

Yet presidential determination can overcome dissent in most if not all cases. Just as President Bush was supported in his determination to expel Saddam Hussein from Kuwait and in his decision to deploy troops on a humanitarian mission to Somalia, so too was President Clinton supported in his sure and swift decision to launch a cruise missile attack on Baghdad.

Observers have begun to herald this period as the end of the Westphalian era when nation-states dominated the international scene as the main strategic actors. If these observers are right, then we must hope that whatever may ultimately replace states—international organizations, ancient tribes, or some new creation—can prevent our common dissolution into anarchic violence. Responsible states must act to control the growing wave of conflicts that now challenge so fundamentally the world's destiny.

ACKNOWLEDGMENT

I am indebted to the following individuals for their assistance in the preparation of this essay: Rachel Epstein, Alexander George, David Hamburg, Dan Kaufman, John Stremlau, and Jim Reed. Its strengths reflect their insights; any shortcomings are my own.

NOTES

1. Policy-makers have repeatedly tried to formulate guidelines for U.S. military action. For example, on November 28, 1984, following the bombing of the U.S. Marines in Beirut, former Secretary of Defense Caspar W. Weinberger outlined six principles that he believed should inform a democratic nation's decision to go to war: 1) the United States should only go to war if U.S. vital national interests or the vital interests of allies are at stake; 2) the United States should only commit forces if those forces are commensurate with stated political objectives; 3) in each case, the military and political objectives must be clear; 4) each contingency must include ongoing monitoring and adjustment to ensure military capabilities match the political objectives; 5) the public and Congress must support military intervention before U.S. troops are deployed; and 6) force should only be used as a last resort. For the complete text and analysis of the principles, see Alan Ned Sabrosky and Robert L. Sloane, eds., *The Recourse to War: An Appraisal of the "Weinberger Doctrine"* (Carlisle Barracks, Pa.: Strategic Studies Institute, U.S. Army War College, 1988). See also Christopher Gacek, *The Logic of Force: The Dilemma of Limited War in America* (New York: Columbia University Press, 1994). More recently, the Clinton administration released its policy on U.S. participation in peacekeeping. In a sharp departure from Bill Clinton's campaign position, the new policy establishes strict conditions for creating peacekeeping operations and for U.S. participation in those missions. See *The Clinton Administration's Policy on Reforming Multilateral Peace Operations.*, Presidential Decision Directive (PDD)-25, Department of State Publication 10161, May 1994. For an explanation of Clinton's shift to a cautious policy on U.S. participation in peacekeeping, see Mats R. Berdal, "Fateful Encounter: The United States and UN Peacekeeping," *Survival*, Vol. 36 (Spring 1994), pp. 30–50. Edward N. Luttwak offers a demographic explanation for the trend away from great power military intervention, arguing that postindustrial families characterized by only two or three children are less tolerant of losing a child to armed conflict than previous generations in which families routinely had six, seven and eight children. See Edward N. Luttwak, "Where Are the Great Powers? At Home With the Kids," *Foreign Affairs*, Vol. 73, No. 4 (July/August 1994), pp. 23–28.

2. See Ramses Amer, et al., "Major Armed Conflicts," *SIPRI Yearbook 1993* (Oxford University Press, 1993), p. 81.
3. There is a substantial literature extolling the virtues of preventive diplomacy as an alternative to international intervention after armed conflict has already erupted. In addition to saving civilian lives, Francis M. Deng argues that prevention would also save lives among the intervention forces and would be far less expensive. See Francis M. Deng, *Protecting the Dispossessed* (Washington, D.C.: Brookings, 1993), especially pp. 133-140. Although President Clinton has resisted this criticism, according to many relief workers, the Rwandan civil war is an example in which early action could have mitigated disaster. See Douglas Jehl, "U.S. Policy: A Mistake? Tragedy for Rwanda Seen as Preventable," *New York Times*, July 23, 1994, p. 1. A theoretical framework for conflict prevention supplemented by geographical and organizational examples is put forth by Janne E. Nolan, ed., *Global Engagement: Cooperation and Security in the 21st Century* (Washington, D.C.: Brookings, 1994). For further reading on early warning, see Kumar Rupesinghe and Michiko Kuroda, eds., *Early Warning and Conflict Resolution* (New York: St. Martin's, 1992).
4. During the Cold War, Yugoslavia played a significant regional role in the East-West balance, and one could easily imagine that the West would not have stood by when faced with the prospect of a shooting war in the Balkans. Indeed, in a previous era, the great powers would have intervened to stake out their spheres of influence in the region. See Luttwak, *"Where Are the Great Powers?"*. Now that Yugoslavia's strategic importance has evaporated, however, the United States should be freed to be less concerned with developments there. Yet it has proven surprisingly difficult for states to ignore what began essentially as an internal war in a peripheral country. The piecemeal policies of outsiders toward Bosnia bear out U.S. strategic inclinations: neither directly nor as proxy does war in Yugoslavia threaten vital interests of the world's most powerful states. There is a growing realization of the threat posed to international stability by this and other "small" conflicts resulting from the refugee flows they generate, their spillover potential and demonstration effects, and the hardship they impose on surrounding states (especially when sanctions or other isolation techniques are applied by the international community). Moreover, their proliferation and persistence in the face of international efforts continue to erode the rule of law as the basis for state relations—the deleterious effects of which may be felt dramatically in decades to come. Criticisms of great power passivity have been particularly acute since the end of the Cold War. In the Yugoslavian case, there has been a torrent of articles in the popular press on the West's failure to take decisive military action to bring a peaceful resolution to the latest Balkan crisis. See, for example, Roy Gutman, "U.S. Indifference Crippled Bosnia," *Long Island Newsday*, September 16, 1993, p. 99; and John Steinbruner, "The Quagmire of Caution," *Washington Post*, April 25, 1993, p. C1. Other columnists have argued against intervention, however. See "U.S. shouldn't get involved in

Bosnian civil war," *Austin American-Statesman*, September 27, 1993, p. 8. For more recent commentary on the expected failure to act now, even in the wake of the Serb parliament's rejection of the latest peace plan and promised reprisals by contact group nations, see Anthony Lewis, "Bosnia Without End," *New York Times*, July 22, 1994, p. A27. The media have been similarly divided over U.S. intervention in Somalia. See, for example, Leslie H. Gelb, "Not Set in Stone," *New York Times*, December 6, 1993, p. 19; Helen Dewar and Kevin Merida, "From Congress, More Questions," *Washington Post*, October 5, 1993, p. 25; Jurek Martin, "Pressure in US for troops to leave Somalia," *London Financial Times*, October 7, 1993, p. 1; "Stay put, US," *Minneapolis Star Tribune*, October 6, 1993, p. 18; Thomas E. Ricks, "U.S. Raises 'Africa Solution' to Justify Pullout From Somalia, but Policy Has Many Critics," *Wall Street Journal*, October 12, 1993, p. 22; and Michael Elliott, "The Making of a Fiasco," *Newsweek*, October 18, 1993, p. 34. There is also much disagreement on U.S. policy toward Haiti. See William Raspberry, "One Choice In Haiti," *Washington Post*, July 18, 1994, p. A26; "Haitian drift," *Economist*, July 16, 1994, p. 14; and "No Good Reason to Invade Haiti," *New York Times*, July 13, 1994, p. A18.

5. There is a wide body of literature on the pivotal role of executive decision making. Two important works are by Alexander L. George, *Presidential Decisionmaking in Foreign Policy: The Effective Use of Information and Advice* (Boulder: Westview, 1980), and Alexander L. George, ed., *Avoiding War: Problems of Crisis Management* (Boulder, Westview, 1991).

6. George, *Presidential Decisionmaking*.

7. Clinton administration policy on military intervention evolves as each crisis influences attitudes toward subsequent crises. Commentators have frequently predicted that U.S. difficulties in Somalia constricted the conditions under which the United States would be willing to deploy forces in Bosnia, for example. See Paul Lewis, "Reluctant Peacekeepers: Many UN Members Reconsider Role in Conflicts," *New York Times*, December 12, 1993, p. 22, and Stephen Engelberg, "U.S. Envoy Meets Clan Leader's Kin in Somali Capital," *New York Times*, October 11, 1993, p. A1. Reporters made the linkage again between Somalia and U.S. inaction in the early phases of the Rwandan civil war. Jehl, "U.S. Policy."

8. Richard K. Betts argues that there tends to be an ongoing tension between civilian leaders and their military counterparts over maintaining political flexibility and ensuring military victory. While politicians may be inclined to use limited force in hopes of achieving a political settlement in the midst of calculated escalation, the military's agenda inevitably involves military victory in the swiftest, surest fashion possible. See Richard K. Betts, *Soldiers, Statesmen, and Cold War Crises* (Cambridge: Harvard University Press, 1977). The decision-making process that led to the absence of armor in the fatal firefight in which a Somalian militia killed eighteen U.S. soldiers is an example of political objectives clashing with perceived military needs. Although military commanders requested additional equipment to protect U.S. troops, then Secretary of Defense Les Aspin

reportedly denied the request because such a delivery would have signaled escalation as the Clinton administration was trying to scale back its operation in Somalia. Secretary Aspin took full responsibility for the fiasco that precipitated the U.S. withdrawal in March 1994. For an account of the civilian-military com-munications surrounding these events, see Barton Gellman, "The Words Behind A Deadly Decision: Secret Cables Reveal Maneuvering Over Request for Armor in Somalia," *Washington Post*, October 31, 1993, p. A1. For an analysis of shifting U.S. political objectives in Somalia, see Ken Menkhaus and Terrence Lyons, "What Are the Lessons To Be Learned From Somalia?" *CSIS Africa Notes*, Center for Strategic and International Studies, No. 144 (January 1993). Bob Woodward also discusses the U.S. military's initial reluctance to engage in a Kuwaiti military operation against Iraq in 1990 in *The Commanders* (New York: Simon & Schuster, 1991).

9. A more extreme case of this is the German experience with re-armament following World War II. See Donald Abenheim, *Reforging the Iron Cross: The Search for Tradition in the West German Armed Forces* (Princeton: Princeton University Press, 1988).

10. For example, on the eve of the ground war, the American public was prepared to support military action far beyond the liberation of Kuwait. Seventy-two percent of the respondents to a Gallup poll held the view that the United States and its coalition partners should keep fighting to remove Saddam Hussein from power or to destroy Iraq's war-making capability. See *The Gallup Poll Monthly*, February 1991, p. 18.

11. See the case studies and analysis provided by I. William Zartman and Francis Deng, eds., *Conflict Resolution in Africa* (Washington, D.C.: Brookings, 1991); I. William Zartman, *Ripe for Resolution: Conflict and Intervention in Africa*, 2nd ed. (Oxford University Press, 1989); Roy Licklider, ed., *Stopping The Killing: How Civil Wars End* (New York University Press, 1993); and Paul R. Pillar, *Negotiating Peace: War Termination as a Bargaining Process* (Princeton: Princeton University Press, 1983).

12. See the U.S. Army's doctrinal manual, *Field Manual 100-5 Operations*, 1993.

13. Indeed, the UN Security Council's recent vote to approve Russian peace-keepers in Georgia legitimizes this unprecedented use of Russian forces in the former Soviet spheres. See "U.N. Endorses Russian Troops For Peace-keeping in Caucasus," *New York Times*, July 22, 1994, p. A2.

14. This list draws in part on Alexander L. George, *Forceful Persuasion: Coercive Diplomacy as an Alternative to War* (Washington, D.C.: United States Institute of Peace, 1991), and Michael Lund, "Europe's Tool Box for Conflict Prevention," in *Post–Cold War European Security and Conflict Management: The Roles of Multilateral Organizations*, draft manuscript, U.S. Institute of Peace, 1993, ch. 10.

15. Indeed, this concept of the use of force provides the conceptual underpinning of Chapter VII of the UN Charter.

16. *The Clinton Administration's Policy on Reforming Multilaterial Peace Operations*, PPD-25.

17. Many critics wondered why the United States sent troops to Somalia but not to Bosnia. See, for example, "Choosing Wars of Conscience," *New York Times*, December 17, 1992, p. A34, and Leslie H. Gelb, "Never Again," *New York Times*, December 13, 1992, p. 17.
18. See President George Bush, *National Security Strategy of the United States*, The White House, January 1993.
19. See Anthony Lake, Assistant to the President for National Security Affairs, "From Containment to Enlargement," *U.S. Department of State Dispatch*, Bureau of Public Affairs, Vol. 4 (September 21, 1993).

5

The People, the Press, and the Use of Force

Andrew Kohut and Robert C. Toth

The irony that use of force has emerged as such a prominent issue now has been noted by many observers. With the end of the Cold War and the election of Bill Clinton, resort to "coercive violence" as an instrument of U.S. foreign policy was expected to be less salient than in previous decades when the potential for nuclear escalation loomed whenever one or the other super-power used armed forces in the world.[1]

The single, well-defined global threat of the former Soviet Union has been replaced by many smaller, more diffuse, less urgent situations where the use of force might be contemplated. Small nations, ethnic groups, and even tribes are now less reluctant to demand long-denied aspirations. In addressing such threats, the external constraints on the United States to use military force have become fewer and weaker because the danger of nuclear escalation has all but disappeared. Internal domestic constraints, however, have increased.

The American public now demands that its president spend more time and resources on problems at home rather than abroad. One of our recent studies found little support among the public or U.S. elites for many of the values that animated the foreign policy of the post–World War II years, including export-ing democracy, defending human rights, and supporting self-determination. In contrast, foreign ventures that advance the U.S. domestic agenda of economic health and growth are now promised the greatest chance of public support.[2]

133

Finally, because national survival is not at stake, because economic issues are more prominent, and because foreign policy elites are more divided, public opinion and foreign policy are more closely linked today. "There is now no domestic consensus on the organizing principles of U.S. foreign policy," the American Assembly concluded earlier this year. "The challenge of establishing new, post–Cold War foreign policy priorities is further exacerbated by the role of the international media, which can play a major if often unpredictable role in determining what gets on the national agenda."[3]

While domestic conditions constrain U.S. foreign intervention, other pressures are working in the opposite direction. A more enlightened view of what constitutes the "national interest"—defense of the homeland, access to oil and other key raw materials, security of lines of communication to resources, markets and allies—is expected of nations as the world ends not only the Cold War but also the twentieth century. Much of the Western public seems prepared, in principle, to defend the oppressed in the name of a larger morality and to shed international legal concepts that made national borders sacrosanct and barred foreign interference inside of them.

As a result, new norms for intervention seem to be emerging. Some deal with safeguarding the "global order" and establishing "global standards (e.g., mass humanitarian catastrophe)."[4] Others are concerned with barring weapons of mass destruction. "It is now often argued that the world community has a right to prevent countries like Iraq, Libya, and North Korea from developing nuclear capabilities—by force if necessary, many would add," Marc Trachtenberg writes.[5]

A new phrase, "humanitarian intervention," has been coined in connection with debates about U.S. policy in Somalia, Bosnia, and elsewhere.[6] With the lesson of Vietnam and Lebanon still fresh in military minds, the Pentagon has been remarkably reluctant to engage in such ventures. General Colin Powell, the former chairman of the Joint Chiefs of Staff, cautioned that whenever committing armed forces is contemplated, a host of "relevant questions"—more like hurdles to be leaped—should be first evaluated.[7]

The Clinton administration, for its part, has put forward guidelines on the conditions under which the United States would support and participate in United Nations "peacekeeping and peace enforcement operations." The first of seven conditions for U.S. participation is that it must advance U.S. interests at an acceptable level of risk, and the last is that "domestic and Congressional support exists or can be marshalled."[8]

Opinion polls can offer some help to policy-makers on when and why such public support can be marshaled. In addition, pollsters have devoted a considerable amount of time and effort in recent years to assessing the public's international priorities. We shall review their work and also present a new poll that we at Times Mirror recently conducted specifically to elucidate these issues. In the end we will offer a model that may better help policy makers predict the attitude of the electorate when use of force is contemplated.

Since the end of the Cold War, the American public has shown three different faces with regard to using U.S. military force abroad: full support in the Gulf War, transitory support in Somalia, and no support in Bosnia. An examination of public opinion and media coverage of these cases provides material for a paradigm of the opportunities and obstacles faced by policy-makers in seeking to assess the likely public response to U.S. involvement in the future.

In this paper we examine in detail public response to these situations as measured by national opinion polls. The analysis pays careful attention to the scope and nature of media coverage of each crisis and to the interplay between it and the dynamic of public opinion. Subsequently, we attempt to draw inferences from these three cases about the American public's inclination to use force and the way news media coverage plays on that inclination. Finally, looking to the future, we set forth some principles of public opinion about military intervention based upon these analyses and the findings of recent Times Mirror polling on this topic.

THE GULF: STRONG SUPPORT

Ultimately, the Gulf War enjoyed popular support because it was relatively cost-free and because it ended well. Even in the earliest stages of the crisis, well before the outcome of the war was certain, public opinion was sufficiently positive to permit policy-makers to feel comfortable that Americans might get behind a war effort. Examination of relevant nationwide polling from the outset of the Gulf crisis through the war itself reveals at least a half dozen reasons for the public's resolve in the Gulf.

First, from the start, there was strong belief that the United States should play a significant role in helping to defend the Saudi oil fields and in evicting Iraq from Kuwait. Second, the Bush administration did a very good job of communicating to the public the purpose of the Gulf deployment, including its initial defensive mission and later offensive mission. Third, multilateralism—money as well as manpower—added significantly to public support for a military option. Fourth, the congressional debate and vote to authorize use of force in the Gulf significantly fortified American opinion. And finally, extensive media coverage of the Gulf crisis and later of the war served to solidify public opinion and keep public attention focused on the crisis. The public's connection to the Gulf through real time news coverage was intense for the brief duration of the war; this connection contributed to a suspension of the public's reservations about the intervention and also contributed to its tolerance for dissent.

From the outset, the news media shaped the public's attitudes toward the deployment of U.S. troops in the Gulf, which were materially different from its reactions to previous major U.S. military involvements. The attentiveness of Americans to the events there was due largely to unprecedented levels of television coverage. As early as August 1990, interest in news of the Gulf not only topped our News Interest Index of that period, but public attention to the crisis registered as one of the five most closely followed stories in the then data base of one hundred and fifty news stories at the Times Mirror Center.[9]

Much of the coverage was about the military buildup in the Gulf, an aspect of the story that attracted great public interest. As

The Tyndall Report said: "When a nation goes to war historic levels of news coverage are appropriate. . . . Moreover, the majesty of the Navy, the wizardry of the hi-tech gadgets, the human interest of the GI sending greetings home to loved ones are all much more telegenic than boring old embargoes and diplomatic dealing."[10] *The Tyndall Report* found that the amount of all Gulf-related news aired on the three U.S. broadcast networks in 1990, "before the war even began," was nearly four times that of the top story of 1989 (Tiananmen Square). And *network* news coverage was not the key media element in this war. Real time news viewing on CNN played a well-recognized, crucial role in the public's continuous connection to the Gulf from August 1990 onward; CNN was overwhelmingly the medium of choice in this respect. Although it was available in slightly more than half of U.S. households, a continually increasing percentage of the public told Times Mirror that throughout the war period, CNN was doing the best job of covering the Gulf. By late January 1991, when the air war started, 61 percent of the public said CNN's coverage was the best. The three broadcast networks *combined* did not achieve that level of applause.

Figure 1   Network News Coverage of the Gulf War

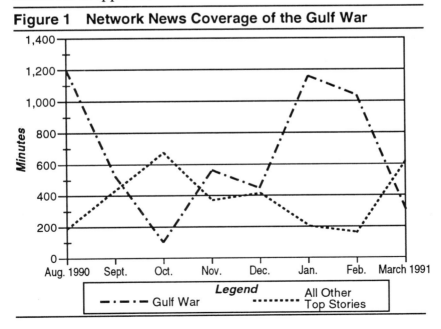

More Opinion Than Ever Before

Against this background, it is not surprising that more Americans had an opinion about the decision to commit U.S. forces to Saudi Arabia than they did about the comparable decisions on Vietnam or Korea. Within a matter of days after George Bush's announcement, 92 percent of Americans had an opinion about his order.[11] "More than two decades earlier, only 78 percent told Gallup they had formed an opinion about Lyndon Johnson's decision to send troops to Vietnam in January 1965. Similarly, fewer Americans, 85 percent, expressed opinions about the dispatch of U.S. forces to defend South Korea in the summer of 1950 according to Gallup in August 1950.

First reactions to troops in the Gulf (and Panama and Somalia as well) were also more positive than first reactions to troops in the field in Vietnam and Korea. Gallup polling in January 1965 found only half of the public supported the Vietnam decision, and in August 1950 two-thirds approved of Americans being sent to Korea.

Initial reactions to each of the United States' post–Cold War military actions were much more enthusiastic. An NBC/*Wall Street Journal* poll found that fully 72 percent supported the invasion of Panama in January 1990 and several months later in August 1990, 75 percent told Gallup that the United States had not made a mistake in sending troops to Saudi Arabia. Similarly, first reactions to Somalia were greeted with the same positive response, as measured in a December 1992 NBC/*Wall Street Journal* poll.

These comparisons strongly suggest that the American public's propensity to rally around a presidential decision to use force has not diminished with the end of the Cold War. If anything, there is more support for such decisions in recent years compared to thirty or forty years ago. One can only speculate about how much of that increased support is the effect of watching events unfold on television as if the audience felt it were taking greater part in the decision.

It must be emphasized that these data record only initial reactions, not ultimate judgments. Certainly first reactions to troops in the Gulf were only a part of the story. As the public was

Table 1   First Responses to Decision to Send Troops

	Positive Response[1]	Negative Response	Don't Know
Korea[2]			
Aug. 1950	65	20	15
Vietnam[3]			
Jan. 1965	50	28	22
May 1965	52	26	22
Nov. 1965	64	21	15
Grenada[4]			
Nov. 1983	63	29	8
Panama[5]			
Jan. 1990	72	18	10
Iraq/Kuwait[6]			
Aug. 1990	75	17	8
Jan. 1991	77	15	8
Somalia[7]			
Dec. 1992	74	21	5

1. Positive response refers to "should be involved," "not a mistake," "a good idea," and "right decision." Negative response refers to the opposite.
2. Question phrasing: mistake or not a mistake to defend Korea (Gallup).
3. Question phrasing: should or should not have become involved with U.S. military forces in Southeast Asia (Gallup).
4. Question phrasing: mistake in sending troops to Grenada or not (Gallup).
5. Question phrasing: American invasion of Panama a good idea or a bad idea (NBC/*Wall Street Journal*).
6. Question phrasing: 1990—United States made a mistake in sending troops to Saudi Arabia or not (Gallup); 1991—right decision or wrong decision in using military force against Iraq (Times Mirror).
7. Question phrasing: should U.S. military forces be involved in the situation in Somalia or should they not (NBC/*Wall Street Journal*).

telling pollsters that it approved of the Desert Shield decision, it was also expressing significant reservations about further military engagement there. First reactions about taking the offensive against Iraq were quite negative. By a margin of 59 percent to 27 percent, an ABC poll in early August found that the public opposed bombing Iraqi military targets to force Saddam Hussein out of Kuwait.

A broader Gallup question at that same time found the public divided about whether the Gulf was worth fighting for. In fact, the public remained ambivalent about going to war right up until Bush made the decision to begin the air war. Questions that asked if the allies should use force to drive the Iraqis out if they did not observe the January 15, 1991, deadline found majority support by the end of the prewar period. However, questions in those same polls that asked if economic sanctions should be given more time to work found the public closely divided on whether to pull the trigger.

Reasons and Resonances

In the end, however, the public's belief that the use of military force in the Gulf was justified overrode its basic reluctance to go to war. As early as August 1990, Americans disagreed with most of the arguments opposing intervention, and agreed with most reasons for taking a hard line with Saddam Hussein. A CBS/*New York Times* poll of that month found many more Americans saw a parallel between the Gulf and stopping Hitler (yes, 61 percent; no, 33 percent) than between the Gulf and the Vietnam quagmire (yes, 42 percent; no, 52 percent). The same survey found two out of three Americans agreeing that the United States should have a say in who controls Mideast oil, and only 30 percent believing that the trouble in the Gulf was a dispute between Arab states from which the United States should stay aloof.

Indeed, throughout the prewar period, there was strong support for the *general* proposition that the United States should do what was required to drive the Iraqis out of Kuwait, including the use of force. Approximately seven in ten Americans agreed with that broad formulation as it was periodically tested by the ABC/*Washington Post* poll throughout the fall of 1990. Often when pollsters asked more pointed questions about military operations, they got more dovish answers, especially early in the crisis. For example, a mid-November *Los Angeles Times* poll found 53 percent of the public saying that based on all they had heard or read, the United States should not go to war against Iraq over the Mideast.

One of the most important turning points in response to the "hard questions" about the use of force was the UN Security Council November vote that set the January 15, 1991, deadline for

Table 2   Gallup Trend on Forces in Gulf

View of U.S. Going to War with Iraq to Drive the Iraqis out of Kuwait

	Favor	*Oppose*	*No Opinion*
1991 Jan. 11–13	55	38	7
1991 Jan. 3–6	52	39	9
1990 Dec. 13–16	48	43	9
1990 Dec. 6–9	53	40	7
1990 Nov. 29–Dec. 2	53	40	7
1990 Nov. 15–18	37	51	12

Iraq to withdraw from Kuwait. The Gallup organization's polling best captures the impact of that UN decision on American public opinion. Prior to the decision, 51 percent of the American public opposed going to war against Iraq if it did not meet the deadline. After the decision, majorities favored going to war every time Gallup asked the question.

Other more direct survey findings illustrate the importance of Bush's multilateral approach to the public. For example, a December NBC/*Wall Street Journal* survey found 58 percent of its respondents saying that the United States should take no military actions if other nations refused to commit significant military forces to the Gulf effort while only 34 percent favored unilateral military action.

Congressional Consideration

As the United Nation's imprimatur added to public support for a war effort and as allied and friendly governments kicked in with soldiers and money, the congressional debate in Washington in January also helped prepare the public for war. All of the major polls found large majorities supported Bush's desire to seek congressional approval before using force. In January, for example, a *Newsweek* poll found fully 82 percent of the public approving that approach. Probably as a consequence, after Congress gave its approval, the ABC/*Washington Post* poll observed a sharp increase in the percentage of the public agreeing that the situation in the Gulf required immediate military action.

Table 3   ABC/*Washington Post* Gulf War Poll Trend

Should U.S. go to war with Iraq:[12]	*13*	*9*	*January 1991* *4–8*	*4–6*	*2–6*	*2*
Yes	69	68	62	63	62	65
No	26	29	31	32	33	29
Don't Know	4	2	6	6	5	6
N=(sample size)	(781)	(511)	(1003)	(1057)	(1007)	(352)
How long should U.S. wait before going to war?						
Go now	37	27	19	18	14	16
< 1 month	21	29	30	31	32	37
Longer	8	10	9	9	10	7
No/Don't know	33	34	41	42	44	40

While the United Nations vote and Congressional approval were important specific milestones in the development of the public's commitment to the use of force, the Bush administration's skill at public communication helped all along the way. For example, in the first week of August, a CBS/*New York Times* poll found the public divided by a margin of 50 percent yes, to 41 percent no, about whether George Bush had "explained clearly what's at stake and why he is sending troops to Saudi Arabia." However, by as early as the first week in September, no fewer than 77 percent in an ABC/*Washington Post* survey said that they did have a clear idea on the matter. Further, at no point during the buildup and debate about military action did Bush's approval ratings for handling the crisis fall below 55 percent. His combat experience in World War II may have given the public greater confidence in him in this respect.

Nonetheless, public perception of the coming war was not particularly rosy. The American public expected to win relatively quickly but also to pay a significant price for victory. Polls in January found the public anticipated as many as 5,000 U.S. casualties. Three in four Americans in a Times Mirror survey said they expected Iraq to use chemical weapons on the battlefield, and two in three in a CBS/*New York Times* poll in mid-January thought that Mideast terrorists would kill civilians in the United States These fears were as prevalent among those who favored immediate actions in the Gulf as they were among those who wanted to give sanctions more time to work.

Polls at this time also found a significant and growing minority dissenting from the use of force as the January 15 deadline approached. The proportion of Americans who said the United States had made a mistake sending troops to the Gulf increased from 17 percent in August to 29 percent by January in the Gallup poll, and that same month, as many as 42 percent told Times Mirror that *not enough* was being heard in the media from those who opposed a military involvement in the Gulf.

Public Opinion on a War Footing

The conduct of the war itself and the public's electronic connection to it created a climate of opinion that was not hospitable to dissent during the brief duration of the war. While virtually all Americans said they were following news of the war, half of Times Mirror's respondents in a late January 1991 poll described themselves as compulsive viewers who "could not stop watching news about the war." By a 79 percent to 16 percent margin, the public thought news censorship was a good thing not a bad thing, and unlike only a few weeks earlier, the public complained that it was hearing too much, not too little, from those who opposed the war. Despite restrictions on coverage, few Americans thought that much information about the war was kept from the public, and the only contentious media issue was whether U.S. news organizations should have been allowed to broadcast from Baghdad.

SOMALIA: TRANSITORY SUPPORT

The East African state, in virtual anarchy for a year, was suffering mass starvation in mid-1992 when the United Nations approved a peacekeeping operation and the United States airlifted the first aid. As the first post–Gulf War overseas commitment of U.S. forces, the operation in Somalia began with an American public more positively disposed toward, and confident in, its military than at any time since the Vietnam era. The nature of the original mission in Somalia, providing humanitarian aid, was also one that the public could easily embrace. These factors, combined with the very positive media coverage accorded the arrival of U.S. forces in Somalia, suggested little potential for the abrupt reversal of public opinion that was to occur in less than a year.

The rapid development of public disillusionment with Somalia reflects the degree to which opinion about an overseas military mission can change when there is not sustained communication with the public, especially when a new policy direction occurs. It also illustrates the power of international media coverage to shine brightly on an operation one moment, and the next moment to bring graphic illustrations of its human costs directly into U.S. homes.

Clearly at the earliest stages of the mission to Somalia, when President Bush dispatched U.S. troops, the public response was highly favorable and media coverage was extremely supportive. Immediately after the deployment was ordered, in a December 1992 *Newsweek* poll, 66 percent of the public approved sending "American military forces to assure distribution of relief supplies." And after the explosion of coverage of the marines actually landing on the beaches—there had been virtually no television footage on Somalia before that—the mission was approved overwhelmingly (84 percent, of whom 53 percent "strongly approved"—according to a *Los Angeles Times* poll in January 1993).

Nonetheless, warning signs also appeared in the polls. The public overwhelmingly understood the mission to be humanitarian aid, not fighting: 59 percent told Gallup in December 1992 that the main objective was "to deliver relief supplies"; only 31 percent said it was to "also attempt to bring a permanent end to the fighting." The public also expected the mission to be short. A majority of those polled by ABC/*Washington Post*, 62 percent, believed the United States would not get bogged down in Somalia but would get out quickly; and in a *Los Angeles Times* poll, 51 percent said it would be over within six months and 69 percent said it would end within a year.

As early as January, marines had clashed with warlord Mohammed Farah Aideed and the first Americans were slain.

Still, Americans remained behind the effort. At the end of March, fully 84 percent of Americans approved (56 percent "approved strongly") of the use of U.S. forces for humanitarian reasons.[13] Even in June, after the mission had broadened dramatically with a full scale attack on Aideed camps in retaliation for the deaths of twenty-three Pakistani peacekeepers, Gallup found two-thirds of Americans (65 percent) approved of U.S. participation in UN efforts against a warlord.

The Screen Goes Blank

The public probably did not fully understand the wider peacemaking mission, however. The first significant raid on Aideed's camp, which occurred January 7, before Bush left office, was portrayed by U.S. officials as a shift of tactics rather than strategy, and the Clinton administration subsequently embraced it as such without either trying to sell it to the public as a necessary change or warning of its potentially deadly consequences.

The U.S. television screen had been virtually blank on Somalia since the troop landings in December, and public interest had plummeted from 52 percent who said they followed the issue "very closely" in January to 16 percent in June, as measured in Times Mirror and Gallup surveys. President Clinton referred to the changed mission only in passing three days after a huge raid on Aideed (following the death of Pakistani UN troops). During an impromptu news conference called to rebut charges of weakness in foreign policy, he said: "We cannot have a situation where one of these warlords, while everybody else is cooperating, decides that he can go out and slaughter 20 peacekeepers."[14]

A monthly running tally of network news coverage devoted to Somalia charts the episodic nature of communications to the public. It illustrates the extent to which Americans initially tuned into one kind of mission (in December 1992), largely forgot about the operation through the spring and summer as coverage dropped toward nil, and rejoined the story in the fall when the nature and danger level of the mission were entirely different from eight months earlier.

By September, as the U.S. death toll mounted gradually and amid increasingly violent incidents involving U.S. forces, a

Figure 2   Television Coverage and Attention Paid to Somalia and U.S. Economy

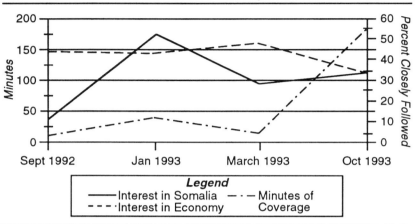

Yankelovich/*Time*/CNN poll found the public was evenly divided (46 percent disapprove versus 43 percent approve) over "the presence of U.S. troops in Somalia." A Gallup poll the same month found a majority saying U.S. troops should leave altogether (53 percent) rather than stay in a limited capacity to preserve peace (46 percent); it found a larger majority, 57 percent, said military combat against warlords should stop. Fully 69 percent told Yankelovich that U.S. troops should be responsible only for food delivery.

The next month brought the Ranger tragedy that precipitated unequivocal public opposition to the Somalian operation. Eighteen U.S. soldiers were killed, some of their bodies were violated by crowds, and a battered helicopter pilot was captured and interrogated, all shown on television news. In an October 1993 Times Mirror survey, the proportion of Americans who followed Somalian events "very closely" jumped to 34 percent, and the amount of television coverage leaped out of the doldrums.[15]

Now 69 percent called for withdrawal of U.S. troops (43 percent right away, the rest gradually) as reported in a Gallup/CNN/*USA Today* poll. At the same time, ABC/*Washington Post* found that belief that U.S. forces would not get bogged down dropped to 44 percent (versus 62 percent a year earlier), and in a concurrent NBC/*Wall Street Journal* poll, approval of U.S. involvement "in the situation in Somalia" was halved to 34 percent compared to 74 percent a year earlier.

A Humanitarian Impulse Survives

It is important to point out that despite the failures of this operation, the U.S. impulse to use force for humanitarian reasons appears to have survived the Somalia experience. In October, after the Ranger tragedy, Times Mirror found that 56 percent of the public still approved "of sending U.S. military forces to Asian or African countries in order to prevent famines and mass starvation."[16] And in December, a year after the first U.S. landing, 62 percent of the public said in a CBS poll that the United States did the "right thing" to send troops to Somalia to "make sure shipments of food got through." Even when the question was framed in terms of the costs incurred, a plurality of 48 percent said yes, the intervention was worth the "loss of American life, the financial costs and other risks involved," while 44 percent said it was not.

Although Somalia failed to eradicate public support for the use of force for humanitarian purposes, it underscored U.S. aversion to the use of force for peacekeeping and nation-building. Asked whether the United States should keep troops there "until the situation is peaceful" or get out "as quickly as possible," the public said "get out" by a two to one margin (61 percent versus 33 percent).

Further, the same Times Mirror poll that found continued support for humanitarian missions one month after the death of the Rangers showed large majorities opposing the use of U.S. forces to restore law and order if governments break down in Africa or Asia (60 percent) or in Latin America or the Caribbean (53 percent).

In the end, the Clinton administration failed to sell the change in mission of the U.S. forces in Somalia to a public that was ready to entertain broader goals at first. President Clinton, however, cited two other lessons learned in Somalia: do not promise a quick military operation to a humanitarian crisis "because there are almost always political problems and sometimes military conflicts which bring about these crises," and do not try to be "a policing officer" in a situation where "there is not political process going on" because you soon appear to be choosing sides and become a target.[17]

BOSNIA: NO SUPPORT

With the collapse of the Soviet Union, Yugoslavia began to break up into ethnic republics in 1991 with the independence of Slovenia and Croatia. Significant press attention only came with the attempt of multiethnic Bosnia to become separate in April 1992. This set off bloody repression as irredentist Serbs, aided by Serbia itself, embarked on "ethnic cleansing" of Muslims, which continued despite periodic threats by outside forces to intervene.

U.S. reactions to Bosnia and the Gulf could not have been more different. The first public response to the civil war in Yugoslavia was that the United States had no stake or responsibility in the conflict. This was followed by sustained indifference to the extraordinary amounts of coverage given the war by the U.S. media. As the brutality intensified, and perhaps as its weight began to sink in, the longer term reaction has been a growing feeling among many (but not most) Americans that the United States avoided its broader moral responsibility in the Balkans. However, this has not been accompanied by a consensus on what the United States should have done or should do now. Public attentiveness has again eroded.

From the very start, Americans thought the United States had a role to play in the Gulf and a moral responsibility to feed people in Somalia. In contrast, the first polls about the Balkan war told a very different story. A January 1993 CBS/*New York Times* poll, taken as U.S. airdrops of food began, found 67 percent saying the United States does not have "a responsibility to do something about the fighting between Serbs and Bosnians," while 24 percent said it did. A similar result was found at the same time by a Times Mirror survey when the public was asked if U.S. forces should be used "in Bosnia to help end the fighting there"; 55 percent said no, 32 percent said yes. In the same poll, only slightly more support came when the element of fighting aggression was introduced: 47 percent opposed using U.S. forces "to prevent Bosnia from being taken over by the Serbs," while 36 percent favored it.

The Bosnian conflict was unlike the Persian Gulf war in another key respect. Whereas the Gulf war resonated with World War II, Bosnia resonated with Vietnam. In an August 1990 CBS/ *New York Times* poll, 61 percent of the respondents said the Gulf reminded them of fighting Hitler, while 42 percent said it reminded them of the Vietnam quagmire. The public split on how U.S. troop deployment in Bosnia might end up: in January 1993, 47 percent said it would be more like the Persian Gulf War, and 41 percent said more like the Vietnam War.

Sustained Indifference

If the Gulf was an example of how media coverage could be beneficial to support for military involvement, and Somalia an example of how it could hurt, Bosnia is an example of how the media can fail to affect public opinion. television pictures of Bosnia failed to create in Americans a disposition to become involved. At the outset of the civil wars in Yugoslavia, in a December 1991 Times Mirror survey, fewer than one in ten Americans said they were paying "very close" attention to news of the conflict in that remote corner of Europe. Indifference remained high throughout the spring of 1992 as the war between the Bosnian Serbs and Muslims was given extensive television coverage. Even reports of "ethnic cleansing," purposive rapes, and other atrocities that recalled the horrors of World War II failed to capture significant attention in the United States.

Indeed, the level of public interest in Bosnia over the course of the conflict has borne *no* relationship to the nature and extent of media coverage. Never did American attention reach a *critical mass* as it quickly did in Somalia and in the Gulf. Only once did the proportion of public who followed news of the Balkan conflict "very closely" climb above 20 percent, and that was in May 1993 when U.S. military action appeared likely. Mostly it hovered at the 15 percent level throughout 1993, dipping to 12 percent in 1994.[18]

Figure 3   Television Coverage and Attention Paid to Bosnia and U.S. Economy

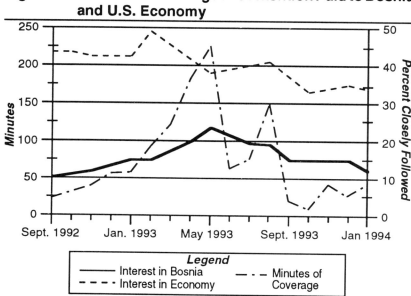

Over the course of 1993, a majority of Americans continued to believe that the United States did *not have* a responsibility to do something about the fighting in Bosnia. Further, most Americans were not even taking sides in the war. An early 1993 Times Mirror poll found just 30 percent of the respondents saying they were more sympathetic to the Muslim side, and 8 percent favored the Serbs. Subsequently in a September 1993 poll to test for possible religious prejudice, we asked the question about sympathy in two forms: whether the respondent was "more sympathetic" to "Serbs" or "Bosnians," and whether the respondent was "more sympathetic" to "Serbs" or "Bosnian Muslims." We found no significant difference; 35 percent said Bosnians and 33 percent said Bosnian Muslims.

By 1994, with the prospects of U.S. air strikes and the slaughter of sixty-eight civilians in an outdoor market in Sarajevo, there was a steady rise in the view that the United States did have a responsibility to do "something." Despite many hours of coverage as well as much importuning commentary in the print media, the *prevailing* attitude remained that this is not an American fight.

Table 4   Responsibility in Bosnia[19]

	U.S. Has Responsibility	U.S. Doesn't Have Responsibility	Don't Know
April 1994	41	49	10
February 1994	36	53	11
December 1993	26	65	9
June 1993	37	51	12
May 1993	37	52	11
January 1993	24	67	9

Question: Do you think the United States has a responsibility to do something about the fighting between Serbs and Bosnians in what used to be Yugoslavia, or doesn't the United States have this responsibility?

Specific questions about the use of force in Bosnia revealed responses along the following lines. Questions that asked if U.S. forces should be employed to *make* peace were rejected. Questions that tested participation in multilateral peace*keeping* generally drew more support unless the wording suggested that U.S. forces might become involved in a shooting war. Questions that tested whether U.S. force should be used to protect UN peacekeepers received strong support.

Even use of U.S. air strikes for humanitarian purposes had drawn little support initially. A Gallup poll in August 1992 found only 35 percent agreeing that the United States should "take the lead" in seeking United Nations–backed air strikes to unblock relief efforts to Sarajevo (45 percent said it should not). Similarly, a CBS/*New York Times* poll found that the use of U.S. planes to bomb targets to get food and medicine to civilians was favored by 39 percent and opposed by 43 percent. Using U.S. air forces not necessarily carrying weapons to keep humanitarian aid flowing was favored by fully 67 percent (35 percent strongly) in a *Los Angeles Times* poll in the same mid-1992 period.

Ambivalent about Air Strikes

Throughout much of 1993, Gallup found U.S. air strikes against Serbian military forces opposed by majorities—62 percent in April and 56 percent in May—who said the United States should not get militarily involved. With rising Serbian attacks and heightened Serbian intransigence toward peace efforts, however, support increased for air strikes more broadly. U.S. air strikes carried out in conjunction with European allies, against Serbs attacking Sarajevo, drew 51 percent and 60 percent support in August 1993 polls by Gallup/CNN/*USA Today* and ABC/*Washington Post*, respectively. A June 1993 CBS/*New York Times* survey found that using U.S. planes to bomb targets that were attacking UN peacekeepers was favored by 61 percent of the public. Using "allied planes" against Serbs threatening UN peacekeepers was supported by fully 85 percent in the previously cited August 1993 ABC/*Washington Post* poll.

Although public attitudes toward U.S. air strikes were somewhat ambivalent, this "American Way of War," as it has been termed[20], was clearly favored over using U.S. ground troops except as part of a peacekeeping force. In early 1993, Times Mirror found that by a 55 percent to 32 percent margin, the public opposed the use of military force to help end the fighting in Bosnia or to prevent Bosnia from being taken over by the Serbs (47 percent to 36 percent). Support for deploying U.S. "armed forces" as part of a UN operation to deliver relief supplies was 57 percent in a December 1992 Gallup poll. Contributing U.S. troops to a UN peacekeeping force enjoyed the same high level of support overall: 68 percent, for example, in May 1993[21] and 73 percent in April 1994.[22]

When the risk of U.S. forces being subjected to sniper fire was introduced into the question, a September 1993 NBC/*Wall Street Journal* poll found opposition to deployment of U.S. forces, even as peacekeepers, rose to 59 percent.

Wariness of ground force engagement notwithstanding, measures of support for multilateral participation grew despite the clear consensus that Bosnia was not an American fight. It is also worth noting that the increasing *minority* view that the United States should take some responsibility in ending the war occurred without either the Bush or Clinton administration taking that position unequivocally. A June 1994 ABC/*Washington Post* poll found 31 percent saying U.S. "vital interests are at stake in Bosnia."

BASIC INCLINATIONS ABOUT THE USE OF FORCE

Looking more broadly at Bosnia, Somalia, and the Gulf, we see that many factors influenced public opinion about military intervention. The public's earliest and most basic attitude toward the situation—that the United States did, or did not, have responsibility to take strong actions—shaped more specific public responses and national policy.

From the very start, the public thought U.S. vital interests were at stake in the Gulf. In Somalia, the public approved the humanitarian objectives in the first part of the mission but rejected the nation-building role for U.S. forces in Somalia in the second part. In Bosnia, despite second thoughts on the part of many, most Americans continue to say this is not an American fight, and the United States shall not be a peacemaker.

General public opinion polling and reactions to these three crises suggest that the public will be disposed to act militarily, if it feels that the vital interests of the United States are at stake, or if U.S. military force can provide humanitarian assistance without becoming engaged in a protracted conflict. Whereas the *peacekeeper* role evokes an ambiguous response, as we have seen in Bosnia, the public strongly rejects the peace*maker* role.

A Narrowing National Interest

In the post–Cold War world, there is not a great deal of consensus about what constitutes U.S. vital interests. In a major 1993 survey, Times Mirror found that protecting U.S. oil supplies and preventing nuclear proliferation were the only foreign policy goals shared by the public and nine leadership groups in the United States. The public's initial, basic feeling that the United States had an important stake in the Gulf, and the consequent support for military action there, reinforce the perceived importance of oil. Public response to the more recent North Korean crisis provides a good indication of the salience of the nuclear issue.

The polls on North Korea have found substantial support for using force to prevent a buildup of nuclear weapons. Tellingly, surveys have found much more support for U.S. intervention to preempt a North Korean nuclear threat than to defend South Korea from North Korean aggression. In late 1993, majorities in Gallup and *Los Angeles Times* polls favored U.S. action to prevent or eliminate North Korea's nuclear capabilities. In contrast, both Times Mirror and Gallup surveys found majority opposition to the use of U.S. military force to repel a North Korean invasion of South Korea.

Reflecting fears of nuclear proliferation, in an April 1994 Yankelovich/*Time*/CNN poll, fully 62 percent said the United States has "a great deal at stake in what happens" in North Korea; and a similar majority—59 percent in March and 58 percent in June in two ABC/*Washington Post* polls—said the United States has a "vital interest at stake" in North Korea. Development of nuclear weapons by North Korea was judged the most serious foreign policy issue facing the United States by most respondents (25 percent) in a NBC/*Wall Street Journal* poll.[23]

In the standoff, Americans overwhelmingly (usually more than three-fourths) support the imposition of a trade or economic embargo to force North Korean compliance with the UN inspection agency. Over the past six months, as administration policy on North Korea has appeared equivocal, public support for military intervention has softened and was essentially split in June. A Yankelovich poll found 46 percent for and 40 percent against "military action to destroy North Korea's nuclear facilities," while a Newsweek poll found 44 percent in favor, 47 percent opposed, to "air strikes against suspected nuclear targets" in North Korea.

Other indications of how Americans define the national interest are evidenced in polls that ask respondents about circumstances that might justify using U.S. military forces abroad by citing specific conditions and nations.[24] Our most recent survey, for example, found in September 1993, that of five situations posited, public approval of use of force ranged from a high of 53 percent "if Iraq invaded Saudi Arabia" to a low of 21 percent "if Russia invaded Ukraine," with 41 percent supporting U.S. intervention if Mexico was "threatened by revolution or civil war."

Other polls have approached the issue in more generic terms, i.e., "if close allies of the U.S. are attacked." A recent Roper poll

(February 1993) found in this respect that virtually all Americans (94 percent) would favor use of U.S. armed forces if the United States itself is attacked. Large majorities also favored the use of force to strike back when Americans in a foreign country are attacked (79 percent), if close allies are attacked (73 percent) and to provide humanitarian relief efforts (74 percent).

Interestingly, the approval rate for military intervention was surprisingly high for causes related to top priority domestic issues: 82 percent favored force to stop the flow of illegal drugs into the country and 70 percent to police the flow of illegal immigration. At the bottom end of the scale or fewer than half of Roper's sampling favored using force to overthrow a foreign government that practices genocide; to stop an invasion of one foreign country by another; or to intervene in a civil war to protect innocent lives.

The Times Mirror Center in May 1994 asked a series of questions of the public designed to elicit preference for use of force along two dimensions: the justification for intervention (national interest, humanitarian cause, policeman role) and the kind of force to be used (air or ground). In addition, we tested attitudes toward use of air power "to eliminate an arsenal of nuclear weapons in an unfriendly country such as North Korea or Iran."

The poll's results reflect the recurring patterns observed in the three cases considered above and in much of the other polling reviewed for this study. It found majority support for the use of force to ensure the U.S. oil supply, to thwart nuclear proliferation, and to provide humanitarian aid. However, little support was evident for military intervention to restore law and order. In every case, there was greater support for the use of air power than for the use of ground forces.

Combining the responses regarding air power and ground troops, we found that majorities of Americans *supported* using force to "make sure U.S. oil supplies are not cut off" by a margin of 50 percent versus 40 percent and to "prevent famines and mass starvation" in Africa, Asia, and Latin American countries by 52 percent versus 41 percent. But a majority *opposed* the use of force "to restore law and order if the governments break down" in Africa, Asia, and Latin America, 51 percent versus 41 percent.

The demographic profiles of respondents who supported use of force, or opposed it, varied across the three missions. Generally, conservative white males supported the so-called national security missions of protecting oil or eliminating nuclear weapons while Democrats, women, and African Americans show greater support for using U.S. force for humanitarian and law/ order causes. Most striking, in this respect, was the degree to which blacks subscribe to a different agenda than whites in justifiable uses of force.

Specifically, the *majority* of Americans willing to use air/ ground forces *for protecting oil supplies* were more often men than women (57 percent versus 45 percent); young than old (60 percent of 18-29 year olds versus 38 percent of those 65 and over); white than black (52 percent versus 44 percent); Republicans than Democrats or Independents (62 percent versus 48 percent or 49 percent, respectively); and Bush than Clinton or Perot voters in 1992 (58 percent versus 47 percent). Politically vocal respondents—those who regularly listen to talk radio and/or communicated with their Congress members within the past year—were more supportive of this mission than the others. (See Table 5)

If we considering the *majority* of Americans willing to use force *to deliver famine relief*, men and women were in the same proportion overall (51 percent and 52 percent) but with more younger women than men (68 percent versus 55 percent in the

Table 5   Military Intervention to Maintain Oil Supply

	Favor(%)	Oppose(%)	Don't Know(%)	N(sample size)
Total	50	40	10	1,206
Sex				
Male	57	37	6	602
Female	45	42	13	604
Race				
White	52	39	9	1,011
Hispanic	50	44	6	64
Black	44	43	13	112
Age				
Under 30	60	33	7	242
30–49	54	37	9	527
50+	42	47	11	412

	Favor(%)	Oppose(%)	Don't Know(%)	N(sample size)
Education				
College Grad.	48	42	10	364
Other College	50	40	10	264
High School Grad.	53	40	7	416
< H.S. Grad.	49	36	15	151
Family Income				
$50,000 +	53	41	6	270
$30,000–$49,999	55	36	9	278
$20,000–$29,999	54	39	7	202
< $20,000	48	41	11	320
Region				
East	47	43	10	241
Midwest	49	43	8	290
South	53	35	12	421
West	51	40	9	254
Community Size				
City	53	37	10	429
Small Town	49	39	12	302
Suburb	52	43	5	241
Rural	48	42	10	215
Party ID				
Republican	62	31	7	356
Democrat	48	42	10	391
Independent	49	43	8	383
Past Vote				
Clinton	47	45	8	389
Bush	58	34	8	283
Perot	47	47	6	124
Other	51	36	13	410
Presidential Approval				
Approve	48	43	9	549
Disapprove	57	37	6	512
Don't Know	36	36	28	145
Political Vocalization				
Regular Listener To Radio Talk Shows	48	48	4	198
Contacted Washington In Past 12 Months	50	42	8	274
Both	58	40	2	76
Neither	52	37	11	810

Question: Would you favor or oppose using American Ground Forces/Air Power in the Middle East to make sure that U.S. oil supplies are not cut off?

18–29 year bracket) in favor; more blacks than whites by a huge margin (69 percent and 49 percent, respectively); more Democrats than Republicans or Independents (59 percent versus 48 percent or 50 percent, respectively); and more Clinton voters than Bush or Perot voters (57 percent versus 42 percent and 51 percent, respectively).(See Table 6.)

Table 6   Military Intervention to Prevent Famines and Mass Starvation

	Favor(%)	Oppose(%)	Don't Know(%)	N(sample size)
Total	52	41	7	1,206
Sex				
Male	51	45	4	602
Female	52	38	10	604
Race				
White	49	44	7	1,011
Hispanic	54	40	6	64
Black	69	25	6	112
Age				
Under 30	61	36	3	242
30–49	57	38	5	527
50+	40	49	11	412
Education				
College Grad.	50	46	4	364
Other College	52	40	8	264
High School Grad.	53	40	7	416
< H.S. Grad.	51	41	8	151
Family Income				
$50,000 +	47	48	5	270
$30,000–$49,999	53	41	6	278
$20,000–$29,999	58	37	5	202
< $20,000	54	39	7	320
Region				
East	48	48	4	241
Midwest	51	43	6	290
South	54	39	7	421
West	54	37	9	254

	Favor(%)	Oppose(%)	Don't Know(%)	N(sample size)
Community Size				
City	56	38	6	429
Small Town	49	45	6	302
Suburb	47	45	8	241
Rural	53	41	6	215
Party ID				
Republican	48	44	8	356
Democrat	59	35	6	391
Independent	50	45	5	383
Past Vote				
Clinton	57	38	5	389
Bush	42	49	9	283
Perot	51	47	2	124
Other	53	39	8	410
Presidential Approval				
Approve	59	36	5	549
Disapprove	44	50	6	512
Don't Know	49	35	16	145
Political Vocalization				
Regular Listener To				
Radio Talk Shows	44	50	6	198
Contacted Washington				
In Past 12 Months	45	49	6	274
Both	40	56	4	76
Neither	55	38	7	810

Question: Would you favor or oppose sending American Ground Forces/ Using the American Air Force in/to Asian, African or Latin American countries in order to prevent famines and mass starvation?

The *minority* that which supported using force *for law and order* was composed differently again. Again there was no gender gap (41 percent for both men and women) in support, but education and income became significant predictors more than in the previous questions: only 31 percent of college graduates approved, compared to 51 percent of those without a high school diploma; and only 31 percent with incomes over $50,000 a year approved, compared to 47 percent with incomes under $20,000 a year. As with humanitarian intervention, blacks were more in favor of using force for this cause than whites by about the same 20 percentage points (59 percent versus 38 percent). Democrats were evenly split on the issue (47 percent for and 46 percent against) but both Republicans and Independents were opposed by large margins (39 percent for and 52 percent against; and 39 percent for and 56 percent against, respectively). Clinton voters were more supportive (44 percent) than Bush voters (33 percent) or Perot voters (38 percent). (See Table 7.)

More of the public favored using air power rather than ground troops for every mission: 59 percent for nuclear targets, 55 percent for protecting oil, 57 percent to relieve famine, and 44 percent to restore law and order. The only unity among Republicans, Democrats, and Independents came in using air power to

Table 7   Military Intervention to Restore Law and Order

	Favor(%)	Oppose(%)	Don't Know(%)	N(sample size)
Total	41	51	8	1,206
Sex				
Male	41	54	5	602
Female	41	49	10	604
Race				
White	38	54	8	1011
Hispanic	43	54	3	64
Black	59	33	8	112
Age				
Under 30	52	44	4	242
30–49	42	52	6	527
50+	33	57	10	412
Education				
College Grad.	31	62	7	364
Other College	41	52	7	264
High School Grad.	41	51	8	416
< H.S. Grad.	51	41	8	151
Family Income				
$50,000 +	31	63	6	270
$30,000–$49,999	41	52	7	278
$20,000–$29,999	45	49	6	202
< $20,000	47	46	7	320

	Favor(%)	Oppose(%)	Don't Know(%)	N(sample size)
Region				
East	38	55	7	241
Midwest	41	51	8	290
South	42	50	8	421
West	42	50	8	254
Community Size				
City	45	48	7	429
Small Town	40	53	7	302
Suburb	35	57	8	241
Rural	42	51	7	215
Party ID				
Republican	39	52	9	356
Democrat	47	46	7	391
Independent	39	56	5	383
Past Vote				
Clinton	44	51	5	389
Bush	33	58	9	283
Perot	38	54	8	124
Other	44	46	10	410
Presidential Approval				
Approve	46	49	5	549
Disapprove	37	56	7	512
Don't Know	34	45	21	145
Political Vocalization				
Regular Listener To Radio Talk Shows	35	60	5	198
Contacted Washington In Past 12 Months	35	57	8	274
Both	35	63	2	76
Neither	43	49	8	810

Question: Would you favor or oppose sending American Ground Forces/ Using the American Air Force in/to Asian, African or Latin American countries to restore law and order if the governments completely break down?

eliminate nuclear weapons; Clinton and Bush voters were also very close in their support, 61 percent and 63 percent, respectively, with Perot voters at 50 percent.

Support for using ground troops averaged 10 percentage points less than air power: 46 percent for protecting oil, 46 percent for relieving famine, and 38 percent for restoring law and order. The demographic profiles of supporters was similar for use of both air and ground forces, with support deteriorating by relatively the same amount among the various categories.

From the Times Mirror survey, we constructed a simple, four-part typology of the American public regarding the use of force. First were those Americans, accounting for 31 percent of the electorate, willing to support the use of force for *both* national security and altruistic purposes (oil and humanitarian aid). The next group, in about the same proportion (29 percent), opposed using force in both situations. The third and fourth groups, in about equal numbers, were either disposed to use force *only* for altruistic reasons (21 percent), or *only* for national security purposes (19 percent).

- Interventionists, who tended to support both missions (31 percent);

- U.S.-centrics, who support the oil mission but not humanitarian aid (19 percent);

- One Worlders, who support humanitarian intervention but not force to ensure our oil supply (21 percent); and

- Noninterventionists, who supported neither of the missions (29 percent).

We observed striking similarities among various groups in this exercise. Interventionists are more likely to be men, blacks, and young people under 30. Noninterventionists are more often women, older persons (over 50), Independents, Perot voters, and the politically vocal.

The One Worlders tend to be women, blacks, and generally liberal—Democrats, Clinton voters, and those approving of Clinton's performance. The U.S.-centrics are more often male, white, and generally conservative—Republicans, Bush voters, those who disapprove of Clinton's performance, and the politically vocal.

CNN, AND OTHER MEDIA EFFECTS

If the public's basic notions about the United States' responsibility to act is the principal driver of response to the potential use of force, media coverage modulates the climate of opinion rather than dictates it. From the very beginning of the Gulf crisis, extensive coverage connected the American public to a situation in which it felt it had a stake. Yet in Bosnia, dramatically graphic television pictures failed to create a disposition to become involved. Public interest in that conflict has borne little relationship to the nature and extent of media coverage. Somalia evidenced the power of international media coverage to shine brightly one moment and the next moment to bring graphic illustrations of the human costs of operational mistakes directly into U.S. homes.

Many have blamed the so-called "CNN effect" for the refusal of the American public to tolerate casualties. Body bags of U.S. soldiers shown in the family living room obviously has an effect on the public's attitude toward use of force. But, for different reasons, neither Somalia nor the Gulf tells us whether the public would tolerate televised casualties for a sustained period in a conflict in which Americans clearly believe their interests are at stake.

With Americans glued to their television sets, would thousands of casualties in the Gulf have eroded support for a war that Americans felt was justified? Would support for Somalia not have evaporated in response to the Ranger tragedy if there were a fundamental base of support for nation-building in Africa?

More often than not, response to media coverage is given credit for the public acting on its deep-seated judgments about the basic wisdom of U.S. military involvement. Perceptively Edward Luttwak points out that the Soviet Union never let its tightly regimented population see any U.S.-style television images of war yet "the reaction of Soviet society to the casualties of the Afghan war was essentially identical to the American reaction to the Vietnam War."[25]

Another reason why the media have had its impact on recent events, according to James Hoge writing in *Foreign Affairs*, is the "absence of articulated policy," i.e., leadership. "The existence of policy that can command public support against emotional swings stirred up by television imagery is key. In the absence of persuasive government strategy, the media will be catalytic. . . . When a crisis erupts and, in the absence of any clear statement of interests and threats, the press raises humanitarianism above more concrete national interests as an exclusive justification for action and intervention."[26] He also observed that "television images usually have a short shelf life, and their emotional effects can be tempered by reason. But that requires political leadership that constructs supportable policy, explains it and knows when to stand fast behind it."[27]

This becomes crucially important and more difficult in an era in which satellite communications give Americans direct access to news of momentous international events. Maxine Isaacs argues that in such an environment, opinion leaders (perhaps even the president) play a less important role in shaping views about foreign affairs as the public can form its own judgments based on firsthand observations.[28] Examining the relationship between elite and mass opinion in response to Tiananmen Square and the August 1991 abortive coup against Mikhail Gorbachev, she concludes:

> The dependence of mass upon elite opinion (expressed either by policy/opinion leaders or by the media), so long presumed by so many authorities to exist, is not total in two important late twentieth century cases.
>
> . . . Scholars should now take into account the fact that the public not only has access to information about remote events, but occasionally, if somewhat unpredictably, pays attention, and makes judgments based on real knowledge about what's going on in the world. It also should be assumed in the future that congruence of elite and mass opinion is possible, but it is not fore-ordained. Indeed, there is ample evidence that public opinion now operates somewhat, if not entirely, separately from elite opinion.[29]

SOME PRINCIPLES OF PUBLIC OPINION
ABOUT THE USE OF FORCE

The experience of the Gulf, Somalia, and Bosnia, as well as the body of post-Cold War polling that we have examined suggest some generalized patterns in public attitudes toward military intervention. Obviously we offer these as guidelines that can be used in judging public opinion rather than as hard and fast rules about how the public is apt to respond to a given situation.

- Early on in a crisis, the public reveals a basic disposition to accept or reject the use of force based on whether significant U.S. national interests *seem* to be at stake or based on feelings that the United States has a moral responsibility to act. This basic disposition or judgment colors response to specific proposals to use force.

- Even when the public feels that the United States has a responsibility to act, large percentages of the public (sometimes majorities) will favor no action unless the disposition to act is stimulated by presidential leadership.

- Even when the public feels that the United States has a responsibility to act, the public will always gravitate to diplomatic or economic options over military force, if they are in play as options.

- Despite the public's low regard for Congress, congressional debate, consideration, and approval make a difference to the American public.

- Generally, equal percentages of Americans can be classified as hard-core interventionists (31 percent) or hard-core noninterventionists (29 percent). The swing vote (40 percent) is similarly equally partitioned between those inclined only to support U.S.-centric missions versus those disposed only to support altruistic missions. The constituencies of each are very different.

- Besides stopping the spread of nuclear weapons and protecting U.S. energy supplies, there is little consensus about the national interests of the United States.
    - However, stopping terrorism, drugs, illegal immigration, international crime, and other global issues with clear domestic consequences are new potential rallying cries.
    - Public support for military intervention for humanitarian purposes survived Somalia.
    - There is very little support for police keeping or nation-building, even in this hemisphere.
    - Public opinion about U.S. participation in peacekeeping operations is less clear-cut.

- Multilateralism plays a crucial role in mustering support, especially when the public is ambivalent about the use of force.

- Surprisingly, the public is *more* likely than in the past to *initially* rally around a presidential decision to use force.

- The tendency of the public to rally around a presidential decision is enhanced by the extraordinary amounts of news coverage of the commission of U.S. troops to the field in the modern era.

- At the earliest stages of a crisis, the public's disposition and the media's coverage frenzy give political and military leadership its single best opportunity to make its case to the public and shape the news agenda.

- Sustained communications with the public about the objectives and scope of an overseas military mission are required to maintain support in a media-crowded environment in which public interest is easily diverted.

- Televised images of death and suffering create sympathy but do not change Americans' basic disposition to shun the policeman or peacemaker role.

- Televised images of U.S. casualties in peacemaking or in police operations or in other exercises in which the public feels it has little stake will have a devastating impact on support. We have no basis for judging the public's tolerance for televised images of U.S. casualties in conflicts that are considered in the national interest or justifiable for other reasons.

NOTES

1. Paul D. Wolfowitz, "Clinton's First Year," *Foreign Affairs*, Vol. 73, No. 1 (January/February 1994), p. 32.
2. *America's Place in the World*, Times Mirror Center for the People & the Press (Washington, D.C.: Nov. 2, 1993).
3. "U.S. Intervention Policy for the Post–Cold War World," Final Report of the Eighty-Fifth American Assembly (Harriman, N.Y.: Arden House, 1994), p. 4.
4. Chester Crocker, "Peacekeeping We Can Fight For," *The Washington Post*, May 8, 1994, sec. C, p.1.
5. Marc Trachtenberg, "Emerging Norms of Justified Intervention," A Collection of Essays, from a Project of the American Academy of Arts and Sciences, Laura W. Reed and Carl Kaysen, eds. (Cambridge, Mass.: American Academy of Arts and Sciences, 1993), p. 15.
6. Michael Mandelbaum, "The Reluctance to Intervene," *Foreign Policy*, No. 95 (Summer 1994), p. 4.
7. General Colin Powell's questions were: "Is the political objective we seek to achieve important, clearly defined and understood? Have all nonviolent policy means failed? Will military force achieve the objective? At what cost? Have the gains and risks been analyzed? How might the situation that we seek to alter, once it is altered by force, develop further and what might be the consequences?" Colin Powell, "U.S. Forces: Challenges Ahead," *Foreign Affairs*, Vol. 71, No. 5 (Winter 1992/93), p. 39.
8. Assistant Secretary of Defense Edward L. Warner III, Opening statement before the Senate Armed Services Subcommittee on Coalition Defense and Reinforcing Forces, April 13, 1994, 3. National Security Adviser W. Anthony Lake, in his policy speech on "enlargement," said that public pressure for humanitarian engagement must be tempered by other considerations, including cost, feasibility, contributions of others, and the likelihood of permanent success. Colin Powell, "U.S. Vision of Foreign Policy Reversed," *The New York Times*, September 22, 1993, sec. A, p. 13. President Bill Clinton, speaking extemporaneously, offered some additional views in discussing the possible use of force in Haiti, listing several reasons to intervene there, including proximity ("in our backyard"), the threat of

massive immigration, the desire to dissuade military coups elsewhere in the hemisphere, the presence of one million Haitians in the United States, and the presence of several thousand U.S. citizens living in Haiti. "Clinton Spells Out Reasons He Might Use Force in Haiti," *The New York Times*, May 19, 1994, sec. A, p. 1.

9. Times Mirror Center's *News Interest Index* periodically asks the public how closely it follows major news stories current at the time of the poll. Responses are very closely, fairly closely, not too closely, not at all closely, and don't know / refused. Only "very closely" responses are tabulated in the *Index*, whose data extend back to 1986.

10. *The Tyndall Report*, Vol. 3, No. 11, (January 1991), p. 3.

11. Also benefiting from instant and exhaustive television coverage during the past decade, comparable numbers of Americans had early opinions about the invasion of Panama (90 percent) in January 1990, and the invasion of Grenada (92 percent) in November 1983.

12. Question: As you may know, the United Nations Security Council has authorized the use of force against Iraq if it doesn't withdraw from Kuwait by January 15th (1991). If Iraq does not withdraw from Kuwait, should the United States go to war with Iraq to force it out of Kuwait at some point after January 15th, or not?

   Question which was asked of respondents who said that the United States should go to war at some point after January 15 1991, if Iraq does not withdraw from Kuwait): How long after January 15 should the United States wait for Iraq to withdraw from Kuwait before going to war to force it out?

13. Market Strategies and Greenberg Research / Americans Talk Issues Foundation and the W. Alton Jones Foundation, March 23–April 4, 1993.

14. "Clinton, Defending His Record, Insists He Hasn't Wavered," *The New York Times*, June 16, 1993, sec. A, p.1.

15. However, it was less than half the amount of time devoted to Somalia when the troops landed. *The Tyndall Report* states that coverage was 423 minutes on the three broadcast networks in December 1992, compared to 183 minutes in October 1993.

16. Times Mirror Center for the People & the Press, *International Policy Opinion Survey*, October 21–24, 1993.

17. CNN "Global Forum" in Atlanta, May 3, 1994.

18. Times Mirror Center for the People & the Press, *News Interest Indexes*, from October 1991 to June 1994; question was twelve times as how closely followed "the civil war in Bosnia"; initial two times asked as "events in the former Yugoslavia."

19. Data from CBS/*New York Times* polls as presented by Alvin Richman, United States Information Agency (USIA), in memorandum dated May 11, 1994.

20. Eliot A. Cohen, "The Mystique of U.S. Air Power," *Foreign Affairs*, Vol. 73, No.1 (January/February 1994), p. 120. Cohen says reliance on air power has been the distinctively U.S. way of war because it is "high-tech, cheap in lives and (at least in theory) quick." While this has been the case for well

over half a century, support for "surgical air strikes" that the public sees as almost casualty-less operations has probably risen since the Gulf War.

21. Gallup, CNN, *USA Today*, May 6, 1993. 603 adults surveyed.
22. University of Maryland, Program on International Policy Attitudes, April 5–8, 1994.
23. Second was the war between Bosnia and Serbia (21 percent), and third was the instability in Russia (18 percent).
24. Gallup for Chicago Council on Foreign Relations, Oct.–Nov. 1990, and earlier. Times Mirror Center for the People & the Press, "America's Place in the World," November 2, 1993.
25. Edward N. Luttwak, "Where Are the Great Powers? At Home with the Kids," in *Foreign Affairs*, Vol. 73, No. 4 (July/August 1994), p.25.
26. James F. Hoge, Jr., "Media Pervasiveness," *Foreign Affairs*, Vol. 73, No. 4 (July/August 1994), p. 138.
27. James F. Hoge, Jr., "Media Pervasiveness," in *Foreign Affairs*, Vol. 73, No. 4 (July/August 1994), p. 142.
28. Maxine Isaacs, "The Independent American Public: The Relationship between Elite and Mass Opinion on American Foreign Policy in the Mass Communication Age," dissertation, 1994.
29. Ibid., pp. 378 and 381.

6

The Limits of Orthodoxy:
The Use of Force After the Cold War

Andrew J. Bacevich

Every nation is caught in the moral paradox of refusing to go to war unless it can be proved that the national interest is imperiled, and of continuing in the war only by proving that something much more than national interest is at stake.
Reinhold Niebuhr, *The Irony of American History*

I

When Reinhold Niebuhr wrote these words, the Cold War—a crisis in international politics touching virtually every aspect of American life—was at its height. Yet the source of the paradox to which Niebuhr referred was not so much political as military. It derived less from the East-West confrontation than from profound changes in the character of warfare, changes that predated by several decades the Cold War itself. The paradox in which the United States found itself enmeshed in the 1950s was a product of what the historian Walter Millis, writing at about the same time, labeled "the hypertrophy of war." These changes in warfare had plunged the military profession into prolonged crisis. That crisis—and the military's efforts to evade its implications—provide an essential point of departure for understanding present-day controversies relating to the use of force.

To Niebuhr and other observers, the conflicts of 1914–1918 and 1939-1945 had demonstrated with awful clarity that war in

171

the twentieth century had become "total." This transformation of war was the product of several converging developments. Advanced societies had evolved vast capabilities to marshal human, industrial, and financial resources for military purposes. The collaboration of soldiers, scientists, and engineers had produced new weapons of extraordinary destructive power. Military staffs had devised the techniques required to bring awesome accumulations of matériel to bear on the field of battle yet in terms of political utility, these impressive achievements had yielded precious little. Although a staggering event in its own right, the bombing of Hiroshima seemed merely to punctuate what had already become evident: that war as an instrument of reasoned policy had seemingly reached a dead end.

Thus by the time Niebuhr wrote in the early 1950s, with the world divided into two hostile camps, each brandishing nuclear weapons, traditional conventions of great power politics no longer provided adequate guidance regarding the proper role of force in regulating international affairs. When the slightest miscalculation might upset the precarious equilibrium standing in the way of a Third World War, only the most important national purposes—true vital interests—could sanction the use of force. War on the periphery might flourish, but the larger powers found themselves constrained in actively employing their military might. As a result, large-scale conflict directly involving great powers in extended combat became increasingly rare.

On those occasions when advanced democracies did engage in protracted conflict, mere national interests could hardly suffice to justify the costs incurred: the havoc wreaked as a by-product of modern military campaigns, the suffering exacted of combatants and noncombatants alike, and the resort to morally objectionable methods in the pursuit of victory. The longer and more brutal the war, the more exalted became the purposes it allegedly served. Thus, for example, in Korea and in Indochina— both wars were raging when Niebuhr wrote—Western belligerents attempted to vindicate their conduct by citing purposes that transcended mere *raison d'état*. During the second Indochina War, this was to prove to be even more the case. Indeed, as representatives of a nation that had fought one world war in order to "end all wars" and "make the world safe for democracy" and whose participation in a second signified the triumph of the ideals informing the first, U.S. political leaders were particularly given to such exercises in national self-justification.

II

If the threat of Armageddon through much of this century has vastly complicated the political leader's problem of when and how to use force, soldiers have for the most part tried gamely to carry on as if nothing fundamental had changed. Military professionals have attempted to evade Niebuhr's paradox, rejecting or minimizing the implications of total war.

They could hardly be expected to do otherwise. After all, the autonomy and institutional authority of the military profession and the status and self-esteem of its members depend upon arrangements very much at odds with Niebuhr's paradox. Three essential elements comprise those arrangements. According to the first of those elements, the international system—"the world"—is composed of competing nation-states, each possessing unambiguous sovereignty. According to the second, the ultimate mechanism for making adjustments to that system and for preventing its breakdown is war, conducted between nation-states and in compliance with certain recognized rules. According to the third, access to the coercive means needed to wage war is permitted only to national elites (of which soldiers form an integral part). For military professionals, a threat to any of these elements constitutes a threat to their rightful place in the proper order of things.

In fact, the century has not dealt kindly with these arrangements. Since the First World War, sovereignty has been progressively circumscribed. Deference to supranational authority has constrained nation-states, even great powers, from acting in pursuit of their own immediate interests. In addition, the lines traditionally demarking war as a realm of activity set apart have broken down. As conflict has assumed virulent new forms, the distinctions between politics and war, between combatants and noncombatants, between what is legitimate and what is impermissible in the conduct of warfare have become increasingly blurred. Nor have national elites succeeded in maintaining their monopoly over the means needed to wage war. Instead, subversives, terrorists, partisans, guerrillas, paramilitary groups, and self-proclaimed revolutionaries have usurped the state's control over the instruments of violence. In short, on several different fronts, the ironies to which total war gave birth have tended to undermine the very rationale of military professionalism.

From time to time, that threat has provoked a sharp reaction. To be sure, hidebound soldiers—and even the travail of experiencing total war firsthand could not guarantee a cure for incorrigible obstinacy—have insisted that war has not changed, that hallowed precepts of military practice should remain unaltered. Yet other soldiers, the clever ones, have sensed that war was indeed being transformed. Furthermore, they understood the imperative of devising a response to that transformation in order to prevent their vocation from becoming irrelevant and obsolete.

During the period following the First World War, for example, the cleverest and most perceptive soldiers by far were the Germans. For the *Reichswehr*, the catastrophe of 1918 was not simply that Germany had suffered a great defeat; it was that the German army had failed demonstrably to fulfill the task that justified its elevated status within German society: securing the decisive victory that would resolve the political crisis of Europe to Germany's permanent advantage. Demonstrated repeatedly over the course of four crippling years of war, this failure had in the end unleashed a host of dangerous social forces that placed in jeopardy values and institutions cherished by the German military caste.

As the historian Michael Geyer argues persuasively, the imperative of stabilizing the social order and upholding their own privileged place within it provided the true stimulus for the outpouring of the German military's innovation and creativity during the 1920s and 1930s. This implicitly counterrevolutionary agenda rather than the narrow technical problem of breaking the stalemate of trench warfare motivated Germany's military reformers. The central intellectual problem confronting the officer corps of the interwar period, notes Geyer, was one of devising ways "to limit war in order to make it, once again . . . purposeful and instrumental." By restoring the possibility of rapid decision achieved at tolerable cost, the German army would once again "make war feasible." By thus reestablishing the centrality of battle directed by military elites, the officer corps would preserve its own status and prerogatives within German society.

The world would come to know the results of these labors as *blitzkrieg*. Yet despite a succession of dazzling operational performances beginning in 1939, the methods devised by German military reformers failed. Instead of limiting war and making it purposeful, German reforms laid the basis for a conflict more horrific than the one of 1914–1918. Once again war jumped the neat institutional boundaries to which military professionals insisted it should properly adhere. Once again the search for that single decisive stroke that would produce ultimate victory—a modern Cannae—eluded the best efforts of generals and their staffs. Once again war became a matter of indiscriminate slaughter, encompassing whole societies and devouring combatants and noncombatants alike. Once again the sheer dimensions and duration of the conflict gave rise to political and social forces that altered the preexisting order in ways neither foreseen nor desired by reigning elites on either side.

Despite this second recurrence of total war in a quarter of a century, the military profession (where it survived) remained steadfast in insisting that the principles of traditional military practice had not outlived their usefulness. Indeed, the effort attributed by Geyer to the German General Staff of the interwar period describes the common enterprise of all military professionals after 1945. In an age when the erosion of national sovereignty continued apace; when weapons of mass destruction continued to proliferate despite their manifest uselessness in waging war; when the failure of national elites to restrict access to instruments of violence had become undeniable and perhaps irreversible; and when real wars time and again exposed the limits of military orthodoxy, throughout this age, professional soldiers persisted in their quest to restore "institutionally contained warfare between armed forces," thereby reversing the revolution set in motion by the onset of total war.

III

In the aftermath of the Second World War, overall responsibility for that enterprise devolved upon the nation that had inherited the mantle of the world's leading military power: the United States. From our vantage point in the 1990s, it may appear that U.S. soldiers were at first slow to take up the challenge. Lacking the stimulus of defeat that had motivated the Germans during the interwar period, U.S. military thinking during the period extending from the late 1940s into the 1960s was lackluster. It derived less from sustained engagement with the implications of total war than from obstinate parochialism and fierce interservice rivalry.

Many will recall this period as a golden age of impressively original thinking about war by Americans. But the innovators were civilians—"defense intellectuals"—not soldiers; their preoccupation was not fighting wars but averting them. In comparison with the sophisticated contours of deterrence theory, efforts by military professionals to devise practical approaches to "warfighting," for instance, the strategic bombing concepts designed under the aegis of Strategic Air Comman (SAC) or the army's ill-conceived "Pentomic" experiment, appear crude and simplistic.

Apart from piling up a massive nuclear arsenal, military efforts to fit nuclear weapons into the traditional framework of campaigns and battles produced little of value. Indeed, U.S. civilian leaders never showed much interest in such doctrinal excursions, indulging them only to the extent that as evidence that military professionals were undaunted by the prospect of fighting World War III they might add credibility to the deterrent posture of the United States. Although President John F. Kennedy's fascination with counterinsurgency and nation-building in the early 1960s stands as the exception to this civilian indifference, it was an exception that disserved the cause of military professionalism.

The premise underlying counterinsurgency doctrine was that by supplementing existing routines with a smattering of novel technique, conventional military institutions could deal with the noxious "brushfire wars" that had become increasingly commonplace after World War II. That premise proved to be false. Instead of allowing soldiers to expand the reach of professional competency, the flirtation with counterinsurgency paved the way for the disaster of the Vietnam War.

Vietnam made it impossible for U.S. soldiers to sustain the pretense that all was well with their profession; in doing so, the war shattered the canopy of intellectual complacency under which the postwar U.S. military had nestled. As a chorus of critics saw it, the military's inability to bring Vietnam to a successful conclusion despite years of prodigious efforts exposed the emptiness of professional claims of mastery in the realm of modern war. So-called strategic weapons, developed at enormous expense throughout the 1950s and into the 1960s, were largely irrelevant to the problem at hand. Even ignoring the political hazards involved, the selective employment of "tactical" nuclear weapons offered little prospect of meaningful operational effect. Concepts of conventional war found no ready application: there were no enemy field armies to encircle, no battle fleets to destroy, no vital industrial centers whose bombardment would cause the enemy's war machine to grind to a halt.

Nothing remained but to engage the enemy on its own terms—waging unconventional war with forces not specifically tailored for the task. Although this U.S. extemporizing produced a harvest of tactical successes, the problem of how to aggregate those successes stymied senior commanders. What was the operational significance of a dozen scattered firefights, of ambushes and patrols, of fire bases defended, of weapons captured and bodies counted? No one knew. So despite the expenditure of U.S. military power on an ever more lavish scale, U.S. soldiers found themselves fighting a war of attrition that they could not win. As had been the case in the trenches of the western front, the sergeants and the captains did their job well enough; the generals failed in their job utterly.

Furthermore, as with Germany's defeat in World War I, the political and social dimensions of the crisis provoked by Vietnam loomed at least as large as the military-technical ones. Although a conflict waged on a far smaller scale than the war of 1914–1918, Vietnam took on some of the qualities of total war, engaging whole societies and producing aftershocks that reverberated through virtually every quarter of American life. Besides nearly ripping apart the U.S. political system, the war gave birth to second order effects that soldiers could only view as hostile to the well-being of their profession.

When it comes to Vietnam, the United States's penchant for swathing troublesome historical events in sentimentality is today much in evidence. In an effort to "reconcile" and to "heal old wounds," Americans seek to smooth the rough edges of memory. But in the collective psyche of serving military leaders, rough edges remain. Although wounds caused by Vietnam are largely hidden from view, they have not healed. Understanding the perspective of today's military leaders on fundamental issues relating to national security—strategy, the proper use of force, the future evolution of their calling and of the institutions they serve—is impossible without first recalling the way the world looked to them twenty years ago when they were subalterns recently returned from a failed and bitter war.

In those days, the national landscape as viewed from inside the U.S. military could hardly have looked more depressing. Vietnam had legitimized mass resistance to war and to military service. To have protested and refused to fight was recognized as a talisman of enlightenment—a view that persists even today in influential sectors of our society. Of those who had fought and who remained in the post-Vietnam military, many felt shunned and unappreciated. Soldiers nursed a smoldering grudge against the media, blaming biased and sanctimonious reporters for puncturing the image of the U.S. fighting man as selfless patriot, casting him instead as either dupe or accomplice to war crimes. Although seldom voiced openly, the experience of having been (as they saw it) used and betrayed by civilian elites imbued the officer corps that came home from Vietnam with a deep-seated cynicism about politics and contempt for politicians. As a result, the war left in its wake an unhealthy residue of civil-military distrust. Even more broadly, the cultural explosion for which the war served as catalyst gave rise to phenomena that soldiers instinctively viewed as antithetical to their traditional ethos. Expectations that the military should somehow accommodate itself to the agenda of black power, feminism, gay liberation, and the cult of the imperial self, evoked dismay and resentment.

IV

To its everlasting credit, the military that returned from Vietnam wasted little time feeling sorry for itself. As with Germany's humiliation in 1918, the U.S. defeat in Vietnam gave way in short order to a period of intense introspection and spectacular creativity. As with the German response, this U.S. reform effort, ostensibly rooted in military-technical issues, had its wellsprings in the imperative of responding to the larger institutional crisis that Vietnam had brought to a head. The overriding task in the 1970s paralleled the one that German officers had faced a half century earlier: reestablishing a basis for military professionalism by affirming that war as an extension of politics remained the special province of a warrior caste that could rightfully claim a distinctive status within society.

In one critical respect, however, the German and U.S. responses differed. German military reform evolved within the narrow strategic framework defined by Germany's position in the heart of Europe. This setting obliged German soldiers to pursue professional rehabilitation by refighting the war they had lost.

Working within the spacious strategic parameters permitted to a truly global power, U.S. military professionals felt no similar compunction to solve the problems of counterinsurgency (solutions that inevitably would have collided with the canons of military orthodoxy). Rather, for U.S. officers, the starting point for retrieving their professional legitimacy lay in avoiding altogether future campaigns even remotely similar to Vietnam. For German soldiers, the western front that had cost them so dearly became an obsession; their aim was to get it right the next time. U.S. soldiers evinced little interest in refighting the war that had caused them comparable anguish. Their response to Vietnam was stunningly simple: never again.

In another sense, the U.S. search for professional redemption after Vietnam did mirror the German approach. In both cases, the aim was inherently counterrevolutionary: to restore limits and boundaries to war, thereby fostering conditions in which the clash of opposing armies not the mobilization of entire societies, would produce decision. U.S. soldiers would have to convince a public and elites scarred by Vietnam that war did not necessarily mean costly stalemate—the notorious "quagmire." They would have to demonstrate the feasibility of achieving decision at tolerable cost and without widespread collateral damage and incidental slaughter. Shoring up the standing of military profes- sionalism required that soldiers demonstrate that—the catastro- phe of Vietnam notwithstanding—orthodox military practice retained its essential efficacy.

Along with the level and scope of violence, the element of *time* was critical. Vietnam had convinced U.S. soldiers that mod- ern democracy's capacity to absorb the strains of war was se- verely limited. In any conflict where success was not soon forthcoming, popular impatience might lead all too easily into support withdrawn from the war with devastating conse- quences for the war's outcome and for those who fought it. Once influential elements within U.S. society mobilized in opposition to war, professional military practice could offer no effective response. Therefore, an overriding imperative in future conflicts was to win quickly, before war weariness could incite discontent. The corollary was equally important: situations where the pros- pect of early decision appeared problematic were to be avoided at all costs.

In short, the officer corps that came home from Southeast Asia devoted precious little energy to dissecting that conflict. Doing so would advance the cause of professional revival mini- mally, if at all. Rather, soldiers threw themselves headlong into an effort to restore the possibility of decision-oriented warfare conducted within a professionally self-contained format—an effort undertaken in the face of skeptics persuaded by Hiroshima on the one hand and Vietnam on the other that all war had become an exercise in futility.

The bind to which these critics pointed was a real one. The post-Vietnam U.S. military attempted to escape it by reasserting the existence, indeed, the primacy, of conflict in the zone between all-out nuclear war on the one hand and unconventional war on the other hand, between apocalypse and people's war. Nor was it absurd to claim that such a zone existed. The unfolding military history of the modern Middle East provided examples that were as instructive as they were fortuitous.

Even as the agony of Vietnam played itself out, the Arab-Israeli Wars of 1967 and 1973 reminded U.S. military officers how wars were supposed to be fought: warrior pitted against warrior in a contest where the stakes, military as well as political, were straightforward and unambiguous; commanders empowered to command and backed by political leaders who refrained from operational meddling; civilian populations that were spared direct involvement as belligerents but that had no difficulty determining whose side they were on. Best of all, within a matter of days these wars ended with an outcome that was unequivocal. In the performance of the Israeli Defense Forces and in their status within Israeli society, U.S. soldiers found inspiration for their own recovery.

The problem was one of adapting the style of warfare exhibited by the Israelis to fit U.S. strategic requirements. For the United States, the "threat" was not Arabs; it had, in fact, never been North Vietnam; it was the Soviet empire. The critical battlefield was not the desert; it was certainly not the jungle or rice paddy; it was the "Central Region," the expanse of industrialized and democratic Europe extending from Denmark south to Switzerland, from the Iron Curtain west to the Atlantic ports. By reestablishing itself as a force that with its NATO allies could win handily any face-off against the Warsaw Pact, the U.S. military establishment might begin to undo the effects of Vietnam. Even without fighting—indeed, the overriding criterion of success was to prevent a fight—the U.S. military profession could recover the stature and legitimacy lost in Southeast Asia.

Thus disposed, U.S. officers categorized the Vietnam War less as a defeat than as a digression from real soldiering, as lost years during which the United States had fallen behind the Soviet Union. Beginning in the mid-1970s and continuing through the 1980s, the Soviet "other" provided both focus and sense of urgency to their campaign of military revitalization. Leaving few parts of the armed forces untouched, this effort manifested itself most prominently in the realm of doctrine, particularly in the AirLand Battle Doctrine devised by the army and endorsed by the air force. AirLand Battle provided the blueprint according to which outnumbered U.S. forces would turn back a full-scale nonnuclear Warsaw Pact attack, relying on superior technology, superior training, and superior personnel to compensate for the enemy's greater numbers.

The Cold War's unexpected end meant that this concept would never be tested against the adversary for whom it had been designed. Even a Battle of Western Europe may not have provided that test: war plans acquired from the former East Germany show that the Warsaw Pact intended from the outset of an attack to employ nuclear weapons on a mass scale. In at least one critical respect, therefore, the assumptions informing the vision of AirLand Battle—that the early stages of war in the Central Region would be nonnuclear—had all along been suspect.

Even though the demise of the Warsaw Pact came not with a bang but with a whimper, the hosts designed to defend Europe from attack did have their day in battle. In one of the great ironies of military history, forces made redundant by the end of the Cold War and soon to be disestablished were handed the reprieve of one final mission, thereby receiving at long last the chance to demonstrate their proficiency in actual combat.

No war is to be welcomed, but if the United States was destined to fight a war in the Persian Gulf, the timing of Iraq's invasion of Kuwait could not have been more opportune. The U.S.-led response to this act of naked aggression culminated in extraordinary and one-sided victory. The strategic consequences of that victory continue to ripple throughout the Middle East. No less important, Desert Storm turned U.S. thinking about war upside down virtually over night. As seen by President George

Bush and others, the nation had at long last kicked the Vietnam syndrome. The war's neat convergence of national interest and international morality combined with an awesome display of military prowess and extraordinarily low casualties fed increased popular expectations about what U.S. power and leadership might accomplish in shaping the new era to follow. Although some theorists glimpsed in Desert Storm the outlines of yet another profound revolution in military affairs—a revolution that promised to change the very nature of war—soldiers saw it as validating the reforms of the previous fifteen years. By liberating a small desert oligarchy from the clutches of a ham-handed aggressor possessed of a large army but no nuclear weapons, they had reasserted the preeminence of "real war." In this sense, Desert Storm seemed to signal the long-sought redemption of military professionalism.

V

Thus, for the United States at least, Desert Storm seemed to herald a release from Niebuhr's paradox. To soldiers, it promised an end to the long crisis of their profession. Yet events subsequent to the Persian Gulf War have dashed all such expectations.

Rather than bringing about an age of harmony, the end of the Cold War gave way to an era in which confrontation and conflict promise to be endemic. Although mostly small-scale and seldom posing a direct threat to U.S. security, post–Cold War military crises such as Somalia, Bosnia, Haiti, and North Korea have proven impossible to ignore. Furthermore, despite U.S. possession of overwhelming military power, these crises have defied ready solution.

To be sure, none of these crises has yet culminated in full-fledged disaster for the United States yet when recalling the confidence and renewed sense of purpose presumed to form part of the legacy of the Gulf War, the difficulty experienced by the United States in bringing its power to bear on these lesser problems is striking. Despite agonizing that has been protracted and almost embarrassingly public, consensus on questions of purpose, means, and method has remained beyond the reach of U.S. policy-makers and their military advisers. At the pinnacle of its military superiority, the United States has seemingly drifted once again into a state of confusion about when and how to employ force.

In short, it becomes increasingly apparent that the end of the Cold War and victory in Desert Storm have not allowed the United States to escape from the implications of Niebuhr's paradox after all. At most, the end of the Cold War has turned that paradox inside out. Previously only vital national interests could justify a decision to employ force. Expectations prompted by victory in the Gulf changed that. The perception that U.S. military power might with minimal risk be employed to serve "something much more than" the nation's immediate interests seemed to oblige the United States to make that effort. The illusion of unchallengeable military superiority magnified the call of conscience. In some instances—both the rescue of the Kurds and the intervention into Somalia are examples—conscience impelled intervention in the near total absence of substantive national interests.

Formerly, according to Niebuhr, once the nation found itself militarily engaged, leaders groped for larger purposes to justify and sustain the commitment they had made. Today, the admirable objectives that provide a compelling argument for going in may not suffice to justify staying there. Americans want to do good in the world, but their willingness to pay for doing good is limited, especially if payment is demanded in American lives. Once U.S. forces are committed to a hostile situation—once the bullets have begun to fly, U.S. soldiers are in jeopardy, and it becomes apparent that success may involve substantial cost—the larger purposes that inspired the decision to intervene lose their resonance. The ensuing debate over how long to sustain a commitment reverts to the question of whether doing so truly serves the well-being of the United States. Failure to answer that question in the affirmative undermines popular and political support for an operation. An enterprise that yesterday seemed expedient is today not worth the blood of a single U.S. soldier. In the case of Somalia, such thinking led the United States to abandon its commitment altogether. In the *Harlan County* incident, it aborted a mission barely under way.

So the bind identified by Niebuhr in 1952 has reasserted itself in a somewhat altered configuration. Its effects remain the same: despite an abundance of available military power, the obstacles confronting efforts to translate that power into political advantage are seemingly insurmountable.

VI

But why is this the case? With the Cold War now history, with the recent example of Desert Storm as a model of how to use power effectively, why is U.S. military policy once again so apparently ineffectual? The interpretation most frequently advanced by critics is the political one: responsibility for bootless U.S. policies can be traced directly to an irresolute leader and the maladroit advisers who serve him. That explanation is incomplete, if not altogether misleading.

Rather, the limited utility of U.S. military power stems in no small measure from the persistent limitations of professional orthodoxy. In an officer corps buoyed by success in the Gulf but still haunted by memories of Vietnam, that orthodoxy has, if anything, entrenched itself more deeply. Adversaries as different as Mohammed Farah Aideed and Radovan Karadzic have all too readily grasped the opportunities implicit in that fact. No doubt they respect U.S. military establishment for its formidable strengths. They are also shrewd enough to circumvent those strengths and to exploit the vulnerabilities inherent in the rigid U.S. adherence to professional conventions regarding the use of force. As long as U.S. military policies are held hostage to such conventions, those vulnerabilities will persist.

None of this is new and most of it is unavoidable. As the preliminary sections of this paper were intended to suggest, the abiding theme of twentieth century military history is that the changing character of modern war long ago turned the flank of conventional military practice, limiting its application to an ever narrowing spectrum of contingencies. Despite expectations to the contrary, Desert Storm did not reverse that trend, nor is the revolution in military affairs to which Desert Storm supposedly pointed likely to do so in the future. On the contrary, as the predicaments posed by Somalia, Bosnia, Haiti, and North Korea suggest, the military history of the post–Cold War era is likely to continue to evolve along the lines of the past several decades.

Unlike the brazen "criminal trespass" that made Iraq such a choice villain in the Persian Gulf, political violence after the Cold War only infrequently takes the form of one state directly victimizing another. Three of the four cases cited above involved some variant of internal conflict. In the fourth case, a state desperate to make up for its own failings has employed nuclear threats to extort political and economic concessions from the international community. Even in this instance North Korea has carefully refrained from overt aggression.

In other words, when political disputes turn violent, seldom does the nexus of conflict take the form of one sovereign entity directly violating another. So long as this is true, the Desert Storm–inspired concept of Major Regional Contingency (MRC), supposedly the template for future U.S. military operations, will rarely prove useful. Indeed, none of the four cases cited has served to validate this planning tool. Perhaps this should not be surprising. Although dressed up in postindustrial garb, the MRC is an attempt to revive a model of limited war more suited for an eighteenth century system of international politics.

Implicit in the MRC model is the expectation of U.S. forces operating in pursuit of clearly defined purposes, waging campaigns of limited duration, and relying on the high-tech weaponry that is the U.S. strong suit. Yet the varied military crises of the past two years have repeatedly frustrated such expectations. Local conditions have undermined efforts to translate political aims into crisp military objectives. What was the mission in Somalia? To feed the starving? To rebuild a failed state? To get General Aideed? Urged to add peacekeeping and peacemaking to their repertoire of missions, professional soldiers bridle, perhaps catching a whiff of rice paddy or triple-canopy jungle in the prospect of assuming open-ended commitments in circumstances where every other party involved possesses the ability to extend the quarrel indefinitely while no one possesses the authority to bring it to a conclusion.

Nor have circumstances on the ground, whether actual as in Somalia or prospective as in Bosnia and Haiti, accommodated the preferred U.S. operational style. Broken terrain and crowded cities do not facilitate the effective employment of ultra-expensive, precision-guided munitions. The intermixing of combatants with noncombatants confronts U.S. regulars with the unwelcome prospect of once more fighting an adversary who is undistinguishable from its surroundings and of being saddled with the blame for civilian casualties that are a by-product of fighting in such circumstances. Even in Korea, arguably the most clearcut of the military problems with which the United States has wrestled of late, Pyongyang's shadowy nuclear capability has vastly complicated efforts to define operational concepts that are feasible and make sense politically. As Roger Molander has commented, North Korea suggests that as a planning tool the nonnuclear MRC may already be a myth.

For reasons such as these, U.S. military leaders have in case after case stood in the forefront of those arguing against direct U.S. military intervention. In a sense, this is not unusual: soldiers are habitually reluctant interventionists. Yet their specific objections—the difficulty of translating political purpose into clear military objectives (Somalia and Bosnia), the lack of a precisely defined operational end point (Somalia, Bosnia, and Haiti), the prospect of conflict involving nuclear weapons (Korea), the risk of casualties beyond a level acceptable to U.S. opinion (almost anywhere)—emphasize the point that the conditions permitting effective military action in the Gulf were the exception rather than the rule. In short, if military professionals saw Desert Storm as restoring "real war" to pride of place, subsequent efforts to apply that experience to the problems actually confounding a turbulent and conflictive world have foundered.

In other words, although soldiers will resist acknowledging the fact, the long crisis of military professionalism continues unabated. This too should not be surprising. No doubt in the aftermath of the Battle of France in 1940, *Wehrmacht* generals congratulated one another on their success at extricating the

German army from the legacy of 1918. They were wrong. So too U.S. officers who saw in Desert Storm a resolution of their own professional dilemmas have deluded themselves. To imagine in either case that a single victory, no matter how satisfying, might reverse historical trends of uncommon power is simply folly.

VII

The point of emphasizing the enduring nature of this crisis of military professionalism is not to condemn or belittle the efforts of those in uniform who wrestle with its consequences. If soldiers cling stubbornly to the premises that have defined the essence of their calling, they are behaving in ways that are predictably human. How could it be otherwise?

On the other hand, an appreciation of the dilemma that soldiers face should temper expectations about how far existing military institutions can be stretched to incorporate situations that depart from conditions ordained by military orthodoxy. Americans may properly insist that their military attempt to adapt itself to new circumstances, but they should do so with the understanding that only modest change will occur. They may question why the nation's vast military capabilities are so seldom relevant to the actual sources of upheaval in the world, but they should not expect their queries, objections, or complaints to have more than modest effect. Given the framework of military professional orthodoxy, reinforced by the U.S. experience of the past twenty-five years, the range of circumstances in which U.S. military power is likely to find application will remain narrow.

No amount of railing against senior officers for their perceived timidity is likely to change that.; nor is foisting some new weapon system on the military or demanding changes in doctrine or force structure. Nor will any so-called revolution in military affairs provide any near term remedy.

Those who would nudge the military toward undertaking a somewhat wider range of contingencies may be most effective by seeking ways to reassure soldiers that in departing from strict orthodoxy the institutional risks that they accept are not excessive. Toward that end, two specific adjustments to prevailing public attitudes about war and the use of force could prove useful.

First, Americans should shed unrealistic expectations about the near term political payoff of even the most successful military operations. When Somalia or Rwanda collapses, military intervention can establish conditions that permit humanitarian operations to proceed. No military action can reestablish them as functioning societies. When Haiti falls victim to military thuggery, military intervention can depose the perpetrators. Military action cannot democratize a nation where the prerequisites of democracy hardly exist. By freeing soldiers from exaggerated requirements about what the use of force is expected to achieve, professional resistance to undertaking such missions may diminish.

Second, the imagery of Desert Storm notwithstanding, Americans should understand that technology is not sanitizing war. Nor is it paving the way toward an era when advanced countries such as the United States will employ the military instrument bloodlessly. With rare exceptions, such as a standoff attack for punitive purposes, the effective use of force will almost invariably carry with it substantial risk of U.S. casualties. Indeed, a capacity for absorbing casualties provides one measure of a nation's military credibility. Toward that end, some modest steps in the direction of desentimentalizing the U.S. soldier are in order.

The United States should never send its warriors in harm's way without good reason. It should train them well and arm them with the best available equipment. It should honor their sacrifices. It should mourn their loss when they fall in battle. If the United States intends to be taken seriously as a world power, the death of U.S. soldiers—volunteers and professionals all—should not in and of itself lead the nation to reverse or abandon stated policy. Americans need not worry that their military leaders will treat cavalierly the lives of those placed in their charge. By conveying their own realistic appreciation that the use of force entails the likelihood of casualties and that the loss of a single soldier does not necessarily constitute unacceptable calamity, Americans will encourage the military itself to evaluate the potential use of force without inordinate anxiety about the institutional consequences of casualties.

Posing no threat to professional orthodoxy, such attitudinal changes might coax U.S. military leaders into becoming marginally more responsive to the world as it is in contrast to the world that they yearn to re-create. If marking no dramatic departure, such heightened responsiveness would at least increase the return on investment for Americans who pay dearly for the privilege of being the world's leading military power.

8

Alternatives to Escalation

Antonia Handler Chayes
and Abram Chayes

Of the three possible approaches available to the international community to deal with violent conflict—military action, economic measures, and intermediation—none has been very useful in the kinds of conflicts endemic to the post–Cold War years. 1) It is difficult to assemble a force with broad legitimacy and sufficient military power in the absence of a threat to traditionally perceived national interests of the United States or other major powers and in the face of high political and economic costs, to say nothing of potential loss of life to those who undertake military action. 2) Economic sanctions are also costly to the sanctioners and take a very long time, if ever, to accomplish the desired impact. They may be easier to launch than military action, but they are more difficult to maintain and make effective. 3) Intermediation seems frustrating and ineffective in dealing with savage and fractionated internal conflict. Too often it is clumsy, unwanted, too little and too late.

The intrastate conflicts that ignited after the restraining pressures of the Cold War were removed, have proven bloody, complex, subtle, and intractable. They do not involve the projection of power across boundaries. Although most have been marked by armed conflict, often as a result of the disintegration of state authority, there has been no military action that could plausibly be termed an immediate threat to international peace and security. In most, there were international ramifications, but the main issues were "internal," played out within the territory of a state or "former state." They looked much like many other chronic problems that had received the fitful attention of the United Nations and other international political actors during the Cold War—Kashmir, Tibet, West Irian, the Sahel—but that preoccupation with the superpower rivalry had kept at the margins of international attention. As that rivalry receded, to be replaced, if only fleetingly, with the prospect of U.S.-Russian cooperation, these conflicts, in part because of their vivid presence through the media in the daily lives of citizens, emerged as major claims on the energy and resources of the international system.

National governments and international organizations have addressed these situations within the framework of a traditional model for dealing with international conflict. We shall call it "the escalation model" because it envisions a sequence of measures, beginning with diplomacy, proceeding to economic sanctions if diplomacy is unavailing, and finally to the imposition of military force. The initial international involvement would be some form of assisted negotiation or mediation. If the talks produced an agreement or cease-fire, traditional peacekeeping would reinforce it. If the talks failed or could not take place because of chaos or anarchy, some form of consensual action would be sought to help alleviate suffering. If that fails, then economic sanctions would be mounted, and finally, military force brought to bear.

It was recognized, of course, that, in practice, the sequence would not be a neat and orderly progression, but the escalation model dominated thinking about the application of pressures not only to contain international conflict but in pursuit of national political objectives. It has roots in the strategic thinking of the Cold War period and, more broadly, in realist international relations theory. It is also reflected in just war principles and in the UN Charter provisions for dealing with threats to international peace and security: first, the methods of peaceful settlement listed in Article 33 or recommendation of the Security Council (Art. 37, 38); next, economic and other sanctions not involving the use of force, under Article 41; and finally, if these measures "have proved to be inadequate, . . . such action by air, sea, or land forces as may be necessary to maintain or restore international peace and security" (Art. 42).

The escalation model, at least tacitly, has dominated the evolution of national and international policy in the former Yugoslavia. Talk, starting with the European Community Conference on Yugoslavia, which created the disastrous recognition policy, through the Vance-Owen and Owen-Stoltenberg negotiations, has been discouraging. Frustration with the inability of negotiation and mediation to put an end to the killing has led, unsurprisingly, to calls for tougher economic sanctions, "leveling the playing field" by eliminating the arms embargo so that the Bosnian Muslims and Croats can put up a more effective fight, using force to protect humanitarian missions, and threatening and ultimately using force to impose a solution that has not been achieved by mediation.

Our first proposition in this paper is that, whatever its relevance in earlier periods as a strategic framework for dealing with *interstate* confrontations, the escalation model is inapplicable to the intricacies of post–Cold War conflict as described above, except under very special circumstances. Coercive military action and effective economic measures remain very difficult to assemble, and the present heavy reliance on their availability in policy analysis and planning is misplaced. When escalation is not forthcoming, as we argue it will not be in most conflict situations, international efforts are criticized as failures and lacking in credibility. Decisions premised on the expectation that such a sequence will occur almost inevitably lead to disappointment and finger pointing.

An alternative strategy would commit the bulk of the effort and much more significant resources of international, regional, national, and nongovernmental organizations (NGOs) attempting to cope with the new types of violent conflict to strengthening the potential for earlier, more effective, and more enduring intermediation. Although in many cases, timely and effective intermediation alone may be able to settle conflicts and forestall violence, economic and military measures will remain necessary as elements of such a strategy in many situations. There, the principal problem is to develop ways to use military forces in support of diplomatic efforts under the constraint that military considerations and objectives are subordinate to political ones, not only in terms of overall strategy but of day-to-day tactics. In particular, the traditional objective of military action—to impose an outcome by force on the enemy—is substantially precluded. There is no magic combination or sequence of measures for every situation. Nevertheless, although every conflict is unique, actual patterns of response provide possibilities for experiential learning. The attempts to comprehend and systematize the experience should be intensified and expanded, given the number and complexity of conflicts that demand the attention of the international community.

NO MORE KUWAITS

In the long period from the end of World War II to the breakup of the Soviet Union, the Security Council invoked its extraordinary power to use coercive military force under Chapter VII only twice, once in Korea at the beginning, and again in the Gulf War just at the end. In the same period, the Organization of American States (OAS) authorized the use of force once in response to the Soviet emplacement of nuclear missiles in Cuba. There is no doubt that the operation of the veto in the Security Council and, more generally, the constraints of the Cold War accounted for much of this paralysis of the United Nations. An examination of those episodes, however, suggests that there were more generic features at work that will continue to inhibit the exercise of these powers even in the absence of the U.S.-Soviet standoff.

1. *The outstanding common feature in all three episodes was the central and indispensable role of the United States.* Each action was precipitated by a sudden disruption of the status quo that the United States perceived as an unacceptable threat to its vital interests. In each case, the United States took the initiative to bring the matter to the international forum and to shape and organize the institutional response. The United States marshaled

the evidence and arguments (and sometimes twisted arms) to convince other parties that the U.S. perception of an unacceptable threat to peace and security was correct.

The United States dominated the military action. All three operations were under U.S. command—by express authorization of the Security Council in the Korea case and de facto in Cuba and the Gulf. The United States did the strategic and tactical planning. Major political-military decisions were made in Washington. Troop commitments of other coalition members were more significant in the Gulf War, and the financial burdens were more widely shared. Nevertheless, in all three instances, the United States provided the overwhelming bulk of the military muscle.

The United States decided when to end the operations. In Korea there were extended truce negotiations, and other countries, particularly some of the developing countries in the General Assembly, played a role in putting pressure on the United States to come to terms. The final decision to conclude the truce, however, was President Dwight Eisenhower's. As to Cuba, an exchange of letters between Nikita Khrushchev and John F. Kennedy ended the crisis without consultation with the OAS on either the timing or the terms of the exchange. In Iraq, four days after the commencement of ground operations and with the Iraqi army in full retreat, President George Bush announced that "all U.S. and coalition forces will suspend offensive combat operations."[1] The timing was such that little more than a perfunctory exchange with the coalition partners would have been possible.

2. *Although unequivocal U.S. commitment was a necessary condition for enforcement action, it was not sufficient.* Twice in the 1980s, in Grenada and Panama, the United States launched small unilateral operations "in our own backyard."[2] For response to major aggression, a broad consensus was necessary not only to enhance the legitimacy of the enterprise, but to provide the facilities and manpower for effective response. Such a coalition is extraordinarily difficult to assemble and maintain. The underlying reality is that as long as national contingents carry out international enforcement actions, decisions to commit must be taken by national governments sensitive to domestic political forces. In all

three cases, the organization did not direct action but rather authorized members to take arms against the offender. The question of whether or not to respond was left to the individual decision of the member states. The foundations of international enforcement action are essentially voluntary.

In Korea, Cuba, and Kuwait, despite the egregious character of the aggressive actions, which could be seen as an immediate and general threat to international stability, the depth and durability of the consensus left something to be desired. Although the United States was able to muster a General Assembly majority in support of Douglas MacArthur's decision to recross the 38th parallel, the action was widely criticized and led to a deepening divergence of aims and policies between the United States and not only the developing world, led by India, but, more circumspectly, with allies as well. Few states stood staunchly with the United States in the end game. In the Cuba case, Brazil and Mexico abstained on the critical paragraph of the quarantine resolution because they thought it was a blank check for further military action. Although North Atlantic Treaty Organization (NATO) leaders provided gratifying expressions of support, they had little stomach for a U.S. invasion of Cuba, if, as many believed, it should prove necessary to force the withdrawal of the Soviet missiles. In the Gulf, Russian commitment was less than wholehearted, and it is not clear how the coalition, to say nothing of U.S. public opinion, would have withstood an extended war. In the follow-on, Arab states and others have increasingly pressed for relieving the burden of economic sanctions on Iraq.

3. *Coercive military action is a high-cost policy.* At the outset of the UN era, an observer reported in somewhat rueful surprise that "the Korean War . . . has shown us that an international enforcement action is, for all practical purposes, a war."[3] Of the three actions, the actual costs of the Korean War were highest to the United States. Apart from South Korea itself, the United States bore most of the financial costs of the military operations and took most of the losses. Over half a million troops were deployed under the UN flag, mostly from the United States and South Korea. Total UN casualties were over 500,000 with 94,000 killed, more than 33,000 from the United States. Chinese

and North Korean casualties are estimated at over 1.5 million, including prisoners of war.[4] The price tag in money was $265 billion in 1991 dollars.[5]

The Cuban quarantine ended without a military engagement, and the only U.S. casualty was one U-2 pilot. The military price paid for the Gulf War was not onerous to the UN coalition. Although the troop deployments matched those in Korea, coalition dead were less than 600, about half from the United States.[6] In each case, the specter of much higher potential losses dominated the planning and decision making. The financial costs were high, approximately $61 billion for the Gulf War, although most of it was paid by others than the United States. These amounts may be small compared to the costs of failure to respond, but in an era of world-wide budgetary stringency, they are very substantial.

Political costs are hardest to measure. Success, especially if achieved quickly and with low casualties, may bring net gains in both foreign and domestic political accounts. All three cases reveal the characteristic U.S. tendency to rally round a presidential show of strength, but this surge is not necessarily long-lived. Although the Cuban missile crisis remains part of the Kennedy legend, in Korea, initial public support eroded, and "Truman's war" became a major political issue in the 1952 election campaign. Iraq gave an immense boost to President Bush and was credited by many with helping to dispel the defeatist legacy of Viet Nam. As the aftermath of the Gulf War grew messy and its long-term consequences remained inconclusive, presidential popularity waned, and caution about putting the U.S. military "in harm's way" reasserted itself.

All this is not to say that this type of enforcement action will never recur. What we argue is that the disappearance of the Cold War confrontation is unlikely to make this type of enforcement action any more frequent than it has been in the past. The concurrence of unequivocal U.S. commitment, the ability to mobilize international consensus, and the willingness to bear (or share) high human and financial costs are sufficiently unlikely that military coercion is not an available option in anything like the range of cases now thought to demand international attention. Strong U.S. presidential leadership might affect this conclusion marginally, but not fundamentally. Without the urgency of the Cold War, tolerance for casualties on international missions that do not directly threaten national security seems to be low, especially among democracies. Nor is there much enthusiasm for bearing the financial burdens of international enforcement actions even if military losses can be kept within acceptable bounds.

MONEY ISN'T EVERYTHING

During the Cold War period, the UN Security Council imposed economic sanctions against South Africa and Rhodesia, but for South Africa, they were limited to arms, military equipment, and spare parts, and for Rhodesia, they were rendered essentially impotent by the refusal of South African and Portugal to join in. Since then, comprehensive economic sanctions have been a feature of the international response in Iraq, Serbia, and Haiti. The dominant lesson of these cases is that economic measures are excruciatingly slow to operate. The end of apartheid in South Africa took three decades from the beginning of the sanctions campaign. Iraq seems to be a classic case for effective economic boycott—dependence on imports for major consumption and industrial needs, few and remote land borders, a single major export that can be easily monitored. Yet, although there is no doubt that the embargo contributed to the success of efforts to discover and destory Iraqi weapons of mass destruction, Saddam Hussein remains in place four years later, and his repression of the Kurds and the Shiites continues. Serbia, too, has suffered from the economic sanctions, and the Milosevic government has agreed to foreign monitors of an arms embargo on Bosnian Serbs, but the war has gone on unabated for two years since they were imposed. The Haitian military showed remarkable resilience to economic measures although, again, the island seemed a classic target for sanctions.

The same requirements that forestall military action—U.S. commitment, broad consensus and willingness to bear costs—

operate in the case of economic sanctions as well. If anything, the requirement of committed U.S. participation is even stronger for economic sanctions. Although it may be that U.S. relative economic power is declining, its markets and financial facilities are still the largest in the world. There is no prospect of a successful economic embargo if access to them remains open. Even technical loopholes in U.S. economic controls, which existed for a considerable period in Haiti, can decisively prejudice the effect of the cooperative effort.

This is also true with the requirement of broad participation. In military enforcement action, if a few powerful states are prepared to shoulder the burden, effective force may perhaps be brought to bear without universal participation, at least against a smaller state. But for economic sanctions, the holdout problem is severe. Even if major trading partners of the target state are prepared to cut their ties, leakages elsewhere can defeat the regime. The defection of Portugal and South Africa undermined the Rhodesian sanctions. Romania's relatively open border thwarted the embargo of Serbia/Montenegro. The absence of the Europeans made a mockery of OAS sanctions against Haiti. Even in nominally complying countries, possibilities and incentives for evasion are large. The Bush administration provided U.S. businessmen with generous exemptions from the economic embargo against Haiti. Congress insisted on buying embargoed chrome from Rhodesia. The resistance of European customers prevented a cutoff of Libyan oil exports.

If the costs of imposing an economic embargo pale in comparison to even limited human casualties of military action, they are nevertheless substantial and seem to grow more onerous as time goes on, with small impact on the behavior of the target state. Moreover, the burden of economic sanctions often falls most heavily on countries less able to bear them. Jordan sustained trade losses in the billions as a result of the sanctions against Iraq, and the frontline African states had to bear the brunt of the sanctions effort against South Africa. Today, the costs of the embargo on Serbia are imposing major strains on Macedonia's weakened economy. Article 50 of the UN Charter provides that states "with special economic problems arising from the carrying out of [enforcement] measures shall have the right to consult the Security Council with regard to the solution of those problems." But the consultations have rarely proven productive.

Finally, the costs of comprehensive economic sanctions to the target state are invariably paid by the poorest and most vulnerable, those least likely to have been responsible for the offensive conduct. This, in turn, feeds pressures for relaxation of the sanctions.

Economic sanctions are much easier to vote than military enforcement, and thus we are likely to see more of them in the years ahead. For all the reasons cited, they are unlikely to be very effective within the time frame set by demands for action in current international conflicts. On the record, they may be useful at best and in varying degrees as a supplement to other measures, rather than as an independent means of resolving international crises, let alone as a way station on the ladder of escalation to military force.

THE NOT-SO-MAGIC SOLUTION

If we are correct that in post–Cold War conflict, coercive military and economic force will almost never be available to impose a solution, the only alternatives is an agreed solution worked out by the parties to the conflict.[7] At best, outsiders, whether national governments, international organizations, or private individuals and entities, can help to create the conditions in which agreement can be reached and help to nudge the parties toward it by a variety of pressures and incentives. What is called for is a mixed strategy combining diplomacy, military deployments, and economic measures in which diplomacy will carry the laboring oar. By hypothesis, this strategy is unlikely to yield decisive results, but often it buys time for feelings to simmer down, for the emergence of moderate forces, for the modification of previously rejected solutions, and the generation of new ones. If these limits are well understood, it will forestall false expectations and might help to minimize the waste of political energy in berating self and others for lack of "political will" to follow through on the escalation model.

1. *Three Is Not Always a Crowd*

It is worthwhile to pause for a moment to examine the basis on which mediation can work. There is some tendency to resist this kind of analysis. Intermediation is the stuff of international diplomacy. It takes place in many forms and forums—formal or informal, visible or secret, official or private, solicited or volunteered. The process is so pervasive that most diplomats believe that they already know how to do it without instruction. In any case, the demand for mediation skills is not confined to diplomats. Ongoing negotiation and mediation are required at all levels in situations of internal conflict—from special emissary to permanent mission head, to a soldier driving a truck bearing food and medicine to a population under siege, to an NGO volunteer. Despite the notion that mediation is an art that cannot be taught, there is now a body of academic theory and some documented practical experience that provides a basis for confidence that the process can work. Much, though not all, experience is in private and public situations of lower intensity, and the transfer to high politics is not simple. Yet there are examples of mediation in highly complex and intransigent conflicts that seem to operate by the same principles.[8]

Academic approaches to third party mediation derive in good part from theories of negotiation since the mediator is dealing with a breakdown in negotiations that has prevented the parties from reaching a peaceful resolution by themselves. Successful mediation, therefore, will require the restoration of a degree of openness and cooperation by the parties to the conflict, and many obstacles exist even then. Thus it becomes increasingly difficult for mediation to work in the midst of violent confrontation where anger and vengeance are the dominant emotions.

The success of the mediative process depends in the first instance on the ability to build enough trust and confidence so that the parties are prepared to disclose their interests and aspirations to the mediator. The foundation of trust and confidence is the impartiality and evenhandedness of the mediator. If there is a perception of bias, the process may well abort. The sense that the French tilted toward the Hutus in Rwanda made their mediative role problematic. In some situations it may be helpful that the intermediary does not have a history of involvement with any of the parties. This was the case with the Norwegians in facilitating the Israeli-Palestinian discourse. Such a mediator is not "disinterested" in the outcome, in the sense of being unwilling to invest enormous effort and exercise influence to achieve a peaceful resolution. On the other hand, it is not necessarily disqualifying that the mediator has some kind of stake in the outcome, for example, to reduce a threat to its vital interests or to restore supplies of needed resources. If this does not mean (or seem to mean) alignment with one of the parties, it need not be an impediment. In fact, mediator interest may translate into the ability to offer incentives to cooperate or punishment for failure to do so. The economic power of the United States was a critical factor in the success of the Camp David accords, for example. But the intermediary must not take sides.

Contemporary negotiation theory rejects the conception of the bargaining process as a zero-sum game. Instead it proposes a problem-solving approach in the effort to create mutual gains. Such an approach stresses the importance of

1) transparency and communication between the parties;

2) a focus on the underlying interests at stake rather than asserted positions;

3) brainstorming to create new options without necessarily committing to them:

4) ensuring that all significant stakeholders are included in the process;

5) careful analysis of the alternatives to a negotiated agreement.

These elements define entry points for intervention of a third party to restore a negotiation that seems hopelessly broken down.

Where there are high emotional feelings and a breakdown in communication, a mediator can help defuse the emotions and restore communication, even if for a long time that communication takes place only through the mediator. That is the classic function of shuttle diplomacy. The parties will not talk to each other, but each may talk to the mediator on the assumption that the message will be conveyed to the other side. Ultimately, as in the case of the controversy between Estonia and its ethnic Russian residents, it may be possible to develop a face-to-face dialogue to work on the management of ongoing issues. The Norwegian facilitation of the Israeli-Palestinian talks that led to the West Bank and Gaza agreements in 1993 exemplifies the mediator's art of nurturing communication where there has been none. There, the long-standing mutual suspicion and hostility made every phrase subject to distortion and required a process of emotional translation before any progress could be made.

Often the mediator can help the parties get unstuck from the bargaining positions that have led to impasse and explore their underlying interests. It is hardest for parties to begin to understand and appreciate the interests of the other side, even if they can articulate their own. A third party can often accomplish what the parties themselves may not be able to do. In the Camp David talks, Israel and Egypt seemed irretrievably fixated on the issue of the location of the borders to be drawn between them. When President Jimmy Carter helped clarify that Egypt wanted a return of its historic lands and the Israelis sought security, it became possible to work out a solution that involved the return of all the disputed territory but on a demilitarized basis. As this case illustrates, to create mutual gains is not necessarily to find common ground, but often to seek trades that exploit differences in values to provide more of what each party wants. In Namibia, after many years of fruitless negotiations among the parties and past failures in mediation, Chester Crocker facilitated a highly creative solution involving a complex series of trades: South Africa agreed to withdraw from Namibia, the Namibians got their independence, and Cuba withdrew its troops from Angola, reassuring both South Africa and the United States.

Brainstorming without commitment to find packages for mutual gain is particularly difficult in an official negotiation. The parties' announced positions are the result of drawn-out internal bureaucratic bargaining, and it is especially difficult to explore possibilities and trades without that exploration being taken as an offer. A mediator can engage in an exploration with the parties separately and tentatively or can organize informal and private talks outside the formal negotiations where it is easier to consider departures from prepared positions.

In contemporary internal conflict, it is more than usually difficult to identify and include all the stakeholders. In some cases, groups are not sufficiently mobilized to have well-defined representation. In others, we may tend to confer on factional leaders a status akin to heads of state, as though they were the legitimate representatives of the entire community when, in reality, there may be other forces that should be at the table. The other side of the need for inclusiveness is the diviseness and additional complexity that a multiparty situation introduces. Moreover, the internal politics of almost any assisted negotiation means that the parties (and the mediator as well) are engaged in a two or more level game, with the need to satisfy multiple constituencies. In a situation of uneasy leadership and shifting factions, progress may be close to impossible if all the parties are at the table. On the other hand, a partial agreement among those parties that are willing may compromise the mediator's neutrality. As the long, drawn out standoff in Bosnia shows, there is no easy escape from this dilemma.

Finally, the mediator may help the parties to analyze what are their best alternatives to a negotiated agreement (BATNA, in the jargon of negotiation theorists). In the civil and legal arena, the BATNA is often the pains and costs of a lawsuit. Even though all the factors are quantifiable, the major obstacle to settlement of litigation is that the parties maintain extremely unrealistic conceptions of the expected value of going to trial. The predictive exercise is even more difficult in complex international disputes, and the tendency to overoptimistic judgments about the alternatives to agreement is correspondingly stronger. It may take a skilled third party to help explain the consequences

of the "no-agreement alternative." One of the serious defects of
the "escalation model" is that it diverts attention from the real
alternatives to negotiation by seeming to specify a programmed
sequence of steps if negotiations fail. In the controversy over with
North Korea's nuclear program, for example, most public discussion proceeded on the assumption that if North Korea was
unwilling to meet U.S. demands at the negotiating table, the
alternatives were first, economic sanctions and then, bombing. If,
as seemed likely, neither of these would have stopped North
Korea's nuclear weapons program (and both entailed serious
additional risks), then the true BATNA was not escalation but a
continuation of both the confrontation and the North Korean
program. A more realistic view of the BATNA might have
induced some rethinking of the negotiating position. Indeed,
Jimmy Carter's third party intervention in the negotiation seems
to have been motivated by a livelier sense of this prospect than
what prevailed in Washington.

In fact, Carter's intervention displays many of the characteristics of effective mediation discussed above. He reopened communication between the parties, first, in his own person and
then by making it possible to reestablish the official channel. He
explored the North Korean interests (other than the continuation
of a weapons program): recognition; a new model light water
reactor and, more generally, assistance with the North Korean
energy program and economic investment. Indeed, his personal
interview with Kim Il Sung by itself satisfied in part the interest
in "recognition." Finally, he developed a new package in which
the parties made a current simultaneous, and monitorable exchange, freezing the status quo and permitting the negotiations
to go forward without either party fearing that the other would
use the period to its detriment.

Mutual gains negotiation has considerable power, and mediators at all levels of activity can be taught some of these
principles. It does not require a rare or charismatic personality to
practice the art, but it must be understood that theoretically as
well as practically there are limits and obstacles to successful
mediation. In the final analysis, the resolution must reflect the
ideas of the parties. A mediator can take the initiative to try to

precipitate agreement. Working from a single text, for example, and successively incorporating the comments of the parties is one technique that has been used successfully. In the end, however, the mediator cannot impose a solution on a "take it or leave it" basis.

2. The Early Bird

Despite the obstacles, there are situations in which some form of third party intervention, without more, can be effective in resolving conflict. Particularly in situations of tension or inter-community conflict that has not reached the stage of sustained violence, there is reason for some encouragement about the potential of early third party intermediation. Since 1990, the Conference on Security and Cooperation in Europe (CSCE) has focused on such activities, and a particularly good exemplar of this form of conflict prevention is its High Commissioner on National Minorities (HCNM), established in December 1992. The design of the High Commissioner's mandate reflects classic mediation principles. The HCNM is authorized to provide "early warning" on tensions involving national minority issues that "in the judgment of the High Commissioner have the potential to develop into conflict within the CSCE area, affecting peace, stability, or relations between participating States." He is free to intervene in such a situation on his own initiative. Although the High Commissioner cannot enter a state without the permission of the government, the pressures on member states of the CSCE to grant permission are formidable and to date none has refused. Once there, the High Commissioner is authorized to consult with "the parties directly concerned"—defined to include governments, local and regional authorities, representatives of associations, nongovernmental organizations, and religious and other groups of national minorities—and to make recommendations for resolving the issues directly to them.

The first High Commissioner, Ambassador Max van der Stoel of the Netherlands, has employed a quiet, low-key approach, first developing the facts of the situation and making contact with the relevant parties in an exploratory vein to develop their confidence in his impartiality and in the potential for intermediation. In the first year of its existence, the HCNM has been involved in situations of ethnic tension in the Baltic states (particularly Estonia), Slovakia/Hungary, Romania, Macedonia, and Albania. In each case, he has made several visits, not only to the capital, but to regions in which ethnic tensions were severe. He has had ready access to the highest levels of government and has made significant recommendations on legislation and policy dealing with ethnic minorities, many of which have been adopted. In most of these countries, he has successfully encouraged the establishment of official commissions on ethnic relations or ethnic roundtables, at which representatives of the affected groups maintain a continuing dialogue with relevant government officials. In Slovakia/Hungary, the HCNM secured the assent of both parties to the creation of an unofficial expert group that visits both countries at stated intervals to advise on the implementation of his recommendations and on further steps to be taken.

Perhaps the most significant, and certainly the best known, of his actions was his mediation of an intense crisis in mid–1993 between Estonia and the one-third of its population who are ethnic Russians, many of whom are long-time residents within its borders. The HCNM's first action in office in January of 1993 had been to visit the Baltic states so he was well acquainted with the cast of characters and had already put forward suggestions about Estonian citizenship and language laws. The passage of a particularly restrictive citizenship law coming at the same time as demands of the Russians in the enclaves of Narva and Sillamae for referenda on autonomous status triggered the crisis. All of the elements of ethnic conflict existed: the Russian population feared expulsion and saw the aliens' law as a vehicle; Estonian nationalists feared separatism and territorial breakup and saw the referendum as its beginning; Russia was weighing in about the treatment of Russian ethnics in no uncertain terms; and the issue of the final withdrawal of Russian troops remaining in Estonia and the treatment of retired officers smoldered in the background.

After reviewing the legislation on his own, the High Commissioner induced President Lennart Meri to submit the law to the Council of Europe and the CSCE for comments before he signed it. The critical comments were perceived as coming from legitimate and more objective European institutions, rather than as Russian intrusion. The law was resubmitted to parliament with several leavening changes although it was still far from ideal. While the HCNM could not dissuade the Russians of Narva and Sillamae from their referenda, he helped defuse the divisive and potentially explosive impact by obtaining reassurance from the government that it would not use force to prevent them, and from the local Russian groups that they would abide by the supreme court's ruling on the legality of their initiatives. Dialogue between the communities continues in a roundtable created at the instance of the HCNM, and the CSCE remains involved. The tension between Russians and Estonians is not over. But, after the final withdrawal of Russian troops from Estonian territory in August 1994, it is well below the boiling point.

The HCNM is a recent and promising initiative, but preventive intermediation is not limited to international organizations or public diplomacy, however low-key. The process has taken many forms. The "second track"—facilitated unofficial meetings on a confidential basis, often including participants who are not even officials of the relevant governments—has brought some high visibility successes, such as the first stages of the West Bank and Gaza agreements and some in the former Soviet republics and in Transylvania. The European Union mediated an agreement under which the dispute between Hungary and Slovakia over the Gabcikovo Dam, a potential flash point in the broader tensions between the two countries, was submitted to the World Court. The CSCE has sent some fact-finding missions and some "missions of long duration" to monitor the situation in a number of countries within its region, including Georgia, Moldovia, Estonia, and several parts of the former Yugoslavia, with at least some contribution to preventing escalation in Moldovia.

The HCNM has been in existence for little more than a year, but its record is not unimpressive. High Commissioner van der Stoel is, of course, an experienced diplomat, but there is little in his methodology and approach that does not seem capable of replication. Yet the investment in the HCNM is minuscule. It began with a staff of four, some of whom were seconded from national foreign ministries. Some of the costs are paid by foundations or underwritten by the Dutch government. The current budget for the office of the HCNM is about $4 million. If even a fraction of the High Commissioner's interventions turn out to have averted more serious conflict, it will have repaid the investment by orders of magnitude. Indeed, the CSCE as a whole is thinly funded. It required the skills of a supply sergeant to collect the necessary basic equipment to operate the missions of long duration.

It is sometimes said that the problem with a strategy of prevention is that there are so many areas of tension and potential conflict without any principle of triage to select among them. Simmering tensions lack drama until they come to a boil. International and regional organizations as well as nations seem to be occupied with full-blown crises, and the lesser conflicts are easily ignored. One experienced UN official remarks that the "curse of Cassandra" operates: Cassandra foretells the future, but no one will believe her. There seems to be enough newspaper and TV reporters to cover all the areas of potential conflict. Why not mediators? There are plenty of retired diplomats and others with mediation training and experience. The problem is to assemble the resources, limited though they are, to put them in the field and to support them there. On the record to date, this would seem to be a very high return investment for the international community.

Once agreement has been reached, a variety of possible strategies will help prevent conflict from recurring. Post-conflict situations are precarious since it is a rare settlement that satisfies all the interests of all the parties, but they also offer the opportunity to turn a tentative peace into a more enduring one. Some of the approaches are mediative, for example, election monitoring, supervising demobilization, helping to settle disputes about the process to which the parties have agreed. These are activities described as "peace building" in the Secretary General's *Agenda for Peace*. El Salvador, Nicaragua, and Cambodia provide impressive examples of such "post-conflict prevention." Certain situations involve an actual peacekeeping function: patrolling areas to keep the parties apart and providing reassurance of compliance—as in Cyprus, the Sinai, and Namibia before its elections. In certain situations, the mediation process as we described it is quite active. In others, simply the continuing presence of an impartial facilitator or observer mission will help prevent conflict from recurring. If the third party presence is withdrawn too quickly, as in Angola, the benefits may be lost. There are models from the private sector worth thinking about in the post-conflict phase. In labor-management relations and, more recently, in large-scale construction projects, the parties have appointed a "life of the project" mediator because they know that a stream of disputes will inevitably be generated. This function has prevented stoppages and delays and works well, even though the exact disputes cannot be anticipated. In a post-conflict situation, an ongoing mediator may serve such a function. This approach is being tried in Cambodia, though as yet without complete success.

However, just as in the conflict prevention phase, it is hard to keep international attention focused on a crisis that is no longer immediate. Again, resource constraints and a plethora of full-blown crises tend to divert implementation efforts from settlements prematurely although it is clear that investment in a robust intermediation at this stage may have a significant payoff.

3. Muscular Diplomacy

In internal conflicts involving significant violence but still below the level of all-out war, the United Nations has frequently organized peacekeeping forces made up of contingents furnished by national or alliance military forces, usually operating under UN command. The forces are made up of lightly armed infantry battalions, often with supporting communications, logistics, engineering, and other specialized units. According to the U.S. Army field manual, Peace Operations, in these operations, settlement, not victory, is the measure of success. Peace operations are conducted to reach a resolution by conciliation among the competing parties rather than termination by force. Military operations are designed principally to create and sustain the conditions in which political and diplomatic activities may proceed.[9] The basic mission is explicitly defined as support of the intermediation process. In principle, the diplomats are on top and the military on tap.

Increasing use of such forces in the years since 1990, however, has raised far-reaching questions about their legal basis, their proper role, their relationship with other kinds of ongoing efforts to deal with the conflict—particularly mediation and the provision of humanitarian relief—and most urgently the circumstances and objectives for which the use of force is appropriate. These questions are not well understood and are currently under intensive analysis and debate at the United Nations, at NATO, and in national military establishments.

The traditional view of the law of the Charter governing the use of military forces by the UN was relatively straightforward. The Security Council has broad authority to take action with respect to situations affecting international peace and security under Chapter VI, *with the consent or acquiescence of the parties concerned.* The International Court of Justice held that even the deployment of UN forces is valid under Chapter VI, provided that the state on whose territory they are to operate consents.[10] Only under Chapter VII, however, can the Security Council take decisions that bind member states *without their consent.*

The post–Cold War pattern of Security Council action conforms to this legal framework, at least formally. The Gulf War, of course, was based on a Chapter VII resolution. The UN forces known as UNPROFOR I (UN Protective Forces for Yugoslavia) and UNOSOM I (UN Operation in Somalia) were deployed pursuant to a cease-fire or other agreement subscribed to by all the parties to the controversy. Thus they could be said to be operating by consent, and Chapter VII action was not required.[11] When, in both Bosnia and Somalia, it became impossible to secure consent, either because the authorities were unwilling to grant it or because there were no constituted authorities, the Security Council resorted to its mandatory powers. UNPROFOR II and UNOSOM II are Chapter VII forces. The enforcement of the no-fly zone over Bosnia was separately authorized under Chapter

VII, as was the effort to capture General Mohammed Farah Aideed in Mogadishu, since these operations were conducted without the consent of those targeted.

In practice, however, all these UN forces (with the partial exception of UNOSOM II in Somalia, discussed below), whether authorized under Chapter VI or Chapter VII, have operated under rules of engagement limiting them strictly to use of force only in self-defense. In Bosnia, in particular, the political and military leadership adopted a very narrow construction of "self-defense," and, although there seems to have been some variation as would be expected among troops of different countries, for the most part UNPROFOR troops were hesitant to return fire even when fired upon.

These stringent limitations depart considerably from the historical pattern. It is true that the traditional limits on peace-keeping forces are that they act with the *consent* of the parties and that they use force only in *self-defense*. But these are not self-defining terms, and in the past they have provided considerable leeway for energetic action by UN forces.

"Consent" to the deployment of the force and to its mission is given by the agreement of the parties in accordance with which the force is constituted. The agreement is ordinarily signed by something that resembles a government or in a post-conflict situation, representatives of the factions and parties involved. That consent, once given, should continue to operate at least until someone at a similar level is prepared to take public responsibility for withdrawing consent, as was Colonel Gamal Abdel Nasser when he demanded the withdrawal of UN Emergency Forces (UNEF) from Egypt in 1967. It is not true, however, that the principle of operation by consent requires the specific consent of local civil or military authorities on the scene, much less irregular forces, to the activities of the UN forces in carrying out their mission.

Similarly, "self-defense" need not be limited to cases where a passive UN unit is fired on by attacking forces. In defining the limits of self- defense for the UN Force in Cyprus (UNFICYP), the Secretary General authorized the use of force against

(a) Attempts by force to compel them to withdraw from a position which they occupy under orders from their commanders, or to infiltrate or envelop such positions as are deemed necessary by their commanders for them to hold, thus jeopardizing their safety.

(b) Attempts by force to disarm them.

(c) Attempts by force to prevent them from carrying out their responsibilities as ordered by their commanders.

(d) Violation by force of UN premises and attempts to arrest or abduct UN personnel, civil or military.[12]

He also authorized self-defensive force to maintain "such unrestricted freedom of movement as may be considered essential by the Force Commander to the implementation of the mandates of the Force" and to enable it "to remove positions and fortified installations where these endanger the peace."[13]

The judicious use of such expanded interpretations of consent and self-defense would permit a peacekeeping force to adopt a much more aggressive posture, when necessary, without moving to large-scale combat. It is true that such a policy is not without risk of some casualties although if the Cyprus experience is applicable, the long-term casualty rate would not be very high. UNFICYP, interposed between two originally warring and still hostile communities, has kept the peace for thirty years. Although the term is much longer than would be ideal, the costs have been far below any alternative.

These technical and legal debates obscure a deeper issue: to what extent is the use of coercive force appropriate in these cases? Or, can "peace enforcement," to use the language of the Secretary General's *Agenda for Peace*, coexist with a primarily diplomatic and humanitarian enterprise? Again, the thrust of the "escalation model" is clear: try to maintain consent, but, if necessary, resort to coercion is appropriate, i.e., shift from peacekeeping to peace enforcement. If local coercion is inadequate, the implicit prescription is to escalate further. But if, as we suggest, the chances of ultimate escalation are vanishingly small, this strategic framework can be dangerously misleading.

The Somalia experience is instructive. UNOSOM I was constituted under Chapter VI to ensure the delivery of food and medicine to the hundreds of thousands of civilians in starvation conditions as a result of the collapse of the state and the descent into unlimited clan warfare. Only 500 Pakistanis of the projected 3,500-person UN force were deployed, and they were essentially confined to their barracks in the airport. The situation continued to deteriorate. At length, in late November, President Bush offered the United Nations up to 30,000 U.S. troops operating under U.S. command. Secretary General Boutros Boutros-Ghali wanted these troops to be used to disarm the warring factions, but the United States insisted that they were there only for the purpose of ensuring the delivery of humanitarian assistance.

The shift to peace enforcement occurred in the spring of 1993 when the United States forces handed off to the newly formed UNOSOM II, an 18,000-man force constituted under Chapter VII with a mission to ensure the disarmament of the guerrilla gangs.[14] To this end, UNOSOM II was to operate under more aggressive rules of engagement, and it was not long before they were tested. On June 5, 1993, twenty-three Pakistani troops on patrol were killed in what the United Nations said was a deliberate ambush organized by General Mohammed Farah Aideed, the leader of the largest Somali armed faction. In the firefight, an additional fifty-four Pakistanis and three Americans were wounded and at least fifteen Somalis were killed. The Security Council, with the full support of the United States and the Secretary General, passed a resolution calling for the arrest and prosecution of those responsible, and U.S. forces still in the country led a three-day aerial and ground attack on Aideed's headquarters.[15] Admiral Jonathan T. Howe, the chief of the UN operation, issued an arrest warrant for Aideed, backed by a $25,000 reward.

The impartiality of the force fatally compromised. The fighting in Mogadishu intensified. The United States sent 400 army Rangers as reinforcements in the hunt for Aideed and the pacification of the city. In a search and destroy mission on October 3, they were ambushed, leaving eighteen Americans dead. A roar of congressional and public protest led to a panicky response by the administration. Although the Security Council had maintained the legal niceties, the American public had not been prepared for the implications of the shift from a humanitarian mission to a Chapter VII operation. Political realities prevented the commitment of the military resources necessary to disarm Aideed and impose a settlement. The escalation model had failed. The search for Aideed was called off amid acrimonious exchanges with Boutros-Ghali, and President Bill Clinton announced that U.S. troops would be withdrawn from Somalia before March 1994, willy-nilly. Thereafter, UNOSOM has presided over an increasingly uneasy truce for a year, after which it was finally withdrawn.

This problem of "drift" from peacekeeping to peace enforcement is emphasized in British peacekeeping doctrine while U.S. thinking seems readier to contemplate potential escalation and worries less about the transition. Both countries accept the subordination of military to diplomatic activity and the overriding importance of the impartiality and the consensual basis of peacekeeping operations as essential elements for successful intermediation. But the British argue for a bright-line distinction between peacekeeping and peace enforcement based on the presence or absence of consent while the United States has seemed to envision a more graduated transition from one to the other. UK doctrine contemplates a range of limited coercive actions in support of the force mission, along the lines of the UNFICYP rules of engagement discussed above, but only if the impartiality of the force and the underlying consensual character of the mission is not impaired. It posits an explicit political (not merely legal) decision to move to peace enforcement, including a decision to provide the necessary forces to impose a solution.

If the U.S. approach may be thought not sufficiently sensitive to the problem of "drift," the U.K. position raises a much more fundamental question: can there be any effective use of military forces that does *not* rest ultimately on coercion? This question has not been much addressed because it has only become relevant in the contemporary context of UN peace operations. The accepted

answer seems to be that the use of troops in a consensual context must be energized by at least the threat or possibility of
the application of coercive power if lesser measures fail to
achieve the objective. Without a credible threat of force in the last
resort, the whole structure of respect for and submission to the
will of the peacekeepers, even in limited contexts, would inevitably unravel. The Bosnian experience is cited as evidence for
that conclusion.

Yet there is considerable experience that points in the opposite direction. The history of UN peacekeeping is replete with
instances, some in the former Yugoslavia itself, where military
demonstrations appear to have been effective in achieving limited objectives, even when it was widely recognized that escalation was unlikely. The most obvious is the preventive deployment of a few hundred troops, including 300 from the United
States, on the border between Macedonia and Serbia. They are
often said to serve a trip-wire function, but the likelihood that an
attack on them would precipitate instant and decisive retaliation
is small. The threats of NATO air action at Sarajevo and Gorazde
were similar. In Sarajevo, with an assist from the Russians, the
Bosnian Serbs withdrew their heavy weapons; at Gorazde, a few
bombs were dropped on some straggling tanks. In the fight over
Bihac, more extensive NATO raids on a Serbian airfield in
Croatia failed to stop the ground attack. There was not much
chance that the outside powers would agree on resort to extended air warfare, and little chance that it would have been
effective in the absence of a commitment on the ground. It was
hard enough to carry out the largely symbolic attack at Gorazde.
Yet these clearly limited measures had some effect in blunting the
intensity of Serbian attacks even if not on a permanent basis.
Why? The question can be asked about the whole range of
peacekeeping experience. Why have observer missions, sometimes wholly unarmed, or a thin line of interposing UN forces
been effective?

The answer is complex. Often, as the British accept, it will be
necessary and possible to use force in a localized situation—to
secure the passage of a convoy or to deny access. The effect will
be to shift the burden of escalation to the resisting party, which

may find it not easy to overcome. In part, the answer may be that, despite repeated demonstrations that the United States and the other military powers are unwilling to intervene massively in these situations, there is a residual uncertainty that at some point a threshold may be crossed. In the later years of the Cold War, a school of strategic thought maintained that deterrence did not require the certainty of retaliation; some finite probability, however low, was enough.

Two other factors deserve consideration. The first is the effect of the agreement under which the force is operating. This may take many forms: a general cease-fire, a truce between local commanders, or a formal governmental agreement accepting the intermediating force in the first place. No doubt many of these are broken before the ink is dry. If the agreement can achieve a modicum of stability, it subtly changes the situation, even for parties or groups who have until then been engaged in murderous combat or haggling about minute details of drafts. In the first place, a senior political leader has signed the agreement and taken responsibility for it. To violate it is to challenge the leader's authority. The ramifications for intra-faction or intra-party political strife are inevitably an inhibition on action. More important, the agreement may establish an equilibrium where none existed before. Game theory has emphasized that in mixed cooperative/competitive situations, it may be more important that there be a rule than what the exact content of the rule is. The parties will coordinate their activities with respect to such an equilibrium, provided there is assurance that others are doing the same. The presence of military personnel with a primarily mediative mission but with some limited ability to respond with force will supply the transparency and therefore the reassurance necessary for the equilibrium to hold.

The second factor is the symbolic effect of limited or threatened military action, not as an expression of the determination to carry out the threat or to escalate if necessary, but as an index of the level of concern and disapproval of outsiders that is sharper than mere words. Robert Hudec makes this point in discussing retaliation in the General Agreement on Tariffs and Trade (GATT), an admittedly less perilous arena. "These

actions . . . convey, effectively, a certain severity of protest that
words alone cannot achieve. The quality which enables them to
convey this message is their relative infrequency, and, in a sense,
their acknowledged pointlessness from a commercial point of
view. The attendant economic deprivation is of minimal significance by comparison."[16] The GATT legal system, he concludes in
not one "which relies on the economic sanction as a coercive
force. It uses sanction, and more often the threat of sanction, as
an escalated form of the same, essentially diplomatic, pressure
which its rulings and recommendations create."[17]

It is easy to dismiss this symbolic effect. After all, if Aideed or
Radovan Karadzic were moved by concern for the opinions of
outsiders, they would not have started the fighting in the first
place or carried it on with such intransigence and savagery when
world opinion went against them. Too often, however, we tend
to personify a whole situation by the behavior of one particularly
stubborn or fanatical leader. In fact, particularly in internal
conflicts, without well-established political or military lines of
authority, there is a mélange of viewpoints competing for acceptance, and in a rapidly changing situation, the balance between
agreeing to a less than perfect solution or fighting on is constantly
shifting for all the participants. It is not merely a speculation that
in such a situation, the demonstration effect of the limited threat
or use of force can frequently tip the balance.

There is, of course, no guarantee that intermediation with
limited military force will be able to solve all the problems of
internal conflict. As with unalloyed diplomacy, the possibilities
of successful intervention are inverse to the scale and intensity of
violence. Military escalation, even if it were politically more
feasible, is not always decisive either. The post–Cold War conflicts are no exception to the maxim that we do not solve international conflicts, we outlive them, and the most we can do often is
to figure out how best to live with them in the interim.

NOTES

1. "Transcript of President Bush's Address on the Gulf War," *New York Times*, February 28, 1991, p. 12A, col. 1. George Bush, Address to the Nation on the Suspension of Allied Offensive Combat Operations in the Persian Gulf (Feb. 27, 1991), *Weekly Compilation of Pres. Doc.*, March 4, 1991, at 224–225.
2. Rwanda is a similar case where a determined and capable military power, pursuing basic national interests within its sphere of influence, was able to force UN approval of what was essentially a small unilateral operation. Haiti may be another.
3. J.L. Kunz, "Legality of the Security Council Resolutions of June 25 and 27, 1950," *American Journal of International Law*, Vol. 45 (January 1951), p. 137.
4. Walter G. Hermes, *United States Army in the Korean War: Truce Tent and Fighting Front* (Washington, D.C.: Office of the Chief of Military History, United States Army, 1966), p. 501.
5. Robert J. Samuelson, "Don't Worry About the Cost," *Newsweek*, February 4, 1991. p.63.
6. Douglas Waller and John Barry, "The Day We Stopped the War," *Newsweek*, January 20, 1992, p. 16. Iraqi losses were much higher of course. Military deaths were estimated at 70,000 to 100,000; and although civilian casualties during the war were between two and three thousand civilian deaths in civil unrest or war-related ailments in the aftermath were put at 100,000 to 120,000.
7. There remains the possibility of bluffing, but that is not highly recommended because it is easily called.
8. For example, Howard Raiffa, *The Art and Science of Negotiation* (Cambridge, Mass.: Harvard University Press, 1982), and Lawrence Susskind and Jeffrey Cruikshank, *Breaking the Impasse: Consensual Approaches to Reolving Public Disputes* (New Yor, N.Y.: Basic Books, 1987).
9. Department of the Army, FM 100-23: *Peace Operations* (unedited revised final draft, April 26, 1994), pp. iii–iv.
10. *Certain Expenses of the United Nations (Article 17, Paragraph 2, of the Charter) Advisory Opinion of 20 July 1962*, (1962) I.C.J. Reports 151.
11. The same was true of Cambodia, Angola, and El Salvador, in none of which was Chapter VII invoked.
12. *Note by the Secretary General Concerning Certain Aspects of the Function and Operation of the United Nations Peacekeeping Force in Cyprus*, April 11, 1964. 19 UN SCOR, Supp. April–June 1964 at 12, UN Doc. S/5653 (1964).
13. *Report of the Secretary General to the Security Council on the United Nations Operation in Cyprus.* Sept. 10, 1964, 19 UN SCOR, July–Sept. 1964 at 280, UN Doc. S/5950 (1964). The force was already authorized to interpose "where specific arrangements accepted by both communities have been, or in the opinion of the commander on the spot are about to be, violated, thus risking a recurrence of the fighting or endangering law and order." *Note by the Secretary General Concerning Certain Aspects of the Function and Operation of the United Nations Peacekeeping Force in Cyprus.*

14. S.C. Res. 814, Mar. 26, 1993, U.N. Doc. S/RES/814 (1993). Twenty-four countries contributed to the force. Donatella Lorch, "U.N. Reinforces in Somali Capital and Vows Punishment for Attack," *New York Times*, June 8, 1993, P. A1, col. 1.
15. S.C. Res. 837, June 6, 1993, U.N. Doc. S/RES/837 (1993).
16. Robert Hudec, *The GATT Legal System and World Trade Diplomacy*, 2d ed. (Butterworth Legal Publishers, 1990), pp. 199–200.
17. Ibid., p.200.

9

The United Kingdom and the Use of Military Force

Bruce George and Nick Ryan

U.K. DEFENSE POLICY: PAST, PRESENT AND FUTURE

The United Kingdom's defense policy has, since time immemorial, been subject to a failure of long-term planning. There has been no long-term view of the security needs of the United Kingdom, so that short-term solutions are constantly under review leading to further short-term solutions. For much of the nineteenth and twentieth centuries, this circumstance has not prevented Britain from fulfilling its home defense needs or its international obligations although, as was seen at the beginning of the Second World War, the readiness of the United Kingdom has on more than one occasion been far short of ideal. As British economic power has declined since 1945, it has been obscured by an attempt to maintain first-rank power status. Yet the reality has forced successive governments to rein in commitments and resources, leading to a "uniformly sporadic" contraction of British defense policy, measured in expenditure, resources, and commitments.

While meeting international obligations to multilateral organizations, the United Kingdom's defense establishment is currently undergoing a further contraction, and some observers worry that the United Kingdom is failing to provide the necessary level of resources to be able to cover the range of scenarios that could present themselves in the emerging security

221

environment. That shortfall has been recognized, reluctantly, by the government, but the restitution of resources is possibly not enough to prevent a crisis of U.K. defense priorities between the minimum necessary for home defense and the requisite amount to fulfill the range of obligations arising from U.K. multilateral positions.

On the other hand, the emergence of conditions favorable to the U.K. position within the North Atlantic Treaty Organization (NATO) and the European Union (EU) could mitigate such a crisis. The Combined Joint Task Force proposal put forward at the NATO summit of January 1994 together with the "joint action" approach to the EU's Common Foreign and Security Policy (CFSP) both favor the United Kingdom's pragmatic approach and could allow sufficient breathing space to navigate an uncertain period with little trauma. If the Treasury is permitted to maintain its disproportionate hold on defense policy, however, by further reducing defense spending, the United Kingdom could be seriously hampered in its ability to meet its commitments. Unique features of U.K. defense policy, principally Northern Ireland, dictate a relatively high level of defense spending for the foreseeable future.

Defense and Security Policy prior to 1945

Throughout the nineteenth century, British foreign policy had a dual focus, the two strands of which were nevertheless heavily interrelated: looking outwards towards empire and askance towards continental Europe. Mainland defense demanded its unavoidable share of attention although, as has tended to be the case since the demise of the Jacobite rebellions of the eighteenth century, there was little demand for war-ready troops on the mainland. Ireland made its demand on British forces, but overall the major requirement for troops other than for empire and continental operations was to suppress popular unrest.

The British focus on the continent centered on the intrigues and ambitions of the four other major powers of the time—Russia, Austria, Prussia, and, most importantly, France. Britain tried to play a balancing role, withholding itself from the more interventionist tendencies of the continental powers but holding out the prospect of intervention in a constantly shifting pattern of alliances depending on who was doing what and how this affected British interests. Throughout most of the century this role meant keeping tabs on France, which was seen to be the major source of instability.

This almost obsessive concentration on France lasted throughout the half century following 1815 but was supplanted by an equally obsessional preoccupation with German power. Following the Franco-Prussian War of 1871, Bismarck's diplomatic skills and adept manipulation of power had created a "dynamically stable" system of agreements, the "Bismarckian Web," which could prove potentially very costly to a power to break out of. When Bismarck fell and revealed the fragility of his alliance system, the major issue in European international relations became the threat of German power. For Britain the period also involved an enormous growth in German industrial output, which brought the two countries into increased commercial rivalry, especially with regard to overseas trade. It has been said by one historian[1] that the predominant foreign policy concern of Britain at the turn of the century was a slowly growing awareness of the gradual diminution of Britain's relative imperial, industrial, and financial power, and a consequent struggle to adapt. This can probably be said to summarize British foreign policy well into the following century until the United States sealed the issue at Bretton Woods.

Of course, an integrated and overlapping factor in British foreign policy was the empire. If the "hands-off" approach to the continent meant that there was no commitment to permanent forces in Europe, the maintenance of empire demanded a considerable military commitment in troops and naval forces. The costs of this maritime empire were not as high as they would have been had it been a land empire, due to factors such as the use of the navy, which was much less manpower-intensive than the army, and the creation of an Indian army to take on many military tasks throughout the far-flung empire. There was a bargain struck between the British people and the Crown also, which saw a large measure of public support for Britain's outward role and any consequent military action, in exchange for the benefits of empire.

Alarm about the growth of German power came to a head in 1914 and was not settled until 1945. Even then, moreover, Britain came out of the struggle having to admit, grudgingly, that U.S. and Soviet assistance was decisive. For all the diplomatic effort to secure Britain's preeminence in the postwar order and thereby maintain the vestiges of empire, it was ironic that Germany had eclipsed British power by raising the United States and the Soviet Union to competitive dominance. The profound change in the global balance of power would have deep repercussions for British foreign and defense policy.

British defense policy 1945–1989

Elements of continuity. NATO has been the core concern of the United Kingdom's defense policy throughout the postwar period. The 1989 Defense White Paper stated that "the mutual commitments of NATO membership have been fundamental to the defense of the United Kingdom for 40 years, and we place the highest priority on providing effective forces for the Alliance." This claim is becoming strained, but it remains true that, subject to the vagaries of the Northern Ireland situation, the United Kingdom's NATO contribution can be described as its "irreducible commitment" and the most enduringly consistent feature of postwar defense policy.

In some ways, it might be said that the "irreducible commitment" to NATO and the further major continuity of the United Kingdom's strategic nuclear force are themselves derivative from the underlying planning rationale of the "special relationship" with the United States. The relationship emerged from the war years when Winston Churchill and Franklin Roosevelt, and then Churchill and Harry Truman, undertook to forge a postwar order, which they largely recognized would involve at least competition, if not hostility, between the West and the Soviet Union. The relationship served the purposes of both the United Kingdom and the United States well for forty-five odd years, taking the occasional dip, as in the case of the Suez debacle, but generally holding up well. The close friendship of Margaret Thatcher and Ronald Reagan, and George Bush after him, was as indicative of the health of the relationship as was the friendship of Harold Macmillan and John Kennedy thirty years earlier.

The postwar Labour government, through Foreign Secretary Ernest Bevin, knowing Western Europe's weakness, expended a great deal of diplomatic energy in founding NATO with the express intention of harnessing a U.S. commitment to Europe's defense. The United States, as it forged a global policy out of George Kennan's "containment" proposals, saw the strategic importance of the United Kingdom in Europe and was more than willing to foster special ties in the construction of "Fortress Europe."

The British strategic nuclear effort began as early as 1941 when a Cabinet Committee recommended a U.K. nuclear weapons program. The effort to acquire and maintain an independent strategic force has been a permanent feature of U.K. defense policy ever since. Since the Second World War, the rationale has been multifaceted: to maintain the United Kingdom's "great power" status and keep its seat at the head table despite greatly reduced economic clout; to preserve an ability to influence U.S. policy as a second center of decision making and thereby to complicate Soviet planning; to make an independent contribution to NATO's nuclear posture; and to act as a deterrent in the purely national interest.

The U.K. nuclear force has existed since 1952 and was plagued for many years with technical difficulties. Problems throughout the 1950s and 1960s with the V-Bomber force and with development of an intermediate-range ballistic missile and a standoff missile (Blue Streak and Blue Steel, both of which were shelved) were finally solved by the purchase of Polaris missiles minus warheads on very agreeable terms from the United States. Polaris provided the backbone of the strategic force until recently, carried in four Resolution Class submarine-launched ballistic missiles (SSBN), but technical difficulties persisted with the domestically produced Chevaline warhead.

Studies were conducted throughout the 1970s for a replacement for Polaris, whose shelf life would not extend safely past the 1990s. In 1980 the decision was announced to replace Polaris with a four-boat Trident fleet, whose missiles (Trident 2 D5) would again be purchased from the United States with warheads and hulls domestically built. The first of these Vanguard Class SSBNs is due to be fully commissioned by the end of 1994 or early 1995.

In addition to the strategic nuclear force, a small sub-strategic force has been maintained, which has consisted mainly of WE-177 free-fall bombs, to be carried by nuclear-capable Tornado GR1/GR1a aircraft; the Royal Navy's Sea Harrier and anti-submarine helicopters have also been nuclear-capable. The army had, until the mid-1980s, operated the Lance short-range missile, but after protracted debate over the "follow-on to Lance," no replacement system was deemed necessary.

From the mid-1980s or so there was further debate over a tactical air to surface missile (TASM), which could provide a standoff capability to replace the WE-177 as a result of significant improvements to Warsaw Pact air defenses. This idea was dropped as it was considered to be beyond Britain's requirements in the security environment that began to emerge in the late 1980s. The sub-strategic role has now been allocated to the Trident fleet in addition to the strategic role. The government's deliberate vagueness over the actual numbers of warheads to be deployed under the recently revised ceiling of 96 warheads per submarine allows both roles to be played simultaneously.

There are several further continuities of the postwar period. Consensus has been the hallmark of defense planning in the United Kingdom since the Second World War, with only relatively minor departures—the most significant of which was the Labour party's jaunt along the path of unilateral nuclear disarmament (and an associated anti-NATO stance) in the early 1980s. Otherwise, disagreements over government defense policy have usually come from all sides and been directed at the government, or, more specifically, at the Ministry of Defense (MoD).

Northern Ireland has become something of an unwelcome continuity in the United Kingdom's defense planning and takes up a disproportionately large share of defense resources. British regular troops (in addition to the normal peacetime garrison) returned to Northern Ireland in force in August 1969. The numbers built to a peak in 1972 of about 22,000 troops, or 26 major units, and tailed off until the late 1970s since when there has been a roughly steady level of 11,000 regular army troops together with around 5,600 Ulster Defence Regiment (UDR) part-time troops. (The UDR was merged with The Royal Irish Rangers in July 1992 to become the Royal Irish Regiment, a mix of part- and full-time troops, whose level remains roughly the same as that of the UDR, about 5,600.) In January 1991, there were 17,762 regular troops in Northern Ireland. Since then there has been a further increase of two battalions. According to the 1994 Defence White Paper, six resident infantry battalions (accompanied), six infantry-roled roulement battalions (unaccompanied), six Home Service battalions of the Royal Irish Regiment, with air support from the Royal Navy, Royal Air Force (RAF) and Army Air Corps, plus considerable engineering, technical, and logistic support are deployed in Northern Ireland. In addition, it should be remembered, units undergo training for four to six months before going to Northern Ireland and must be retrained for their primary role when they return, effectively removing them from the order of battle temporarily. This amounts to a very considerable slice of an armed force that can boast only forty regular battalions but that has substantial commitments.

Finally, a major continuity in the United Kingdom's defense policy is a general willingness to "slug it out" for the national interest. On numerous occasions since 1945—not always too successful—British forces have become engaged in hostilities: Korea, for instance, in 1950; Suez in 1956; Aden in 1968; and the Falkland Islands in 1982. Such actions illustrate a relative constant in U.K. defense planning: the maintenance of intervention capabilities. Yet, as we shall see, if the principle of maintaining those capabilities was more or less universally accepted, the practice of maintaining them was far from uniform.

Elements of change. It has to be admitted that the seeming clarity of a division between continuities and changes is false. The continuity often has to be qualified; likewise it can be said that in change there lurks continuity. Defense expenditure is a striking example. On the one hand, there has been a massive change in defense expenditure between the early 1950s and the 1990s. From a peak of 10 percent of gross national product (GDP) between 1951 and 1953, it has plummeted to around 3.4 percent at present and is projected to fall further to 2.9 percent by 1996–7.[2] This represent a major change in the resources of defense, but it has been a gradual decline, one accompanied by a series of reviews reluctantly reining-in military and political commitments. It is this long-term, constant decline that makes it a "continuity in change."

With a fall in expenditure there has been a complimentary fall in manpower. In 1951, the United Kingdom had roughly 825,000 men and women under arms. The single greatest change in these figures came with the abolition of National Service in the early 1960s, but personnel numbers have continued to fall since and in 1991 were down to 298,000. A comparable contraction of the civilian defense sector has occurred, but unlike the military reductions, the major civilian reductions occurred in the 1980s: from 290,000 in 1979, the figure fell to around 180,000 by 1988.[3] Manpower is usually the most expensive component of running costs, and civil servants are especially so, commanding relatively high wages. It is no surprise, then, that the public expenditure obsessed Thatcher government would look to areas such as civilian support to provide significant savings (a trend which the Major government has continued).

Such contractions could not be accomplished without a marked change in the United Kingdom's global role. Emerging from the Second World War as one of the Big Three diplomatically, Britain was nevertheless exhausted economically, and it was soon clear that the empire was on the wane. Again, though, it was not immediately obvious to everyone. In the decade after 1947 there was a 50 percent increase in colonial service recruitment,[4] there was a four-fold increase in the number of troops stationed in Aden in 1957–9,[5] and the withdrawal from empire turned out to be something of an uneven process until the 1960s and 1970s when the reality of the situation really began to be grasped.

There were, of course, strategic considerations beyond simply maintaining the empire for status's sake. When the United Kingdom, under the first Wilson government in 1964–5, committed 68,000 servicemen and one-third of the entire surface fleet to assist Malaysia against the Indonesian insurgency, the reasons for becoming so heavily involved included persuading Malaysia to keep its foreign earnings in sterling as well as showing strength in a turbulent part of the world.[6] Furthermore, the three services had their own reasons to lobby for a maintenance of the "East of Suez" policy, which was, in effect, the threshold of globalism for Britain.

The decolonization process would present opportunities for a contraction of expenditure and commitment by a weak economy, but it was also a dilemma for the bulk of the British politicians and diplomats who had been brought up with empire. It was felt that globalism was the manifest destiny of the British, and the creation of the United Nations Security Council with Britain one of its five permanent members, together with the development of the United Kingdom's nuclear weapon capability, could have done nothing to erase residual delusions of imperial grandeur. However, the reality surfaced in the form of intervention capabilities. Notwithstanding the enormous deployment to Malaysia, which Britain could not afford to withhold, a series of defense reviews and inconsistent interventions revealed the lack of understanding over what the United Kingdom's global role should be.

Suez, for instance, revealed an enormous gap between intervention policy and reality. The deployment was the very antithesis of rapidity, with the task force taking as long to reach its destination as a previous one had under Admiral Horatio Nelson a century and a half earlier. The debacle also revealed the extent of military overstretch that existed. Indian independence had stripped the United Kingdom of a major source of military manpower, but there had been no reduction in commitments: when the Suez crisis broke, many of the troops necessary to retake the canal were engaged in colonial garrison details (Malaya, Cyprus, Kenya, British Guiana, British Honduras).

The debacle led to the Sandys review of 1957, which proposed a number of measures, some more sensible than others, to relieve military overstretch and to reduce the strain of commitments on the struggling economy: increased reliance on the nuclear deterrent as a substitute for ground forces; creation of a

Central (Strategic) Reserve, wholly air-transportable with pre-positioning of stockpiles for mobility; upgrading of air and naval transport; and more emphasis on interservice command and control coordination. It did not resolve overstretch or the burden of commitments, but it greatly improved contingency capabilities. Intervention in Kuwait in 1961 showed these improvements but revealed how continued effort needed to be put into areas that the Sandys review had identified, i.e., strategic airlift and interservice coordination. The 1962 Defence White Paper said that outside Europe, joint service task forces would be used, while a Joint Service Staff was created within the MoD to advise on all aspects of joint service operations.

By 1964, several conflicts already revealed the fragility of these reforms and again highlighted overstretch so that another review became necessary. A desire to maintain a globalist capability remained, but there was serious danger that the economy could not support the weight of far-flung commitments and capabilities. An acknowledgment by the Wilson government in the mid-sixties of this reality was not matched, however, by any significant attempt to tailor resources to commitments or vice versa. The globalist aroma was too heady, it seemed, to be abstemious. In reality, the Treasury would not provide the resources and the Foreign Office would not give up the commitments, and they are, in the pecking order, the two senior departments of the U.K. government.

In 1968 the government announced that it would no longer rely on special capabilities for use outside Europe, but that domestically stationed forces (i.e., 8th Field Force) would be earmarked for use outside Europe when necessary. Many of the Sandys's proposals and those in subsequent White Papers were reversed: a rundown in strategic airlift; reductions in military manpower; ending of overseas stockpiling; and emphasis on the support of governments being assisted for bases and transit assistance (the Sandys's proposal to substitute nuclear for conventional forces never, thankfully, having received much support). The protracted debate between continentalists and globalists was, it seems, settled in favor of the continentalists—the 1968 Defence White Paper saying that "Britain's defence effort will in future be concentrated mainly in Europe and the North Atlantic area"—a statement that has held up since.

Such a process of review and counter-review continued into the 1970s, producing a series of contractions in fits and starts. The 1970s also saw a continuous retrenchment from overseas and the reassignment of forces to NATO. While the United States and the Soviet Union were busy sculpting the "policy" of détente, the United Kingdom continued to face crises throughout its former empire. The rot had taken firm hold by now, however, and there were few serious attempts to re-create an intervention capability requiring anything remotely comparable to the resources of an "East of Suez" policy. By the end of the 1970s, U.K. rapid deployment forces were almost exclusively allocated to NATO in the Allied Command Europe Mobile Force (AMF) and the U.K. Mobile Force. By 1979 the only two tri-service deployments were in Belize and Hong Kong while small detachments remained elsewhere.

The 1981 Defence White Paper, entitled "The Way Forward," reinforced this tendency, announcing drastic reductions in naval out-of-area capabilities: the phaseout of the amphibious assault ships *Intrepid* and *Fearless* without replacement; the selling off of the aircraft carrier *Invincible* to Australia; and the phaseout of the commando carrier *Hermes*. This action, taken under the short tenure of Defence Secretary John Knott, would temporarily finish off the United Kingdom's out-of-area amphibious capability.

However, partly as a result of the Iranian hostage fiasco and the Soviet invasion of Afghanistan the early 1980s also saw renewed interest in the out-of-area issue in NATO. The United States responded with a Rapid Deployment Joint Task Force, mainly for contingencies in the Gulf area. This required European NATO partners to be able to commit forces to fill in for diverted U.S. forces, which had been earmarked as NATO reinforcements. At the same time, notwithstanding the amphibious capability cutbacks described above, the new Thatcher government decided it wanted a revival of a British overseas capability (mainly in transport, logistic support, and equipment improvements for units such as 5 Infantry Brigade, the renamed 8th Field Force). Such improvements were designed to enhance the out-of-area capabilities of the armed forces with only modest increases to the defense budget. Rumors that changes would bring back "special capabilities," as referred to in the 1967 White Paper, proved to be false; only "general capabilities" were being considered, comparable to the 1968 changes. Again, the emphasis was firmly on NATO, while in the event of an extra-European emergency, forces could be identified from within the existing U.K. order of battle, which would be most appropriate for a force configured according to the demands of the specific situation.

The Falklands conflict of 1982 served notice on the U.K. government that without some serious attention to intervention capabilities, the ability of the United Kingdom to dedicate resources to defense of far-flung territories could be severely jeopardized. There were compelling reasons why the government could not abandon the Islanders, but also this was a demonstration of British prestige under a prime minister who was determined to make Britain "great" again. Yet, according to David Reynolds: "Without crucial U.S. logistic support the outcome might well have been in doubt."[7] The Pentagon was, he says, channeling vast quantities of essential supplies to the task force as well as offering crucial intelligence and use of U.S. facilities on the island of Ascension. The task force also involved all four of the amphibious vessels designated to be withdrawn in the review of the previous year. Finally, however, it illustrated a gulf between military doctrine and reality which has existed since at least 1952; as Richard Rosecrance observed even in 1968: "Doctrinal tendencies have emphasised strategic air power, reliance upon nuclear weapons, and a smaller army. Practice has paid less heed to strategic strength, but has frequently demanded battalions, air lift, and conventional naval forces."[8] The major lessons to be drawn from the conflict—other than the specific lessons about weapon systems, some of which had never been tested in warfare previously—were those of readiness and mobility, but more poignantly, the value of amphibious assault forces for out-of-area operations was shown in stark relief. All four amphibious and carrier ships previously earmarked for withdrawal were reinstated (although *Hermes* was sold to India in 1985).

As lessons were learned throughout the 1960s, 1970s, and 1980s, and then quickly forgotten, one aspect of power projection, which has changed dramatically, remains to be mentioned. Although the United Kingdom has never had a significant strategic airlift capability—NATO being heavily dependent on the United States for this capability—it has always prided itself on its merchant marine, which performed heroically during the Second World War, and which has always been seen as a reserve pool for the Royal Navy in times of crisis. However, since 1979 the merchant marine has been halved because of prohibitively high costs; ships have been progressively "flagged out" to foreign governments, permitting them to operate more cheaply.

The planning for NATO throughout the Cold War assumed high-intensity conflict with NATO's forward-based forces playing a holding role until a massive reinforcement operation, delivering some 90 percent of NATO's reinforcements and supplies by sea, would put the forces into place for a counterpunch. The U.S. merchant marine would be critically important to these plans. Likewise, the Falklands demonstrated the importance of the merchant marine to the United Kingdom's national intervention capability yet no attempt was made in its aftermath to reverse the decline. Some commentators pointed to potential foreign monopolization of merchant shipping as a possible source of U.K. vulnerability in time of crisis. It is by no means clear that monopolization would occur to that extent, but it remains, arguably, an important aspect of the United Kingdom's out-of-area weakness.

U.K. Defense Policy and Intervention Capabilities since 1989

The upheavals of 1989, 1990, and 1991, beginning with the divorce between the Soviet Union and its satellite states, taking the unification of Germany, and ending (nominally) with the collapse of the Soviet Union itself, have had profound repercussions for U.K. defense policy. First, and, most obviously, the threat of a massive invasion from the East is gone, and according to most estimates, it would take many years for Russia to be able to regenerate that threat. Few in the West now believe that Russia would choose that path. Even Vladimir Zhirinovsky, the self-styled savior of sleighted Russian greatness, is widely believed to be unable to undertake the sort of revanchist foreign policy agenda that he espouses, even if he were able to get into the driving seat.

Nevertheless, as is frequently pointed out, Russia retains a huge army and, with three other former Soviet states (Belarus, Kazakhstan, and Ukraine), continues to possess nuclear weapons. The latter gives reason to continue taking a keen interest in the United Kingdom's erstwhile adversary; but that, for the time being, is about all. The United Kingdom is still feeling its way into a new strategic relationship with Russia, and few would dare to prejudge the outcome. Therefore, the United Kingdom can detarget Russia its nuclear weapons, and it can reduce nuclear programs, but compelling reasons remain to keep a minimum deterrent capability. Nuclear weapons cannot be disinvented; until there are secure means to safeguard a nuclear-free world from the reappearance of nuclear weapons, they cannot be disposed of without the residual and profoundly destabilizing threat of a race to reinvent. As long as NATO possesses nuclear weapons, it can operate a war prevention policy, whereas it gave them up, it could only operate war limitation—this is part of the NATO ladder of response and should not be given up. That is the U.K. government's view, and that will remain U.K. nuclear policy for the foreseeable future.

A consensus has reemerged around this policy, or, at least, there is an absence of dissensus. In terms of defense policy more generally also, a greater degree of consensus than has existed since prior to the split of the early 1980s has emerged. Partly this is because the ideological standoff of the Cold War has thawed, allowing less dogmatic approaches to defense and security policy. In the United Kingdom, the major consensus currently is that defense spending is falling too far, and the odd ones out this time are not the Labour Left, but the Conservative government—previously self-styled guardians of the British national interest and defense. Since, 1990, when the program of defense cuts entitled "Options for Change" was announced, the government has found itself at odds with its own backbenchers, and where in previous years the Thatcher government was able to score decisive points off Labour's rift over defense policy, in the 1992 general election, after initiating swinging defense cuts, the Major government was unable to make any electoral capital off defense.

An aspect of the consensus that has yet to make itself felt is the public's reaction to casualties sustained by British servicemen on, for instance, UN peacekeeping duties. The British contingent in UN Protection Forces for Yugoslavia (UNPROFOR) in Bosnia has taken few casualties, including seven fatalities. If the Serbs attacked UN troops and increased those causalities, what implications might that have for future operations? Under the high-intensity assumptions of the Cold War and mutually assured destruction (or the myth of it), a different contract was being made between governments and the public over defense and the likelihood of casualties. We have yet to see the public's reaction to significant casualties from low-to medium-intensity warfare under the spotlight of instant telecommunications and where British national interests are not immediately obvious.

A gradual sea change has been under way since 1989 in the strategic importance attached to different countries under these changed conditions. Many U.K. commentators have predicted a lessening of the strategic importance of the United Kingdom to the United States when the latter has been drawing down its forces in Europe, and NATO planning no longer has to be predicated on massive reinforcement via the Atlantic. The primary focus of strategic thinking has shifted to the fringes of Europe and away from the Central Region and particularly to the eastern part of Central and Eastern Europe. President Bill Clinton specifically acknowledged this shift during a two-day visit to Germany on July 12 and 13, 1994, when he stated that the United States would seek a strategic partnership with Germany to manage change across Europe. President Clinton acknowledged the historical links between the United Kingdom and the United States, but Germany's centrality in Europe and its economic preeminence make it the natural partner for the United States in a renewed European policy.

It remains to be seen whether this development will knock a leg off the table of British defense policy. The personal friendships of premiers has less effect than before. Despite coming from outside the political elite and despite staying overnight at the White House, John Major is hardly the confidant of Bill Clinton, but then again, if the issue is one primarily of strategic relationships, the centrality of NATO to U.K. defense planning and to U.S. European policy will keep the two countries hitched to the same cart for the foreseeable future.

It could just be that the United States looked at the United Kingdom during this period as a second-rate power, which was determined to become third-rate, and one that would be an unreliable strategic partner for a longer-term European policy. The already mentioned "Options for Change" defense cuts, initiated at the beginning of 1990 (somewhat prematurely, in the eyes of critics) have almost certainly affected the United Kingdom's ability to respond with the required flexibility of forces of the major European power. According to the House of Commons Defence Committee (HCDC),[9] the decision to limit the United Kingdom's contribution to the United States-led multinational force in Somalia to two RAF Hercules transports was because there were insufficient infantry battalions—a consequence of Options for Change, which critics, including the HCDC, had been warning of since the government set out in detail its proposals for reductions in July 1991.

The defense budget has been trimmed consistently ever since the inception of Options for Change, and it has particularly irked critics that the Treasury has repeatedly modified projected future defense spending downwardly. The HCDC has stated that it is unhappy with the process of cut upon cut, saying that "there has been no period of financial calm: just the opposite. No plan seems to survive the next public expenditure round. Every activity is reviewed and revised again and again, The priority in PES 94 (the Public Expenditure Survey) must surely be, as never before, to leave defence expenditure well alone."[10]

Since those words were written, a statement on July 14, 1994 by the Secretary of State for Defence, Malcolm Rifkind, has listed further cuts in defense spending without further reducing defense expenditure—cuts in one area are intended to free resources for the front line. Under the rubric "Front Line First," this efficiency drive is to cut military manpower (mainly in the RAF) and civilian manpower within the MoD—uniformed personnel by 11,600 and civilian staff by 6,200, a significant further cut in an establishment already reduced significantly. There are worries, however, that the Treasury will see these efficiencies as a justification for further cuts in the defense budget. It is feared that armed forces morale could be severely undermined by the instability of defense spending when no longer-term level can be predicted.

The implications of current turmoil in defense policy for the United Kingdom's intervention capabilities are uncertain. Going by the Gulf experience, however, there is much to be learned. The decision to make a significant contribution to the coalition was made for a variety of reasons. There was contrary to later developments, a desire to reaffirm the "special relationship" with the United States in the aftermath of the Cold War. There was also, as a former imperial power, a "natural tendency towards globalism in British foreign policy," a by-product of which was that "readiness to take on aggression was an important part of the national self-image."[11] There was some concern in Whitehall that a substantial contribution could be used to obstruct the cuts in Options for Change, which had been set out in detail only eight days prior to Saddam Hussein's invasion of Kuwait and there were fears for the viability of support for a large contribution over such a distance. Nevertheless, it was felt to be politically important to make a contribution as an input into U.S. decision making, and senior military opinion pressed for a significant armored contribution, arguing that logistic shortcomings and technical problems could be overcome.[12]

The large contribution lobby got its way although the shortcomings were seriously highlighted, for instance, the cannibalization of Challenger tanks in Germany to maintain those in Kuwait. The Gulf operation also highlighted the inadequacy of U.K. sea lift: both the National Audit Office and the HCDC pointed out the United Kingdom's heavy dependency on "expensively chartered foreign ships," reflecting an unease over heavy lift since the decline of the merchant marine and emphasizing the dichotomy between deployability of forces (which is receiving considerable attention) and the means of deployment (which is not).[13]

In the previous section the decline of the United Kingdom's global commitments was discussed yet equally demanding commitments were established to NATO and in Northern Ireland. The NATO commitment would undergo change after 1991, when the New Strategic Concept was unveiled, but it and the Northern Ireland commitment, which has been discussed previously, remain, as do certain residual commitments from the colonial era. Additionally, however, commitments to the United Nations and to a nascent European Security and Defense Identity (ESDI) have been forged.

With the receding threat from the East and the realization, especially through the ex-Yugoslav wars and conflicts such as those in Nagorno-Karabakh and Georgia, of resurgent sources of instability such as nationalism, religious hostility, terrorism, the drug trade, and massive population movements, NATO began to fundamentally review its strategy and force structures. The New Strategic Concept, unveiled at the Rome summit of November 1991, called for a broad approach to security—recognizing a diversity of risks and a wider security arena—as opposed to the prior collective defense rationale of the alliance. This would provide a foundation for the dismantling of the geographical limitations of the defensive alliance and would give a strategic rationale for the alliance's subsequent force restructuring.

The restructuring of NATO forces begins geographically. The layer cake concept, which divided the Central Region into national sectors has gone, and there has been a reorganization of major and subordinate commands although the reasoning was entirely strategic. Three former major NATO commands have been reduced to two, Supreme Allied Commander Europe (SACEUR) and Supreme Allied Commander Atlantic (SACLANT), with CINCHAN (Commander in Chief, Channel) lapsing. This former British command has been supplanted, however, by the creation of Allied Forces Northwest (AFNORTHWEST), a major subordinate command based at High Wycombe, which takes in the United Kingdom, the U.K. Air Defence Region, Norway, and most of the surrounding waters. AFNORTHWEST combines with two other major subordinate commands, AFCENT and AFSOUTH, under SACEUR.

The new force structure also creates new functional formations, the most important of which for the United Kingdom is the ACE Rapid Reaction Corps (ARRC), which, together with Rapid Reaction (air) and maritime) forces, makes up ACE Rapid Reaction Forces. There also continues to exist the ACE Mobile Force (AMF) while maritime reorganization has created three standing naval forces: Atlantic (STANAVFORLANT), Mediterranean (STANAVFORMED), and mine counter-measures (STANAVMINFOR), the latter of which had been the Standing Naval Force (Channel) under CINCHAN.

The United Kingdom's major commitments to NATO can be summarized as follows:

- 1(U.K.) Division in Germany, consisting of 3 armored brigades and assigned to the ARRC;
- 3 (U.K.) Division, assigned to ARRC, consisting of 5 Airborne Brigade, 1 and 19 Brigades (mechanized), and being able to subsume, for instance, 3 Commando Brigade for potential out-of-area operations, and providing, in addition, a national Strategic Reserve;
- 24 Airmobile Brigade, assigned to ARRC Multinational Division (Central) (MND[C]), also able to operate nationally with logistic support from resources of 3 (U.K.) Division;
- 3 Commando Brigade, a light, mobile, self-contained amphibious infantry brigade, trained for cold weather, mountain, jungle, and desert operations; a major subunit is the U.K. Amphibious Force, which with a Dutch commando unit makes up the United Kingdom/Netherlands Amphibious Forces. This can be part of NATO Rapid Reaction Forces as part of a contingency force together with U.S. naval and Marine Corps units but is also a Western Europe Union (WEU)-designated force. It has traditionally been committed to Norway but is deployable, presumably, anywhere with ACE Rapid Reaction Forces;
- One battalion group is committed to Immediate Reaction Forces (land) as part of the ACE Mobile Force;
- Naval ships allocated to NATO Immediate Reaction Forces include one frigate or destroyer for

STANAVFORMED, one frigate or destroyer for
STANAVFORLANT and one mine countermeasures
vessel (MCMV) for STANAVMINFOR. These contributions can be increased to give the Standing Naval Forces
more depth as Rapid Reaction Forces if required.

The extreme mobility of these NATO-committed formations
illustrates the nature of the change in alliance force structures
since 1991. Gone is the heavy armor and forward presence
emphasis of the Cold War (although armour will continue to play
its role in future NATO formations). If the United Kingdom is
basing its force structures on mobility, in accordance with its
NATO planning assumptions, does that also suggest a heightened role within the United Nations, given that the UN Secretary
General, Boutros Boutros-Ghali, has asked member states to
identify forces that could contribute to UN peacekeeping operations (favoring light, mobile formations)?

It would be well to set out the United Kingdom's current
commitments to the UN. Apart from its permanent seat on the
Security Council, the United Kingdom has recently made a
heavy contribution to peacekeeping and humanitarian aid. In
1992, for instance, the United Kingdom was the UN's second
largest troop contributor. Some of the commitments have fin-
ished since then, but there has been a substantial increase in
the commitment to Bosnia following the appeal for extra troops
to patrol the safe areas. A second battalion group was deployed
following that appeal. This commitment to UNPROFOR is
by far the United Kingdom's biggest, involving in total 3,350
ground troops plus extensive support. The United Kingdom also
participates in the Iraq/Kuqait Observer Mission (UNIKOM)
with fifteen observers and in INFICYP, the disengagement force
in Cyprus, to which the United Kingdom contribution has fallen
to 425 personnel. There is also the small deployment of fifteen
customs and excise officers to assist with the sanctions enforcement operation against Serbia and Montenegro on the Danube.
Since 1989 the United Kingdom has been involved in Un relief
and peacekeeping missions in several other cases, including
Namibia, Western Sahara, and Cambodia. For a time the United

Kingdom/Netherlands Amphibious Force was also deployed to southern Turkey and northern Iraq as part of Operation Provide Comfort, in support of UN Security Council Resolution (UNSCR) 688. This saw 5,000 troops (Dutch and British) under the command of 3 Commando Brigade with supporting army units and 34 helicopters of the Royal Marines, Royal Navy, and RAF.

The Armilla, established in 1980, continues to patrol in the Gulf with the United Kingdom contributing one frigate/destoryer and support while another remains within twenty-four hours sailing time; there is a carrier group in the Adriatic, together with three Royal Navy auxiliary vessels to provide logistic support and reinforcement for the two infantry battalion groups in Bosnia; and frigates and destroyers are part of the joint NATO/WEU patrol in the Adriatic. Sea Harriers on the *Ark Royal* and RAF Jaguars in Italy are able to provide close air support to UNIPROFOR if necessary, and together with RAF Tornado F3s and Tristar and VC10K tankers patrol the Bosnia no-fly zone. RAF Tornado GR1/1A patrol the southern no-fly zone in Iraq while RAF Harriers fly reconnaissance missions in the northern Iraw no-fly zone in support of UNSCR 688.

The United Kingdom also continues to have commitments arising from bilateral or multilateral agreements outside the NATO/UN/EU context. These commitments, mainly deriving from former colonial obligations, include Belize, whose government has this year taken over responsibility for defense—in the event of a threat to Belize's security, the United Kingdom has "assured" the government of Belize that the United Kingdom shall consult with Belize; the Five Power Defence Arrangements (FPDA) commits the United Kingdom to consultation in the event of a threat to Malaysia or Singapore and has seen a considerable joint exercise commitment. One recent exercise, ORIENT 92, saw the largest ever U.K. contribution, involving seven ships, RAF Harrier, Tornado, and VC10K aircraft and one army battalion headquarters group; and finally, one Gurkha battalion is committed to Brunei until 1998 at the expense of the sultan, and, in the event of a threat to Brunei's integrity, the battalion is tasked to fight with the Royal Brunei Armed Forces.

The battalion also serves as an acclimatized reserve for the Hong Kong garrison until its withdrawal in 1997.

A creeping aspect of U.K. defense and security policy, which has, by and large, remained undefined but which promises to be a significant factor in the future, is the European Union's Common Foreign and Security Policy and the Western European Union. The United Kingdom has traditionally had an Atlanticist orientation, and many would want to keep things like that, yet membership of the EU suggests an irresistibility about the United Kingdom's contribution to creating a CFSP. There is a not-unconnected ambivalence in the United Kingdom's attitude to the WEU; the United Kingdom was a founding signatory, but after NATO's inception, and in the political and strategic climate of the time, the United Kingdom preferred to look towards the alliance and to let the WEU hibernate—the main task being to tie the United States into Europe politically and militarily. This having been done for forty years, it is not surprising that there was something of an uncertainty over the importance of the WEU to the United Kingdom when it began to rehabilitated after 1989.

The United Kingdom's initial view, notwithstanding the WEU's London location, was suspicious. The Thatcher government continued to be the most ardent apostle of caution after the revolutionary events of 1989, preaching the continued validity of NATO when some argued that it would not be able to justify itself with the collapse of the Warsaw Pact threat. The simultaneous attention, meanwhile, especially after the Single European Act of 1986, being paid to European economic and political union held a possibility of greater European defense integration, but in the absence of an understanding over the mechanisms or even validity of such a project, the United Kingdom was in no mood to be too enthusiastic. It was with some relief, therefore, that the United Kingdom signed the Maastricht Treaty, knowing that it created a mechanism for the CFSP of "joint action," but did not try formally to define the relationship between the member states and the WEU. This relief matched the United Kingdom's general hostility towards federalism, which was seen to be the route towards loss of national sovereignty in areas such as defense. The Yugoslav debacle gave ample evidence of how far the European Community (EC) had to go in the field of foreign policy and might have played a considerable part in damping CFSP fanaticism.

The United Kingdom's suspicion of the WEU was also allayed somewhat by the simultaneous NATO review of strategy and force structures, the pace and depth of which have been astonishing. As it became evident that the WEU would be both the defense component of a developing CFSP and the European pillar of NATO, the United Kingdom could breathe easier, knowing that this aspect of the developing European security "architecture" matched its own intentions to a far greater degree than it had previously feared. The announcement by President Clinton that the United States and Germany should be the major joint managers of European change does not, given the above, give great cause for alarm as the developing structures of European security maintain the consensual approaches of NATO and the WEU and keep the United Kingdom tied into joint decision-making procedures.

It might be said, then, that the United Kingdom remains committed in a variety of ways to multinational security organizations, to overseas defense commitments, and to national force structures, which favor mobility and flexibility, i.e., which call for the United Kingdom to retain a power projection or intervention capability. On the one hand, U.K. membership of and commitment to NATO assures the United Kingdom that multinational force structures are largely developing consistently with its own preferences, that is, towards flexible and mobile formations in a decision-making context that the United Kingdom, as an Atlanticist-oriented country, prefers to all-out Europeanism, no matter how consensual. The disposition of the United Kingdom's armed forces reinforces this tendency. As well as the major commitment of Northern Ireland, the United Kingdom has forces in Bosnia, Germany, Cyprus, the Falklands, Turkey, Gibraltar, Hong Kong until 1997, Brunei, Belize (as a training location), and small detachments in a variety of locations. An element of mobility and flexibility must remain in U.K. forces to accommodate far-flung commitments. The additional aspect of the WEU presents the United Kingdom with a further multinational defense decision-making forum, which will, eventually, present commitments (the United Kingdom already has units earmarked to the WEU).

There is no evidence that the government understands the sheer variety of tasks that are being heaped upon the armed forces in this defense and security context. The annual Defence White Papers map out the specific commitments of the units and pay lip service to the diversity of tasks to be performed, but critics remain to be convinced that the United Kingdom's armed services can perform as expected under the ongoing pressure of the Treasury without a serious crisis of morale, effectiveness, and, eventually, national political credibility. There have already been indications that this situation is not being imagined by the paranoid or the parochial. The HCDC observes: "The evidence available to us suggests that the United Kingdom's contribution to operations in Somalia was dictated as much by availability of forces and funds as by an assessment as to the best contribution from a military standpoint: that the United States did indeed seek the commitment of British ground forces: and that an opportunity for a valuable contribution from both a military and humanitarian perspective was lost.[14] The future of the United Kingdom's defense policy looks decidedly uncertain, but there are certain areas we can point to as looming large.

The Future of U.K. Defense Policy

Several possible future conditions have enormous potential ramifications for U.K. defense policy. One is the future demand placed on forces by existing commitments. The most obvious is Northern Ireland. For all the talk of peace at the moment, if there were an escalation of hostilities by the Irish Republican Army (IRA) of significant extent, it could actually draw more British forces into the province than are committed already, and the United Kingdom is stretched as it is. However, even without a flare-up in Northern Ireland, it is not inconceivable that over the next few years, as defense expenditure falls to below 3.0 percent of GDP and heads towards 2.5 percent, a significant conflict could arise that would demand concerted NATO action while the United Kingdom is committed to, perhaps, several substantial UN commitments. The United Kingdom has to hope that the forces required to deal with the variety of possibilities in such a vague scenario are not multiply allocated to the different rapid deployment forces required to deal with this range of contingencies and are not in the process of going to or coming back from Northern Ireland.

As the divisions between defense roles become less clear in some cases, the forces required to perform them become more similar. Malcolm Rifkind announced on July 14, 1994, as part of the "redistribution" of resources from the Ministry of Defense bureaucracy and support areas to the front lint, that a Joint Rapid Deployment Force would be created "building on the capabilities of our existing rapidly deployable forces to enable them to deploy and operate together more speedily and effectively."[15] This partly amounts to the creation of a joint headquarters, which is welcome news, but it leaves a question mark over whether the existing rapid deployment forces are to be further multi-tasked by this exercise or whether it amounts to a paper force, which cannot be assembled because of their other commitments. It leaves the possibility that certain commitments will be dropped to honor others, in which case the United Kingdom's commitment can be questioned. Such questions are not answered by the way the current government reveals its policy decisions. Most of the strengthening of the front line that the Defense Secretary announced on July 14 amounts to a reversal of earlier equipment cancellations or withdrawals while personnel are reduced.

Another factor in the future of British defense policy is the burgeoning role of the UN in crisis management, peacekeeping, and humanitarian intervention. There has been considerable debate over the last few years about the viability of UN standing forces or national continents of UN-earmarked forces. The United Kingdom favors neither of these approaches. The HCDC has succinctly summed up the majority position.

> In the event of a general need to support the UN, it seems to us that the best criteria for involvement in peacekeeping operations are that it should be an operation which requires the particular skills and strengths of British

forces; that the United Kingdom should be seen to be an active participant in a substantial number of such operations; and that there is a serious chance of a successful outcome. In general terms, those peacekeeping operations in which the United Kingdom is currently engaged meet those criteria.

There are also steps which could usefully be taken to clarify and reinforce the United Kingdom's existing commitment to provide peacekeeping and related forces where possible. The principal one would be for NATO to reinforce its earlier offers to make its structures and forces available for such duties as mandated by the UN or Conference on Security and Cooperation in Europe (CSCE). . . .

It would therefore be no more than reflecting reality for the UK to emphasise to the UN that, as had already been demonstrated, UK forces assigned or committed to NATO will normally be available for peacekeeping duties where other commitments permit.[16]

This, in effect, allows the United Kingdom to continue the planning course that it has mapped out following the NATO strategy review: that is, to support fully the force structure implications of the strategy review, to make sure that U.K. forces are adapted to these requirements across as wide a cross section of the national force posture as possible, and to push for the convergency of other possible commitments, such as the UN, with the same planning criteria.

The attractiveness of this course is that it seems to allow for a substantial amount of double, even triple hatting of tasks for units, allowing a wide range of commitments to be maintained. The worry is that, in a volatile world, several conflicting commitments could call the bluff of the United Kingdom; it is a form of creative accountancy with armed forces.

There are other uncertainties, also, in this deployability question: for instances, where does the strategic lift capability come from? The United Kingdom's C130 fleet is rapidly approaching the end of its credible life cycle, and the United Kingdom is heavily dependent on agreements with the United States or charter arrangements for outsized load movement. This has forced the question of strategic lift onto the agenda. In studying the future replacement of the C130 fleet, the MoD has stated that it has no requirement for outsized loads. Warrior, AS90 self-propelled howitzer, and the DROPS tracked logistics vehicle, not to mention the Challenger II tank, are all outsize loads and would have to be "rapidly deployable" through some extra-national means, either at great expense, with the goodwill of a generous ally, or slowly (but still at great expense), depending on the specific nature of the deployment. The HCDC has called for funding to maintain the European Future Large Aircraft program, which should eventually lead to an outsize load capability with employment benefits for Europe. And, although it is less desirable, the C-17 aircraft already exists. Combined with the decline of the merchant marine, to put U.K. lift requirements into the hands of foreign (albeit allied) or commerical hands is, potentially, to leave the United Kingdom vulnerable in time of crisis, and the credibility of a national intervention capability can surely be questioned in the absence of strategic lift.

As multinationality becomes the norm for rapid deployment, there are also unresolved questions about the levels of role specialization, which are commensurate with a national intervention capability. Three examples will suffice to demonstrate the point: air superiority, strategic lift, and amphibious vessels. The first simply does not exist until Eurofighter 2000 becomes available to fill the gap. The second has been discussed above. As to the third, after the lessons of amphibious operations were learned from the Falklands, there was a real worry about the provision of "amphibiosity." There was no decision on the replacement of the aging *Fearless* and *Intrepid* for an agonizingly long time, and only this year is it expected that an Invitation to Tender for the first replacement will be issued.[17] There have been worries also about the credibility of the United Kingdom's amphibious capability in the absence of a helicopter carrier (LPH), which alone can provide the accommodation for amphibious forces stationed offshore for any length of time and which would possess sophisticated command and control for amphibious operations. An order was placed last year for the LPH, but in the meantime, a significant gap remains in the United Kingdom's amphibious capability. To rely on allies for these capabilities is fine if the allies are willing and available, but U.K. national capability remains impaired in their absence. Malcolm Rifkind's reference to a Joint Rapid Deployment Force surely begs this question of gaps in the national capability.

Looking at the future of U.K. defense policy, we cannot avoid a fleeting mention of the European Union although a separate book could be written on this matter. The United Kingdom, whether it likes it or not, is now deeply entrenched in the European Union. The question is not whether the United Kingdom is a member, but how it would like to see the Union develop, and how the United Kingdom approaches this could have considerable ramifications for U.K. defense policy. In this regard, it is interesting to note Foreign Secretary Douglas Hurd's observations on this matter.[18] Briefly, his proposals are to keep CFSP within the intergovernmental, consensual pillar of the European Union, which would avoid the necessity, contained with the rules and procedures of the Treaty of Rome, of procedural votes to overrule the objections of partners. There are, of course, problems with this approach, which we have seen exercised by John Major all too recently: the veto, which could be more problematic with the expansion of the Union and will require considerably more consensus than recent years have witnessed. Nevertheless, the up side is that consensuality has been the hallmark of NATO and EU for years, and CFSP would sit alongside those organizations much more comfortably if such an approach were maintained. It would likely fit more comfortably with the emerging planning assumptions of NATO and the EU, of which Combined Joint Task Forces are a significant recent upshot. These have yet to be fully elaborated, but a range of possible contingencies based on diverse risks and scenarios and with a range of participation and contribution by members is a credible approach, which would harness the strengths and particular preferences of members.

There are many questions about the future of British defense policy, therefore, not the least of which is how much is the United Kingdom willing to pay for? Much of the credibility of the defense posture of the United Kingdom will depend on either how much it can juggle within economic constraints, how many commitments it is willing to trim or where it intends to find extra resources to ease the pressure that is building on the armed forces. In addition, the United Kingdom is a member of multinational organizations that have a bearing on its defense policy, and whether the United Kingdom will require a more significant national intervention capability or can safely depend on multinational burden sharing will depend to a considerable extent on the development of those organizations.

The Multilateral Dimension of U.K. Defense Policy

Briefly, then, it remains to mention the ever-shifting multilateral context of the United Kingdom's defense policy. It hardly seems to require saying that there existed, until the recent past, a concept commonly referred to as "mutually reinforcing and interlocking institutions," but the multilateral world has been changing so fast over recent years that perhaps a quick reminder might not go amiss. This now obscure phrase represented a short-lived idealism in the ability to manage the security environment through a hierarchy of organizations, the UN, CSCE, NATO, EC, WEU in Europe, for instance, whose relative authority and competence is clearly distinguished and the linkages between which are efficient and evident. The post-Yugoslav wars soon put an end to any such ideal as all the European security organizations contributed their expertise and came away scolded, while the war raged on.

The duplicate NATO/WEU Adriatic flotillas were held aloft as the epitome of the failure of the ideals of the new multilateralism(with a suspicious squint, in most cases, towards the WEU) while a general failure of member states to provide NATO with figures and details of available forces to implement the Vance-Owen plan was pointed to, rightly, as a contradiction between the alliance's strategic and operational development on the one hand, and the political priorities of its members on the other. The North Atlantic Assembly Political Committee Report of November 1992 argued that "that relevance of the Alliance will be measured in direct proportion to its ability to act upon actual risks to peace in Europe as a whole, even if no vital interests of any NATO nation may be at stake, and even if not every NATO nation chooses to take part in a military operation;"[19] while a more alarming (but at the time common) view of the situation was give in *The Times* of July 29, 1992: "With the evaporation of the threat that called it into existence NATO is falling apart, and the rift between the Anglo-Saxon Atlanticists and European continentalists grows steadily wider."[20] NATO was focused on particularly as it had something to prove in the new era: its right to exist in successive historical epochs. The UN came in for similar treatment, and the difficulties over command and control arrangements in UNPROFOR between NATO force elements and UN headquarters gave critics particular satisfaction as both organizations could be castigated.

What is remarkable is that many of the difficulties that signaled the death of multilateralism and the rebirth of great power intrigue have been overcome to a large extent. UN-NATO working groups discussed the command and control difficulties and quietly reduced their significance, even if they did not eliminate them, while suggestions continue to be made on how to improve working mechanisms—as in the suggestion by Douglas Hurd, for instance, in an address to the UN General Assembly on September 28, 1993, that the planning and operations staff at the UN Headquarters be expanded to create a general staff for UN peacekeeping for the purposes of unity of command and clarity of relationship between the UN headquarters and operational headquarters.[21] While the warning of NATO's relevance still stands and national interests still exist, the headlong force restructuring that has followed the November 1991 Rome Summit and that has determined contingency planning has shown an alliance able to adapt remarkably swiftly to an emergent security environment.

The January 1994 Brussels summit at which the Partnership for Peace proposals were extended to Central and Eastern European countries and the concept of Combined Joint Task Forces was endorsed shows a continuing adaptability. Partnership for Peace was greeted in some quarters as a failure to grasp the nettle of NATO enlargement. It reflects the reality of the security situation in Central and Eastern Europe, both in terms of the variance in defense sophistication and economic potential between countries and in terms of the uniqueness of the Russian foreign policy predicament where firmness is required to prevent Russia from claiming *carte blanche* in its near abroad, but where strategic interests require a realization of the unique importance of Russia to stability across a large arc of potential conflict.

The alliance's adaptability demonstrates also—to the benefit, hopefully, of CFSP—the flexibility of the intergovernmental process and consensus although it might be pointed out that the interests of members look rather more united in NATO than they do in the EU. That can be traced largely to the U.S. link to Europe in NATO—a link that was reaffirmed by President Clinton at the January summit when he gave the assurance of a continued U.S. presence of around 100,000 personnel for the foreseeable future.

The foregoing observation might hold some significance for the United Kingdom and its defense policy, as it implies a longer-term relevance for NATO's planning process and force structures than might have been estimated a year or two ago and suggests a defense planning process for the United Kingdom, which is generally more favored and familiar than the uncertainties of CFSP. It allows most contingencies other than Northern Ireland and dependent territories to be based on assumptions about NATO force structures so the United Kingdom can continue to argue, as has the HCDC, that its contribution to UN peacekeeping should be predicated on its NATO membership. It also allows some leeway to influence the development of the European Union and a European Defense and Security Identify so that CFSP might develop more along the United Kingdom's preferred evolutionary, gradualistic path, and less along the formal, constitutional path favored by some continental states. It also gives some space for adaptation to an enlarged Union.

There are, then, reasons to be optimistic about British defense policy in its multilateral context although it is a volatile environment, and across a variety of scenarios, there could be any number of problems for the steadying relationship between and within international security organizations. However, significant decisions remain to be made by the United Kingdom about what level of contribution it is willing to make and therefore what level of authority and responsibility it can credibly claim in the future. It must recognize that the commitments it has in common with other countries are supplemented by substantial unique commitments; the willingness of the United Kingdom to enter into dialogue with the IRA and Sinn Fein in Northern Ireland is partly a recognition of the expense of that commitment. It cannot, however, be assumed that the commitment will disappear in the near future. Sufficient resources must be dedicated to U.K. defense policy to maintain the multifaceted tasks allocated to the armed forces, or the United Kingdom must rein in its commitments. That has been said, loudly, since 1991 in the United Kingdom and will be repeated until a hard decision is made.

NOTES

1. R. Albrecht-Carrié, *A Diplomatic History of Europe Since the Congress of Vienna* (London: Methuen, 1958), p. 154.
2. House of Commons Defence Committee (HCDC), "Statement on the Defense Estimates 1994," Sixth Report, Session 199394, June 22, 1994, paragraph 14.
3. Statement on the Defence Estimates 1994, Command 2550 (London, Her Majesty's Stationery Office (HMSO), April 1994), Figure 13.
4. D. Reynolds, *Britannia Overruled* (Longman, 1991), p. 228.
5. Ibid., p. 225.
6. Ibid., p. 228.
7. Ibid., p. 260.
8. R. Rosecrance, *Defense of the Realm* (Columbia University Press, 1968), p. 179.
9. HCDC, "United Kingdom Peacekeeping and Intervention Forces," Fourth Report, Session 199293, June 9, 1993, paragraph 59.
10. HCDC, "Statement on the Defence Estimates 1994, paragraph 13.
11. L. Freedman, and E. Karsh, *The Gulf Conflict* (Faber and Faber, 1994), p. 110.
12. Ibid., pp. 113–114.
13. HCDC, "United Kingdom Peacekeeping and Intervention Forces," paragraph 24.
14. Ibid., paragraph 59.
15. Ministry of Defense, "Front Line First: Investing for the Future," Supplementary Report, July 14, 1994, Section III.

16. HCDC, "United Kingdom Peacekeeping and Intervention Forces," paragraphs 58–66.
17. In fact, a letter from the Minister of State for Defence Procurement, Roger Freeman, dated August 18, 1994, states that Invitations to Tender (ITT) have been issued for the design and build of two landing platform dock (LPD) ships and one further ship and an option price for a second. The decision on the number of ships to be ordered will be finalized once responses to the ITT have been examined.
18. D. Hurd, "Developing the Common Foreign and Security Policy," *International Affairs*, Vol. 70, No. 3 (July 1994), p. 421.
19. B. George, "NATO and the New Arc of Crisis—Dialectics of Russian Foreign Policy," North Atlantic Assembly Political Committee General Report, November 1992, paragraph 32.
20. Cited in ibid., p. 3.
21. Foreign and Commonwealth Office Background Brief, "Britain and UN Peacekeeping," June 1994, p. 5.

10

Intervention in French Foreign Policy

Dominique Moïsi

One the May 24, 1978, the *Times* of London carried an article entitled "We Used to Behave like the French." The second Shaba operation in which French forces deployed to maintain order in Zaire, had just taken place, and it was apparently with a mixture of bafflement and envy that the other European nations, especially those with a colonial past, reacted to this spectacular high point in what could be described as a pattern of intervention in French foreign policy.

Today, again from Bosnia to Rwanda, France maintains a highly visible interventionist stance. To explain this characteristic of their foreign policy, the French often put forward their tradition of chivalry from the crusades. From their struggle against the ottoman Empire to their support for the American Revolution in the eighteenth century or for the independence of Greece in the nineteenth century, France has been generous with the blood of its children. Such a generosity may be the result of the encounter between a demographic situation—France was the most populated country of Europe in the seventeenth century—and had a military tradition. Whereas the British, protected by their insularity, were keen on using the strength of others in what the French would describe as "pragmatic cynicism," the French liked to engage themselves directly. The French also have something distinctive of their own, celebrated in the parting words of Cyrano de Bergerac in Edmond Rostand's play: "C'est mon panache."

Beyond panache there is, of course, the search for national interests and—nations being what they are—the exploitation of the weaknesses of others. It is this mixture of romanticism, chivalry, spirit, and power politics that constitutes the essence of the French approach to intervention.

After looking at the African policy of France—the ideal setting for French interventionism—I will discuss the impact of the end of the Cold War and of the emergence of humanitarian interventionism on the French tradition of intervention.

FRANCE AND AFRICA

If one takes the classical legal definition of intervention, i.e., "dictatorial interference in the national affairs of another State," which I intend to do in order to focus upon the specific characteristics of the French case, French intervention as such, in spite of its symbolic importance, is dually limited in time and in space.

One cannot really speak of French intervention before 1960, and the granting of independence to the African states or 1962 and the end of the Algerian war. The was in Indochina, the war in Algeria, and, more generally, French military action in the Maghreb cannot be described as interference in the national affairs of another state since they were colonial struggles within French territory or within the French empire. Even the unhappy Franco-British intervention in Suez in 1956 can be described historically as the last of the truly European colonial operations, an unsuccessful and anachronistic attempt to replay the Crimean War, one hundred years later. It is nevertheless important to assess what the Suez affair represented for France. The canal takeover by the Egyptians jeopardized, of course, substantial economic interests since about 48 percent of French oil supplies came through the canal. Moreover, some eighty thousand French investors held about half the shares of the Canal Company. Yet deep antagonism to Gamal Abdel Nasser was the prime factor in French policy. For the French, to dispose of Nasser was a way of defeating the Algerian rebellion. Beyond that, there was the urge to wipe out the memory of a succession of humiliating failures: the defeat of 1940, Indochina, Morocco, and Tunisia. The French desperately needed a victory to bolster their self-esteem. Interviews made at the peak of the Suez crisis are highly revealing of that state of mind. What were the French elites saying?: "We are trying to turn history back . . . to wipe out the strains of Munich which led to our defeat in 1940, and of our failure to prevent Hitler from taking over the Rhineland in 1936. . . . Nasser is the symbol of all France's enemies . . . of all France's humiliations in the past.[1] The Suez affair, in its deep psychological motivations, but also in its final result—the humiliation of the old European powers both by the superpowers and the new Third World leader—is of extreme symbolic importance. Together with the Indochina and Algeria wars, the Suez crisis translated France's reluctance either to abandon its empire or to stop playing an imperial role.

The Suez crisis accelerated the French decision to build an independent nuclear weapon, but it acted as a moderating force in limiting the scope and therefore the geographical extent of French intervention. From then on, French intervention would be limited to francophone Africa. (The French police intervention in Mecca in 1980 involved no more than ten French gendarmes used, if one may say, on a "consulting" basis.)

The other cases of direct military intervention by France recent years—in Lebanon under the United Nations peacekeeping force or in the Sinai in an ad hoc European force or the presence of French troops in Bosnia today—do not belong to the same category. French troops are present in these cases in compliance with an international treaty and within the framework of international agreement, even if France's acceptance in playing such a functional reveals French determination to have a world, and not only a regional, role.

Let me come back to my definition of intervention, "dictatorial interference in the national affairs of another State." So described, the French policy of intervention is in many respects an artifact of a specific situation—that of the African continent, its natural weaknesses aggravated by the legacy of decolonization and in particular, by the artificiality of its divisions into too many states. In addition, there were also the closeness of the cultural links between France and francophone Africa, and French ambition. That ambition is a mixture of idealism and cynicism, of sense of duty and outright exploitation of the weaknesses of others. It corresponds to a desperate and somewhat successful attempt to refuse and to adapt at the same time to the international system after 1945 and France's newly reduced international status.

France's claim to independence, the building of an independent nuclear force, (the *force de frappe*), the coming out from the military body of the Northe Atlantic Treaty Organization (NATO), and the maintenance of close and privileged political, military, economic, and cultural links with francophone Africa have been the two pillars of the same policy, of the very claim to international existence. Independence as conceived by the French and intervention are therefore closely linked. One may consider them both as comfortable pretexts. What can the meaning of independence be, for a middle-size power such as France after 1945, in an increasingly interdependent world, which was dominated and divided by the superpowers up till 1989? The shrewd use of a "nuisance value" policy by Charles de Gaulle on East-West questions has, in that sense, the same significance as the French policy of intervention in Africa. Such a policy of intervention corresponds ultimately to a refusal to accept the diminished sense of self stemming from the loss of an empire. But the pursuit and, to a large extent, the success—of such a neocolonial policy could not be explained without an understanding of francophone Africa and of the context and the nature of the links existing between local and French elites.

France's relations with the African continent date back more than two centuries. Eighteen out of the fifty members of the Organization of African Unity (O.A.U.) are former French colonies or French territories. If one adds Zaire, Rwanda, Burundi, and the Mauritius islands, French is the official language in twenty-two states. The elites of these territories have not only adopted the French language but, for many, French culture; and some of them have ultimately participated in the political life of metropolitan France before independence: Lépold Senghor, Houphouët Boigny, and Modibo Keita were ministers in the

Fourth and even in the early years of the Fifth Republic. One tends to forget that Sékou Touré of Guinea was a vice-president in the National Assembly. All these rulers felt that at least one of their ancestors had been a "Gaulois." These close personal ties explain the willingness of the African governments to retain their links with the Metropole not only at the economic level with France and, through France, with the European Community, but also politically, thanks to the mechanism of the Communauté, which set the grounds for political autonomy.

There was also another reason francophone Africa was an ideal continent in which the French ambition could play a world role. It was weak and seemed to call for outside interference, one that would not be dangerous for France because of Africa's relative seclusion from world politics and the superpower rivalry (at least until the 1970s). Given the weakness of the African nation-states, French military means were perfectly adequate. For the French, intervention in the Middle East would have been too costly and above their means, as the Suez adventure had clearly shown. Africa, given the archaic state of its armies, was within French reach, a continent ideally fitted for the small interventions that France specialized in, where a small but necessary counterweight could make a decisive difference.

Not only was Africa within French reach and its leaders willing to accept the preservation of French influence, but the African continent itself had been, from the early colonial days, perceived by the French as a key instrument of French diplomacy. Following France's defeat in the Franco-Prussian war, the conquest of Africa took on the character of a national compensation through which the country could regain its rank in the European concert. It was with Europe in mind that France went to Africa.[2] As a result, the defense of Africa—the largest part of the French empire—became closely associated with the defense of France itself. This geostrategic association was reinforced during World War II when Africa became a major theater of operations and a crucial source of manpower and support for de Gaulle's Free French Forces.

After 1946, the Fourth Republic emphasized the role of Africa in rebuilding France as a great power. In the late 1940s and 1950s, some French strategic writings stressed the importance of Africa for the defense of Western Europe. They warned that since the Soviet Union was being contained by NATO in the European theater, it might attack the West through Africa. Red arrows were drawn on maps of the world to show the new grand design of Soviet strategic planners.[3] Therefore when, starting in 1975, intervention by proxy of the Soviet Union took place in Africa, it could be integrated in an old French scheme. At long last, French action could be presented not as a remanent of colonialism through a neocolonial attitude, but as a responsible Western answer to Soviet imperialistic ambitions, as the two were compatible.

Let us now turn to the characteristics of French intervention in Africa. First, this policy has been implemented through ad hoc institutions, largely outside the purview of traditional diplomatic channels. French intervention in Africa has been a highly personalized, presidential venture, a modern incarnation of the eighteenth century *"secret du roi,"* which often replaced the official policy of the Foreign Ministry.

Under the Fifth Republic, such decisions were made by the president himself with the help of two ad hoc institutions, the Ministry for Cooperation until the late 1970s; and the "Secrétariat Général pour les Affaires Africaines et Malgaches," whose role was to maintain a permanent personal link between the French president and the francophone heads of states. The role of the Quai d'Orsay consisted mainly in selling abroad a policy decided elsewhere, hence its traditional reluctance to support decisions for intervention as much out of prudence or out of frustration for having been left out of the decision-making process.

A second feature of France's policy of intervention is its formally legal character. The French have legitimized their military interventions under two legal umbrellas: one has been the *"accords de défense,"* formal bilateral defense agreements that provide for French military intervention conditional upon the request of the local governments and the approval of the French authorities, even if often, in reality, such defense agreements were signed when the intervention forces had already landed on the ground. The other "umbrella" under which France has intervened is the military technical assistance agreement (*accord d'assistance militaire technique*), which provides for French aid in the organization, equipping, and training of the national armies and police forces of the new African states.

A third important characteristic of French intervention is its limited scale. If one excludes the 3,500 men stationed in Djibouti, which was a French territory until its independence in 1977, there were never more than 10,000 French troops in francophone Africa, never more than 2,000 in one place at the same time, and, in most cases, they were there for short periods only. Therefore the expression used in the late 1970s, describing France as the gendarme of the West, must be viewed in perspective.[4]

Within this policy of intervention, important distinctions have to be made. One should distinguish between interventions that are taken in response to purely internal destabilization and those that are reactions to external aggression, even if the origins of the troubles are internal. The second type of intervention is easier to justify in the eyes of the world because it constitutes a response to another external intervention.

Historically, most interventions—at least until 1974—were aimed at stabilizing regimes that had gained their independence from France. The numerous interventions in Cameroon, Congo, Gabon, Chad, Niger, and Mauritania between 1960 and 1964 fall under this rubric. They were at the time justified by the French on the grounds of needing to protect the newly created regimes. "It is not possible that a few gunman be left free to capture any presidential palace at any time, and it is precisely because such a menace was foreseen that the new African States concluded agreements with France to protect themselves against such risks," to quote the Minister of Information of the time, M. Alain Peyrefitte,[5] France's nonintervention was not often also a form of intervention, passivity representing a conscious choice to abandon a disappointing leader. Such was the case with Fulbert Youlou in Congo in 1963 or with Hamani Diori of Niger in 1974. Usually, the reasoning behind these nonactions was the lack of credibility of the deposed leader. Looking at the evolution of Congo and comparing it with the stability of Gabon where the French intervened to save Léon M'ba and where his successor Albert-Bernard Bongo is still in power, some French officials are still wondering whether they should have intervened in Congo. Nonsupport to an endangered leader may sometimes take a more active form, as in the case of the Central African Republic, where the French, after having supported—for too long, many people would say—the Bokassa regime, actually intervened to replace Jean-Bédel Bokassa, with the man whom Bokassa had deposed, David Dacko. When Africa became, following the Portuguese decolonization, a theater of superpower confrontation with Soviet-Cuban penetration on the one hand and Libya's African ambitions on the other, the rationale for French intervention shifted from internal to external threats. French destruction of the Polisario insurgent forces, which attacked Mauritania in 1977, French involvement in Chad, and, above all, French intervention in the Shaba provinces of Zaire in 1978 fell into this second category. French intervention in Kolwezi, Zaire, in 1978, which was undoubtedly a success, had the dual ambition, apart from its humanitarian justification of saving the lives of white civilians, first, of drawing a line against further Soviet-sponsored destabilization in a geostrategically key country, (particularly since, at that time, no other Western nation and the United States in particular, was ready to enter the African struggle), and, second, of reassuring France's clients of its willingness to honor its commitments. In the minds of many African leaders, French military disengagement from Chad in 1979 endangered the credibility of France's guarantee. In African eyes, Chad was the equivalent of what Iran represented for Arab clients of the United States.

It was remarkable that France's repeated military undertakings have imposed so few costs on France at a time of strong Third World nationalism and reluctance in much of the West to carry out military interventions. Yet this policy had its own limits and contradictions. Even if the policy reinforced French prestige in the West, there was clearly a contradiction between France's claim that Africa's problems were primarily economic in nature and its emphasis on military action.

Another form of French intervention, the promotion of foreign arms sales, has also contributed to the relative isolation of France on African issues. Other examples of French policy that have stigmatized France include its arms sales to South Africa, which continued on a large scale until the end of the seventies; covert action to support the Biafran succession in order to weaken the threat of Nigeria to francophone African countries; and, more recently, France's military involvement on the side of the former government of Rwanda. This was why Nigeria denounced France's intervention in Shaba as modern version of nineteenth century imperialism; as General Olusegun Obasanjo said, "Just as our ancestors could not accept the gunboats of the last century, we cannot accept the dropping of paratroopers in the twentieth century.[6]

Whatever the justification to France's claim that Africa is a continent ideally suited for intervention and that only small counterweights are needed to influence events, France does not have the necessary logistical means (transportation and communication) with which to carry out its modest ambitions without risk. This explains the reluctance of the French military establishment to get involved in new adventures. In the case of Rwanda, intervention was carried out in spite of the opposition of the military establishment. The Kolwezi operation was carried out only with the assistance of U.S. transportation. In Rwanda, France rented Russian transportation planes.

Psychologically, the French are not fully at ease with a policy of intervention whose neocolonial aftertaste is evident, even today. Public opinion has been passively supportive of France's policy of intervention in Africa, understanding its logic, even supporting it in Rwanda on humanitarian grounds. But how would it react to French military deaths? The political impossibility of risking significant casualties constitutes the most formidable limit to French intervention, even if the French have a margin of maneuver infinitely superior to that of the United States.

INTERVENTION IN THE POST–COLD WAR ERA

Since the end of communism and the breakup of the Soviet Union, France, like the rest of the Western world, is an orphan of the Soviet threat. It is also confronted with an international system in search of a new order and guiding principles.

Fast emerging is a competition between the logic of economics entailing globalization, interdependence, and regional integration; and the logic of politics in which, at present, fragmentation seems to be gaining the upper hand. France is also confronted with a world that is united by the communication revolution and that is becoming a global village, such that actions are too often dictated by television images. The opportunities to intervene militarily in the world are multiplying while the rationale to do so is changing completely.

Under the influence of Bernard Kouchner, former minister for health and humanitarian aid in the two previous socialist governments, the French seem to have elevated the principles of humanitarian intervention above the principles of national sovereignty. In Rwanda, it was the combination of the interventionist traditions of France in Africa, the wish to reassure Africans that France was still an African power, and the new humanitarian logic of the 1990s, that explain why France took so many risks.

Although the operation has so far been a relative success, France is painfully aware of its diplomatic isolation, of the open or disguised criticism by its best friends, and also of the total absence of European support in the conflict. France was also aware of the fact that the proliferation of modern military equipment will make military intervention tomorrow more costly than it has been up to now. The intention to create an intra-African force to act as a substitute for French forces reflects this new awareness of France's limitations.

In fact, even if France's intervention in Rwanda proves to be a "qualified success," France's policy of intervention in Africa will never be the same for two reasons; Africa will count less for France, and the Africans themselves will start question the credibility of their old protector. Times are changing.

Ultimately, some lessons on intervention are starting to be learned by the French government as well as by the West in general. These lessons can be summarized as follows.

1. Any intervention that stablizes a long-term conflict may require a long-term military commitment—since the removal of troops would trigger a recurrence of instability.

2. Intervention can be truly successful only when undertaken at an early stage of the conflict in a decisive manner.

3. The longer the conflict is allowed to fester, the more likely it is that intervention will need to be focused on preventing its spread or on a purely humanitarian mission.

4. However, as Laurence Freedman wrote recently,[7] "Successful intervention will in the future more often require the formation of a coalition effort. Yet, in the media age, the point at which opposition can be mobilized to manage a local crisis comes, unfortunately, after the point at which the crisis can be readily managed."

5. The unintended consequences of any intervention will always be as great if not greater than the intended consequences.

6. Staying out is nevertheless a form of intervention.

NOTES

1. Herbert Luethy and David Rodnick, *French Motivation in the Suez Crisis* (Princeton, N.J.; 1956) Institute for International Social Research, p.80.
2. Henri Brunschwig, *Mythes et réalités de l'impérialisme colonial francais,* (Paris; Armand Colin, 1960).
3. These ideas could be found in particular in the articles published in the 1950s by the *Revue de Défense Nationale.*
4. One these questions, see Dominique Moïsi and Pierre Lellouche: "French Foreign Policy in Africa: A Lonely Battle against Destabilization," *International Security,* Vol. 3, No. 4 (Spring 1979).
5. *Le Monde,* February 28, 1964.
6. *Le Monde,* February 21, 1978.
7. Lawrence Freedman in "War and Peace: European Conflict Prevention," *Chaillot Papers* , (Institute for Security Studies, Western European Union, October 11,1993).

11

Military Force and International Relations in the Post–Cold War Environment: A View from Russia

Sergei A. Karaganov

Looking at the growing chaos that has followed the end of the Cold War and the demise of superpower bilateralism, many people may start to long for the "old good times" when international relations appeared dangerous (especially during the last twenty-five years of the Cold War) but seemed relatively predictable and easy to manage. True, the positive effects resulting from the end of the Cold War far outweigh the negative ones for most countries. Central European countries won freedom, Germany was united, and the United States seemed to become the sole superpower.

Even Russia, the main heir to the country that was defeated in the Cold War, seems better off in most respects. Military pressure from the West is virtually nonexistent, and despite the attempts of several groups of politicians and strategists in the West to make a Russian threat the "organizing factor" for post–Cold War policy, few people have accepted this thesis. Russia also no longer needs to subsidize an outer empire. Because of its economic revolution and adoption of a normal price system, Russia is beginning to serve as the economic center for most of the former Soviet republics.

Indeed, for most observers in the outside world, Russia has become a normal country struggling with enormous internal problems rather than the omnipotent and omnipresent demon that it was portrayed as during the Cold War. The one thousand mile border between Russia and the West makes it virtually inevitable that suspicions will remain between the two sides, but for now tensions are low.

Yet even though most individual countries are better off, the international system has become less stable, and a feeling of insecurity has spread over more of the world than in the previous era. We are witnessing now only the first stages of the changes that will take place with the end of the Cold War, and we do not know the ultimate outcome and results.

In part, this is because the demise of communism and the dismemberment of the Soviet Union have started a long-term and profound transformation of the world system. Some aspects of this transformation are evident already. Most of the economic structures from Bretton Woods will probably survive, but the security system created at the dawn of the Cold War has entered a period of inevitable decline. Abbreviations like SEATO (Southeast Asia Treaty Organization), CENTO (Central European Treaty Organization), etc., have almost faded from memory. The loss of the Cold War security system has been reinforced by the creeping (and unfortunate) withdrawal of the United States from Asia in general and from the Far East in particular, and by the abrupt withdrawal of what used to be called the Soviet Union from Europe and Asia.

Most participants in the security debate are willing to acknowledge that this decline cannot be slowed down and certainly cannot be reversed. In the case of NATO (North Atlantic Treaty Organization), for example, the loss of the prime raison d'être of the alliance—deterrence of the Soviet Union—has most probably made the alliance mortally ill. Its life could and should be prolonged, but the results are more or less predictable. Barring a miracle, it is highly unlikely that NATO in its present form and with its present functions will survive.

The weakening of NATO is paralleled by the demise of other security structures created during the Cold War. The Conference on Security and Cooperation in Europe (CSCE), an organization created to deal with the aftereffects of the Cold War, may not be terminally ill, but it is also sick and has shown itself incapable of dealing with the challenges of post–Cold War Europe. The only European political structure that is surviving well, the European

Union (EU), is still too fragile and weak in its ability to carry out foreign policy and security functions.

Similarly, the United Nations has inadequately handled new security challenges. The end of the Cold War raised hopes for the revival of the UN, and the organization took up a plethora of new obligations. The new spirit of agreement between major nations made possible an expansion of UN-sponsored peacekeeping operations in several trouble spots, but almost immediately three major restrictions limited UN effectiveness in peacekeeping. The first was financial, i.e., who will pay for UN operations. The second was the reluctance of many countries, including the United States and Russia, to give an international organization the sovereign ability to make decisions concerning the use of force. The third impediment was also obvious, but less often discussed than the other two: restrictions on the rules of engagement for UN peacekeepers render most UN operations incapable of terminating conflicts. This was made especially clear in the former Yugoslavia.

In the meantime, while the old security structures are fading and the candidate replacements are failing to measure up, most politicians and observers decline to face what is probably the most formidable security and political challenge of the new century—the new role of China. The rapid economic and military growth of China, the weakening of Russia, and the inability of the West to organize itself have effectively immobilized Russia and its Western partners vis-a-vis China.

Currently China is not an expansionist power. It may or may not become one. It could remain stable or it could start to disintegrate. Whatever happens to China, it is already clear that the combination of its economic growth and the increase of its military potential makes it inevitable that the Chinese leviathan will be one of the dominating factors in world politics in the next century. Alas, the established powers in international security affairs are virtually ignoring this factor, not even trying to modify the international security system in order to create a framework for a future Chinese role.

In addition, the demise of the stable two bloc security and political system has unleashed many of the previously suppressed conflicts within the countries belonging to the eastern part of the system. There are more and more signs that this demise is starting to unfreeze many of the international conflicts both within the former two-bloc system and outside of it.

Attempts to create a new security system on the ruins of the old system have brought mixed results. The defeat of Iraq by an international coalition supported by Russia has been the only clear-cut sign that such a new system was being established. At the same time, the failure of the international community to resolve the conflict in the former Yugoslavia and the retreat of UN forces from Somalia have undermined the positive results of the victory over Iraq. The deepening cleavage between the United States on the one hand and Russia and most other major European powers on the other over what to do to restore peace in Bosnia is further exacerbating the situation. The situation could become even worse if Russia is alienated by a decision to enlarge NATO.

The most significant challenge to the model of the new world order may occur if states begin to reject the idea that postindustrial societies do not need to exercise direct control over territory or resources in order to remain secure or to increase their welfare or influence. For example, one of the worst things that could happen to Russia would be for Russia to assume direct control over the former republics of the Soviet Union again. These states are poorer than Russia and could drain its resources. Nevertheless, it is becoming evident that the leaders of certain Asian countries still consider territory, natural resources, or control over population as a prize worth struggling for, if not fighting for.

The Cold War created a two-bloc system that was, in effect, a huge zone within which direct military force became largely unusable (with the exception of internal coercion within the communist bloc). Now this zone is rapidly shrinking, so that very soon it will probably include only NATO countries and European Union countries.

Two brilliant classical strategic thinkers, Zbigniew Brzezinski and Henry Kissinger, have offered different scenarios for the return of traditional geopolitics.[1] They may prove to be right (although, from the vantage point of a Russian observer, they pay undue attention to the possibility of a resurgent Russian threat—

a notion almost laughable for a person living in Moscow). The so-called "return of history" and the reemergence of the historic patterns of international power politics could become a reality. If this return of history occurs and a modern version of balance of power politics returns to Europe, the United States will not be able to return to a policy of isolation.

The coordinated management of security by great powers during the Cold War and, even more promising, the cooperative management of security that occurred during the last few years could provide an acceptable basis for the effective management of conflict in the post–Cold War international system. Unfortunately, at this time the odds that either arrangement can be established do not look good. The challenges are formidable and complex. The political will necessary to make such a system operate is currently clearly lacking. As a result, the world community could be doomed to accept mostly ad hoc and piecemeal solutions to the prevention and management of crises.

The Crisis of Nuclear Deterrence

The profound transformation of the international system triggered by the demise of the Soviet Union and communism has also brought about a profound transformation of the role of nuclear weapons. These changes may even have started to eliminate the main rationale for maintaining strategic nuclear arsenals. The primary justification for these arsenals, ensuring mutual strategic deterrence between the two superpowers, is no longer a pressing requirement and may be virtually irrelevant within the foreseeable future. Unfortunately, most of the pundits of nuclear deterrence, who spent all of their lives dealing with traditional nuclear theology, have not yet started to evaluate the new roles that nuclear weapons may assume in the international system.

It is clear to most people involved in strategic debates that nuclear weapons should be retained for the future. However, refusing to reexamine the old rationale for nuclear weapons may not only undermine nuclear deterrence, but could also weaken the arguments of leaders who favor retaining nuclear forces, as new generations of politicians, not privy to the nuclear debates of the previous decades, start to come to power.

It is clear that the easing of the "balance of terror" and the weakening of the psychological impact of nuclear weapons on international affairs have produced positive effects—most especially, of course, a decrease in the possibility of a nuclear conflict (although we can now admit that the real probability of such a conflict was negligible even before the end of the Cold War). It could also be argued that the end of the nuclear balance of terror, when combined with the lack of creative thinking on the new political role for nuclear weapons, has brought more negative consequences than positive ones.

There are more and more signs that the great nuclear powers are becoming less cautious in respect to regional crises. The laissez-faire approach of the Western powers, especially of the United States, towards the developing civil war in Yugoslavia is only one example but a very pertinent one. It would have been virtually unthinkable during the Cold War that Yugoslavia would be given a chance to disintegrate in a bloody fashion when such a war could have easily escalated into a confrontation between the Western and Eastern blocs, and such a conflict was linked to the balance of terror.

Without the restraints imposed by superpowers motivated to avert the escalation of a conflict to nuclear war, regional powers are proving themselves much freer in using force against each other than in the previous era. This is especially true in Asia. The defeat of the Iraqi invasion by the international coalition with the support of Russia has slowed this tendency toward regional conflict but has not stopped it.

One of the less discussed functions of nuclear weapons is what I would call "value shaping" or the threat of nuclear war to force nations and leaders to act with greater moderation. It has worked on several levels within the nuclear powers and on the international level. The threat of nuclear war gradually washed away the more extremist views from the leadership of the United States and the Soviet Union. Internationally, the potential costs of nuclear war helped to de-legitimize war as a means of achieving national objectives. A generation of politicians in the Northern Hemisphere has grown up with the notion that because a major conventional war could escalate into a nuclear war, wars should be avoided at almost all cost. We do not know how many conflicts were prevented by this delegitimation, and, of course, they were not eliminated altogether, but we have witnessed a remarkable stability in many potential trouble areas because of the background threat of nuclear war.

We could consider the hypothesis that, as the already negligible possibility of nuclear war decreases further, the chances for conventional wars will increase almost everywhere, and, as a result, the stability of international relations could deteriorate rather than improve. Of course, this deterioration is not inevitable, and it could be slowed down or even partially reversed by a set of policies aimed at a creation of a new world order. But we must first acknowledge the risk of deterioration and begin the search for solutions. Indeed, unless we start to change our views on nuclear deterrence and the role of nuclear weapons in the international system, we could be left in the unpleasant situation in which the negative effects of nuclear deterrence, such as the latent risk of nuclear war, remain, while many of the positive effects, such as the stability offered by deterrence, gradually evaporate.

In an ironic twist, while the effectiveness of nuclear deterrence in resolving conventional conflict and the practical usefulness of nuclear weapons are becoming more dubious, Russia is openly embracing nuclear deterrence as the centerpiece of its official policy. Russia's embrace of nuclear deterrence has its logical explanation, of course; the current political and economic crises of the country and the weakening of its position in the international community provide Russia with an incentive to rely on nuclear weapons for status and as an economical alternative to conventional forces. The Russian economic crisis will continue for the coming years, and, even when adverse economic conditions ease somewhat, resources will be needed for civilian purposes and not for military needs. Russia simply has no chance, if it wants to reform itself profoundly, to build up its conventional forces to a level commensurate with all the security challenges it faces, especially that of the potential threat from the Far East.

Thus the primary document on Russian military doctrine states unequivocally that "the aim of the Russian Federation's policy in the field of nuclear weapons is the abolition of the danger of nuclear war by deterrence of aggression against the Russian Federation or its allies." Contemporary Russian military thought considers nuclear weapons as a means of deterrence against not only nuclear aggression, but also against any aggression or major war. Russia has tried to widen the political usefulness of nuclear weapons.

The emphasis on nuclear forces by Russia also has roots in its assessment of the dangers of proliferation along Russian borders. Most potential nuclear proliferators border Russia, from the Middle East to the Far East. Russian military doctrine states: "The Russian Federation would not use its nuclear weapons against any state-member of NPT (Non-proliferation Treaty) of 1 July 1968, which does not have nuclear weapons, with only two exceptions:

a) if a state assaults the Russian Federation, its territory, armed forces or other troops or its allies, and is allied to a nuclear state; and

b) if such a state participates in or supports a military assault on Russian Federation, its territory, military forces or other troops or its allies, and does so in concert with a nuclear state."[2]

Officially, these clauses are explained as necessary to deter all potential aggressors and to limit the scale of a potential aggression, but clearly these provisions were put into the doctrine for at least two additional reasons. One is to deter the creation of anti-Russian alliances. The second, even more interesting reason, is aimed at putting additional pressure on Ukraine or other potential proliferators. The Ukrainian factor has almost certainly made Russian policy-makers more inclined to use nuclear weapons for political purposes.

Although we could understand why Russia has emphasized nuclear deterrence at this time, it is clear that this position is most probably transitional—a detour rather than a long-term policy. So far, most strategic analysts have been looking for old solutions to new problems. The U.S. "bottom up review" of nuclear strategy provided another example of this unwillingness to consider new thinking. The old rationale for nuclear weapons should not be saved, rather, new ones should be developed. Otherwise, the delegitimation of nuclear weapons will be almost inevitable within the next decade or two.

Some steps are already being made, such as the deep cuts agreed upon in START II (Strategic Arms Reductions Treaties), the de-targeting of nuclear weapons, and reducing the alert readiness of strategic systems (or even taking them off alert). These are only limited measures. One step further would be to have the leading nuclear powers coordinate their nuclear policies to ensure deterrence, beginning first with Russia and the United States and gradually involving other nuclear states in this process. Opening a discussion of possible common actions to be taken against proliferators not only in the nuclear field, but also in the field of other weapons of mass destruction is also a consideration. Simply mentioning the possibility of coordinated use of nuclear weapons against proliferators could prove to become a potent deterrent against proliferation. This new strategy of coordinated deterrence could be strengthened by a wide dialogue on the containment of the conventional arms race, especially in unstable regions.[3]

Generally speaking, I believe that in order to strengthen international stability, the major nuclear powers and the community of strategic analysts should try to make nuclear weapons much more visible in international debates and stop the tendency to avoid raising the nuclear issue. Admittedly, this is a self-serving argument for a Russian at a time when Russia would benefit from increasing the visibility of nuclear weapons in order to compensate for its current weakness, but this does not negate the basic validity of the above arguments.

Russian Security and Defense Dilemmas

Russian thinking on the usability of military force is evolving in a direction that is different from not only the thinking of the

United States and other Western powers, but also from that of Soviet and Russian policy-makers of the last decades and centuries. The traditional Western military threat to Russia—that of invasion—is almost nonexistent and will not be revived unless NATO moves closer to Russian borders. The challenge to Russia emanating from the West now has a different character; it is the threat of isolating Russia from the rest of the world community. Such isolation could further weaken the possibilities for cooperation between Russia and the West on a wide variety of issues. Such a policy could also strengthen antidemocratic forces within Russia itself and those who call for forceful reintegration of the former Soviet Union.

In some respects, there is a natural tendency for Russia to isolate itself as it concentrates on internal affairs, as foreign trade by Russia declines, and as the European Union and Germany become more preoccupied with their own affairs. The tendency toward isolation is also reinforced by the enlargement of the EU (which Russia cannot hope to join in the foreseeable future) and the weakening of the CSCE (the only European political organization in which Russia has full membership). This tendency will be a problem if it becomes institutionalized in the coming years.

There is a growing perception within Russia that it is losing respect in world affairs not only because of its economic and societal decline, but also because of its military weakness. As a result, Russian leaders across the political spectrum talk more and more about the necessity to reinvigorate the military although the various proponents of rebuilding the military have more than one motive. Nationalist politicians exploit the issue to promote their program reunifying the former Soviet Union while other members of the Russian elite, including many in the military leadership, are counting on using the defense issue to reverse the isolation of Russia in world affairs and to increase the role of Russia in the international security system.

The debate continues. The second school, those who would exploit the defense issue, has been gradually winning even though Russia has neither the resources nor the political will to increase military spending. It is notable, however, that unlike most other domestic debates within Russia, the outcome of this particular debate depends largely on the policies pursued by the outside world. If the efforts to isolate Russia continue, the nationalists and militarists will be strengthened; on the other hand, if the West pursues a policy of active interaction with Russia, those who advocate the integration of Russia into the international defense and security system will be strengthened.

The most serious potential security challenge that Russia faces emanates from the Far East. Although on a map Russia appears almost as big as the Soviet Union, in fact it retained only a little bit more than 50 percent of the Soviet population. Moreover, after the decline of the economy is considered, the Russian gross national product (GNP) is less than one-half of the Soviet GNP of 1990. By most measures, Russia has moved to the category of medium-sized powers. These facts have changed not only global politics, but also the regional balance of power in Asia.

With Russia, the traditional northern counterweight in Asia, losing a large part of its economic, military, and political power, China has radically increased its own geopolitical status and has become far more powerful. In some respects, it is assuming a potentially hegemonic position in continental Asia. The situation is further complicated by a massive migration of Chinese to the scarcely populated Russian Far East. Estimates of the number of permanent residents who have moved to the region from China range from one to two million people. So far this largely illegal immigration has brought only some ethnic and economic tensions, but if it is not regulated and curtailed, it could also lead to political problems under some future circumstances.

The foreign policies of the current Chinese leadership are mostly responsible and cautious. However, future contingencies need to be considered. During the process of reform, China could become unstable and its leadership could become radicalized. Alternatively, as China moves toward capitalism, it could acquire some of the features of a classical imperialist power. Obviously, this challenge should be dealt with primarily by political means, i.e., by developing friendly relations with China, but political efforts alone might prove to be insufficient. The potential Chinese problem is pushing Russia towards greater political reliance on nuclear weapons and a security partnership with the West.

It is relatively clear that the greatest threat to Russian security emanates from within Russia itself. The situation within Russia could yet fall apart due to a combination of mismanagement and social unrest although this possibility becomes increasingly remote with time. There is also still an existing possibility that some Weimar-type scenario could bring to power a rough authoritarian ultra-nationalist regime, which could provoke an additional wave of conflicts on the periphery of Russia and a hostile isolation. Such a belligerent isolation would very likely break the spine of Russia, in the same way as the spine of the Soviet Union broke under the unbearable burden of an ineffective economic and an inhumane political system and of a military industry that never was drawn down following its buildup during World War II.

At this juncture, the most immediate internal threat to the development of Russian democracy is the wave of violent crime within the country and the growth of terrorism. These developments promote changes in attitudes in the society towards the military and other "forceful structures." Specifically, these institutions could become more popular with the public and gradually erode the natural aversion that societies have towards the use of force within the country and abroad.

The main and most immediate security challenge that Russia is facing from abroad is the instability within the countries on its borders that were created from the territory of the former Soviet Union. The current situation in which fifteen states emerged from the breakup of the Soviet Union is most probably a temporary phenomenon. Some of the states will survive, some could fall apart (Georgia is still on the verge of dissolution, Uzbekistan could follow suit, and Ukraine looks vulnerable), and some could merge into new quasi-state structures.

The most troublesome aspect of this picture is the fact that most of the states of the former Soviet Union (with the exception of the Baltic states and gas-wealthy Turkmenistan) have been growing weaker rather than stronger after assuming statehood.

Three states of the Caucasus were being torn apart by interstate and internal conflicts and by poverty. Tajikistan was already in flames, and only Russian troops were keeping the Tajik disease from spreading. A combination of the absence of reforms, of the refusal of Russia to continue subsidization of the local economies, and of the gradual squeezing of former trade links was pushing the situation even further towards the brink.

In 1992 most of the new states were trying to strengthen their statehood, and it appeared as if they were at least partially succeeding. By the end of 1993, the tendency was reversed. For example, in Ukraine a combination of a refusal and an inability on the part of most elites to initiate economic reforms sent the economy of that country into a free-fall. Under a more or less normal pricing system, Ukraine has become heavy net consumer while Russia has become a net producer—the opposite of the expectations held by the general public only two years ago. It is hoped that the gallant reforms started in late 1994 by the new president, Leonid Kuchma, could reverse this trend.

An arc of instability and conflict has developed around the southern and southwestern periphery of Russia. This instability could threaten Russia in at least two ways. First, it could strengthen the idea of reunification in the minds of many Russians even though the majority of Russians understands that reunification would again place Russia in the position of supporting the outlying territories. The growing instability leads these people to conclude that, at least in certain cases, Russia cannot afford *not* to take over. Second, Russia could be forced to take political or military action to control this instability and prevent it from spreading.

On the surface these developments have created a wave of "great power" or even "neo-imperialist" rhetoric, along with a false feeling of omnipotence. Even some liberals and Westernizers, such as Foreign Minister Andrei Kozirev, have contributed to that wave. However, beneath the surface a much more powerful trend is developing. Russian elites increasingly appreciate the fact that reunification with the other former Soviet states would be forbiddingly costly and that Russia simply cannot afford to merge with such weak economies and turbulent societies. In addition, most of these states are developing in a direction opposite to that of Russia. These views are growing despite the fact that currently only those who participated in the preparation of the *Belovezhkaya Pusha* agreement that dissolved the Soviet Union and an extremely narrow circle of close allies dare to claim publicly that the dissolution of the Soviet Union was in the interests of Russia or a good thing per se.

Taken together, these contradictory factors result in a policy aimed at managing, rather than resolving, crises and conflicts. The military-political component of this policy is peacekeeping. The Russian elite has a variety of views on this policy. Most consider it a necessary price to be paid to prevent the spread of conflict to the territory of Russia proper. These "unwilling peacekeepers" are in the clear majority both among the political and economic elites and among the military leadership. A minority see peacekeeping operations as a way to prop up Russian political influence and eventually to pave the way to some sort of reunification.

The problem of preserving the rights of Russian and other minorities will make peacekeeping more and more important in some of the former Soviet states and even within certain autonomous states within the Russian Federation. In these states, minorities face discrimination and forceful emigration; examples in which this is so include the Baltic states, certain Central Asian republics, Azerbaijan, Moldova, and the Chechen Republic. Two million refugees entered Russia in 1991–92 (mostly from Central Asian states) as a result of these developments. According to some estimates, migration from the former Soviet states could include three million Russians and approximately 1.5 million people of other nationalities by 1996. The flow of refugees could grow even larger in the event of serious deterioration of a situation within some of the Commonwealth of Independent States (CIS) members or in relations among them.

Massive migration would undermine the internal stability of Russia and other former Soviet states and would form a social base for radical movements and interethnic conflict. Moreover, the problem is not limited to Russian-speaking minorities. The majority of the former Soviet republics are multiethnic states. The problem with the treatment of minorities has been hidden for some time. If the international community and Russia permit suppression of minority rights within these countries, the result will inevitably be a wave of chauvinistic feelings in Russia towards minorities from other republics. This would be especially unfortunate as, for centuries, such minorities have been treated comparatively well. The central regions of the Russian Empire, which now form the Russian Federation, did not experience pogroms, and members of the elites from the outlying provinces were able to enter the czarist elite easily. (This was especially true for individuals from the Christian provinces.)

There are already disquieting signs of xenophobia within Russia towards migrants from Caucasus republics. This xenophobia could combine with anti-Russian feelings in the republics with predictable results.

Of course, most members of the Russian leadership understand that the problem of minorities should be addressed primarily through political and economic means, but military force does play a certain role in this strategy, too. First, Russian forces have already been used on several occasions to save civilians, mostly minority groups. Second, Russian authorities, despite predictable negative reaction from some parts of the international community, use the threat of punishment by military force against those who might potentially violate the rights of minorities, especially Russian minorities in the outlying republics. Third, the threat of postponing the withdrawal of Russian forces was used to pressure Latvian and Estonian governments to respect the civil rights of their Russian-speaking minorities.

This is not to say that Russian leaders do not appreciate the limits of military force as a useful instrument to protect minority rights. But it is widely believed that, in the context of the rough and relatively primitive circumstances of most of the former Soviet states, relatively rude instruments could work and deter violence against minorities.

Another serious challenge for Russian security and defense policies is the situation within the military. For several years, the Russian armed forces have been subjected to more pressure on the social, economic, and morale fronts than has any other stratum of Russian society. The level of discontent among Russian officers is great.

Moreover, at the same time, the military is becoming more and more influential in Russian politics. This growing influence is in a way a natural phenomenon for a transitional society. The problem is that the state structures that were intended to control the military have been weakened and that Russian political leaders have become dependent on the military. (For example, President Boris Yeltsin had to call upon the military to storm the Russian Parliament on October 4, 1993, in order to preserve the government.)[4]

The problems within the military and their growing influence mean that they will have an important (and perhaps critical) role in any military reform policy or changes in the Russian force posture. The military's influence and concerns for their future will put very strict limits on the ability of Russia to use military force in support of national objectives, including peacekeeping. The Russian military, who are mainly interested in their survival and in dealing with the many social and economic problems they face, are largely unwilling to participate in any major operations unless they are paid well. Often when they have been willing to support peacekeeping operations (as in the case of Georgia), their willingness has depended less on strategic considerations than on their desire to avoid having to relocate to less comfortable places.

Russian Approaches towards Peacekeeping[5]

The "return of history," or the reemergence of traditional political competition, has also occurred within the former Soviet Union itself. Most of the states that were created from the Soviet Union two years ago are weakening, and the stability of most of them is increasingly fragile as well. At first, the Russian governing elite anticipated that Russia could count on the help and participation of the international community in managing this instability. However, the experience of the last two years has taught Russian leaders that these hopes are largely futile. Past experience in dealing with Western partners has convinced most Russians that it is senseless to count on international support and participation. In most cases, Western support did not materialize (although in many cases this was less a result of decisions by the Western partners themselves than by objections raised by Central European countries and the former Soviet states neighboring Russia). In cases in which Western support was sought, such as the Nagorno Karabakh crisis, the effort proved largely unsuccessful and, some would claim, counterproductive.

As a result, the prevailing view in Russia has changed. Russian elites do not reject international participation in managing conflicts on the territory of the former Soviet Union in principle, and, in some cases they would welcome such involvement if it seems useful and comes along with financial support. However, for the most part, Moscow is drifting towards a more unilateralist mode or one that relies only on fellow members of the CIS.

This move is understandable but presents some dangers. Such unilateralism could encourage suspicion of Russian motives by other countries. It could also lead to a loss of international support for Russian policy. Worst of all, unilateralism could overextend Russian resources if Russia is required to intervene in too many conflicts. The refusal of the world community to share the financial burden and to legalize the Russian role also implies a de facto rejection of any effort to control and to influence this role. Also this rejection strengthens the tendency towards the de facto creation of two security zones in Europe.

Evolving Russian policy toward conflicts within the former Soviet Union seems to be driven by the following interests:

- Preventing the spillover of conflicts to the territory of Russia proper;

- Curtailment of suffering and of loss of human lives;

- Protection of minorities, especially Russian-speaking minorities;

- Supporting the political status of Russia within the international community;

- Preventing potentially hostile forces from filling power vacuums created after the dissolution of the Soviet Union; and

- Creating additional possibilities for influencing the internal development and foreign policy orientation of neighboring states.

After saying all that, I have to stress once more that the majority of Russian elites do not favor involvement in violent conflicts outside of Russian territory. Russia is an unwilling peacekeeper despite the suspicions of most outside observers.

The realities of the current situation in the former Soviet Union and of Russian experience in peacekeeping to date are teaching Russian ruling elites that military force can be used and is sometimes useful. The use of force helps to attain political goals and reduce human suffering. To be sure, although military force is once again proving useful, its utility is limited to only a very narrow range of lower level conflicts, but that does not change the basic lesson.

Russian troops have proved to be relatively effective in enforcing and keeping peace in several conflicts that have flared up on the former territory of the Soviet Union. Russian troops were able to stop wars in both Moldova and Ossetia. The presence of the Russian 201 Mechanized Rifle Division under the CIS banner in Tajikistan keeps the civil war there under control. Most probably the introduction of Russian troops into Georgia will sooner or later end the Abkhazia-Georgia conflict. It is also clear that within the next year Russia will be required to terminate the six-year conflict between Armenia and Azerbaijan over Nagorno Karabakh.

Russian experience in peacekeeping provides several lessons that should be studied. In most cases, Russian peacekeeping operations are more effective than other similar efforts of the international community. Russian peacekeepers are less constrained by established operational concepts. Led mostly by Afghan war veterans, these troops rely heavily on relatively fresh experience accumulated during that war.

Several specific features of the "Russian way of peacekeeping" can be discerned.

- Forces of belligerents are often employed along with the ostensibly neutral Russian forces. That practice was used, for example, in Transdniestria and Ossetia.

- In several instances, Russian peacekeeping troops were introduced before the end of the fighting so that they, in effect, played the role of peace enforcers.

- Russian and CIS troops under Russian leadership often cooperate actively with local field commanders in order to attain objectives such as free passage of humanitarian convoys.

- Even unarmed peacekeepers introduced into a zone of conflict as a police force are usually trained for fighting and keep weapons nearby; this is believed to be a potent deterrent against those who are deliberating the use of force.

- In some cases, the mandate of the peacekeeping forces provides for use of force not only in self-defense, but also for pursuing and destroying armed elements of one or both parties to the conflict.

- The mandate is received either from CIS or from the government involved rather than an international body. (Moscow continues to seek mandates from the UN or CSCE, although with growing skepticism.)

- Russian peacekeeping operations have proved to be more sustainable than similar efforts by other countries because Russian society has proven more tolerant towards the loss of life of military personnel.

However, the Russian experience is unique in many ways. Russian peacekeeping or peace enforcing operations face very weak countries, which in many cases see the Russian participation as not only inevitable, but almost as a fact of life. Also many of these states had not yet secured true independence but rather remained dependent on Russia even after their formal sovereignty was recognized by the international community and Russia.

Russia faces several problems as a peacekeeper. The financial burden of Russian peacekeeping operations is shared neither by CIS countries nor by the international community, even when Russian peacekeeping has a clear-cut legal mandate. Another problem is the legality of Russian involvement. In principle, leaders in Moscow agree to the internationally accepted norms of peacekeeping. The most important of these is that peacekeepers are not to be deployed without the agreement of conflicting parties or an invitation by the government. However, the reality is much more complex. Russian troops participate in the Tadjik civil war on one side (though on the side of the legal government). The presence of the 14th Army in Moldova is only half-heartedly accepted by the Kishinev government. Also Russian forces supported sides in the civil war in Georgia, most probably without direction from Moscow.

The dubious legality in some cases and the obvious fact that Russian involvement contributes to the buildup of Russian political clout in the neighboring areas contribute to the development of suspicions of "Russian imperialism." (Being Russian, I do not want to start proving that "we do not beat our wives.") Yet critics should answer: Do they have an alternative, and what would they do in the shoes of Russian policy-makers?

While Russia moves towards more unilateralist or inter-CIS policies in the zone of the former Soviet Union (though not rejecting international legal norms or a possibility of international participation and not asking for a carte blanche), its approach towards multilateral peacekeeping operations is moving in a less clear-cut direction. In principle, Moscow continues to support enlarging the mandate of the CSCE and of the UN and particularly supports the idea that the planning and operational staff at the UN headquarters be expanded to create a general staff for UN peacekeeping operations. Moscow supported the Desert Storm operation and has been acting hand in hand with the Western powers to curtail the war in the former Yugoslavia. It has also backed the UN efforts in Somalia and the invasion of Haiti.

This continuous support is based on the appreciation of several key interests of Russia:

- Interest of most elites in being friendly to or even allied with the most developed and affluent countries of the world;

- Interest of many elites in being allied with most democratic and capitalist powers;

- Interest in reserving a place in a new security arrangement, which could grow out of the present security order; at this juncture, Russia does not have any significant allies and does not know where it belongs in security terms;

- Interest in keeping levers of control and influence over policies of other major powers in the peacekeeping/peace enforcement/humanitarian intervention field;

- Interest in getting in exchange for Russian support of other great powers an understanding or even backing of similar efforts by Russia within the CIS; in spite of the relative success of Russian peacekeeping and crisis management policies, these successes are in most areas inconclusive; sources of potential instability for many years to come are too numerous for Russia to manage alone;

- Interest in curtailing and deterring instability in the world outside of the former Soviet Union—all the more because most sources of instability and potential proliferators of weapons of mass destruction are located close to borders of the former Soviet Union and are still mostly defended by Russia; and

- Interest of the military (at least some of them) in being "members of the club" and in furthering their professional objectives.

With all the above-mentioned interests pushing Moscow towards active and constructive participation in and support of international efforts in the field of peacekeeping and peace enforcement, more and more signs of wariness if not skepticism towards these efforts are noticeable. Partially these doubts are caused by appreciation of the limits of Russian involvement— due to the lack of financial and personnel resources—and thus of the limits of influence on relevant policy-making. There is also a growing perception, especially after some episodes when NATO went on bombing in the former Yugoslavia in spite of opposition from Moscow, that Russian interests and sensibilities are not sufficiently respected.

The previous policy of unequivocally following Western initiatives provided for a backlash not only among political forces, which are normally called nationalist or neo-communist, but also among the much wider stratum of the elite. This internal pressure is pushing Russian diplomacy towards a variation of a neo-Gaullist posture.

I believe that unless there is an unlikely change in the internal situation of my country—with ultranationalists coming to power and formulating a new set of national interests—the first of the above-mentioned group of considerations will continue to prevail. However, it is unclear whether and how this prevalence of interests will influence practical policies. Much will depend on the readiness of the West to meet Russian concerns and interests halfway, not only to cooperate with but to integrate Russia and the Russian security establishment, even to harmonize and adjust defense policies to meet the challenges of the new era. That is not the most likely outcome, taking into consideration the current growth of anti-Russian feelings in the West and the ambiguity of many Russian interests and policies. Gaullist policies could pay off, if a country is already a member of an alliance. Russia is not there yet.

However, it is clear, at least for me, that the failure to integrate Russia in the security field could only contribute to the growing destabilization of international relations. Historical patterns are returning to world politics; military force in its different aspects is reassuming much of its past utility. At the same time, other factors, such as the diffusion of military power, the introduction of new legal norms in the international community, and the growing influence of public opinion in the age of CNN, make unilateral use of force and political unilateralism less effective than previously.

NOTES

1. Zbigniew Brzesinski, "The Premature Partnership," *Foreign Affairs*, Vol. 73, No. 2 (March/April 1994); and Henry Kissinger, *Diplomacy* (Simon and Schuster, 1994), especially chap. 31.
2. "Osnovnye polozheniya voennoi doctriny Rossiyskoi Federatsii" (Basic elements of the military doctrine of the Russian Federation), *Izvestiya*, November 18, pp. 1 and 4. See also P. Grachev, "Voyennaya doctrina i bezopasnost Rossii" (The military doctrine and the security of Russia), *Nezavisimaya Gazeta*, June 1994.
3. F. Ikle and I have cochaired a group of Russian and American experts and former senior policy-makers, who produced a common report that developed such an argument at some length. See Center for Strategic and International Studies (CSIS), Washington, and Council on Foreign and Defense Policies, Moscow, "Harmonizing the Evolution of U.S. and Russian Defense Policies." Washington, D.C.: CSIS, 1993). (Also published in Russian.)
4. For a more detailed description of the new role of the military see S. Karaganov, "Voyenniye, Politica, Obshestvo" (The Military, Politics, Society), *Krasnaya Zvezda*, December 2, 1993, p. 2.
5. For official Russian views on peacekeeping, see the article of the Deputy Minister of Defense G. Kondratiev, "Mirotvorcheskaya Rol Rossii" (The Peacekeeping Role of Russia), *Krasnaya Zvezda*, June 21, 1994, pp. 1 and 2.